# REMEMBERING

# FORWARD

# *REMEMBERING*

# HAROLD

MERCER UNIVERSITY PRESS

# FORWARD

# G. CLARKE

MACON, GEORGIA  1995

ISBN 0-86554-472-7

*Remembering Forward*
by Harold G. Clarke

Copyright © 1995
Mercer University Press, Macon, Georgia 31210-3960 USA

*First printing, March 1995*
*Second printing, April 1995*

Library of Congress Cataloging-in-Publication Data

Clarke, Harold G.
    Remembering Forward / Harold G. Clarke.
    xvi + 235 pp. (and 16 pages of photographs)   6x9"
    ISBN 0-86554-472-7
    1. Forsyth (Ga.)—Social life and customs. 2. Forsyth (Ga.)—Race
relations. 3. Clarke, Harold G.—Childhood and youth. 4. Forsyth
(Ga.)—Biography.     I. Title.
F294. F66C53     1994
975.8'265042—dc20                                              94-42345
                                                               CIP

# Contents

# List of Photographs

*(A Photo Album: the Clarke Family & City of Forsyth* appears between pages 128 and 129. Illustrations are listed by plate number.)

## Plate

The photographs are courtesy of Harold G. Clarke, except for the cover photograph and detail of the Monroe County Courthouse, circa 1930, and plates 14 and 15, which are courtesy of the Georgia Department of Archives and History, Atlanta. Also, the cover photograph of Harold G. Clarke is courtesy of Southern Directory Publishing, Forsyth, Georgia.

To

*Mama* and *Daddy*

who nurtured me during these years

and to

*Nora*

who has made the rest worthwhile

# A Man of Justice

## by Celestine Sibley

When a thirty-three-year-old legislator named Harold G. Clarke came to the Georgia House of Representatives in 1961, those of us in the press section found that we liked him right away.

He had a friendly relaxed way about him, a durable sense of humor, and, of incontestable importance, he was one of us. Although a practicing attorney, he was also a newspaperman. He had served in all capacities on the family-owned newspaper in Forsyth, Georgia, and had edited the *Stars and Stripes* in the Pacific. Proof positive that he was a gentleman of intelligence and humor, we agreed among ourselves.

Harold Clarke did not let us down then—and he hasn't since.

He had some stormy times in the Georgia legislature during the ten years that he served there. One of his major battles which the press delighted in and gave an unfortunate name was played up in alarming black letters as a bill to "ABOLISH ATLANTA." Actually, Representative Clarke was only trying to do a wise and practical thing, blend the city of Atlanta with the county of Fulton. He had loved Atlanta all his life. It was the big town near his hometown. He didn't want to diminish it in the slightest, but "ABOLISH ATLANTA" caught on and the consolidation of the city and the county didn't. It came within nine votes of passage, and then Harold

Clarke proved that he could listen respectfully to the reasoning of opponents. He withdrew the bill from further consideration at the behest of Fulton County representatives who asked for more time to study it. Representative Clarke gave up his seat in the House in 1971, and, about that time, I stopped covering the legislature. So I lost touch with him—until one day, during the administration of Governor Joe Frank Harris, I embarked on a trip to Washington with some other Georgians to deliver a plaque to the Tomb of the Unknown Soldier. I was walking across the field toward the National Guard plane, which was taking us to the capitol city, and I met Harold Clarke.

We greeted one another cordially, chatted about the intervening years, and sat together on the plane. Finally, I said curiously, "Harold, aren't you some kind of judge?"

He nodded.

I was embarrassed to have lost track and didn't want to pursue the matter in case he was a lowly police court judge or even a justice of the peace. But reportorial curiosity won out. Presently I said, "What kind of judge?"

The answer was mumbled, but I caught it: Supreme Court.

It wasn't until I got back to town and checked with my colleagues at the newspaper that I learned that Harold Clarke was not only a supreme court justice, he was chief justice! It was typical Harold Clarke modesty.

Harold was appointed to the high court in 1979 by Governor George Busbee, and he came to be known as the court's "gentle" leader, a chief who persuaded instead of using a club, a man called "possibly the best leader this court has had in fifty years." During his tenure on the bench, the high court overturned numerous death-penalty cases, gave broad interpretation to open meetings and records law, expanded individual rights, and favored victims of large corporations. On ten occasions, the court overturned capital convictions in death-penalty cases because defendants were poorly represented by their attorneys. On three occasions, death sentences for black defendants were overturned because prosecutors struck blacks from the jury.

On his sixty-sixth birthday in September 1993, Judge Clarke announced his intention to retire, and there was lamentation among members of the bar, whose state association he had served as president. They called him "one of the great chief justices in history," a man of charm and warmth, and a compromiser who could "bring people together" and who attacked racial and gender bias in the courtroom.

None of this is in *Remembering Forward*, his first book. He doesn't tell you that he is a graduate of the University of Georgia, or of his courtship and marriage to Miss Nora Gordon of Commerce. He does mention, but parenthetically, their four children, Lee Ann, Harold, Jr., Julia, and Elizabeth. This winsome story is really an account of what it was like to be a boy in a little Southern town between World Wars I and II. For people who knew that time period, there will be instant rapport with the kid who came from a preacher's family, was "raised nice" by a gentle mother, but did his share of fighting, fishing, and hooky-playing to swim at a forbidden spot called the Blue Hole. He rode trains when he went more than a mile or two from home, and he cherished then—as he does today—kindness and caring and the eccentricities of neighbors. (I like the man in the book who, turned down for a loan at the town's bank, exclaimed, "Damn a bank that won't bank!")

It's not in *Remembering Forward*, and, if Harold Clarke is the one to write it, it may never be. But what newspaper people and lawyers remember with a choky sense of pride in him is what happened in June 1992. Justice Charles Weltner was near death with cancer. Chief Justice Clarke valued him for the same qualities which won him the John F. Kennedy Profiles in Courage Award in 1991. As a young congressman, Weltner had chosen not to seek reelection when he learned he would have to support gubernatorial candidate Lester Maddox, a segregationist. Weltner, Justice Clarke said, was the court's "spiritual leader." It saddened everybody who knew him that Charles Weltner would not live to follow in the footsteps of his great-great grandfather, Joseph Henry Lumpkin, who was the state's first chief justice.

Harold Clarke made it possible. He stepped down as chief justice temporarily in order to allow Justice Weltner to serve before he died in the post he had long desired. When Justice Weltner was sworn in, he went back to his office and found cards and stationary with the imprint of his new title. Harold Clarke provided them.

Denizens of the press section who saw Harold Clarke sworn in as a freshman legislator in 1961 and thought well of him were not wrong about the author, and they will find this book deeply satisfying.

# Small-Town America

## by Eugene Hilburn Methvin

America used to be a nation of small towns like Harold Clarke's beloved Forsyth, described so lovingly in this book. I share his reverence. Forty-three years have passed since I left the enfolding arms of my little hometown of Vienna, Georgia, to enter the University of Georgia in the fall of 1951. For the last thirty-five years, I have traveled America from coast to coast as a Washington-based roving editor for the *Reader's Digest*. Much of my reporting involves crime, law enforcement, and social welfare issues, and I've pounded the sidewalks of Boston, Brooklyn, Harlem, Newark, Philadelphia, Cleveland, Chicago, Seattle, Los Angeles, Houston, Dallas, St. Louis—and many more. But wherever I've been, I've used my hometown and county in Georgia as the measuring stick against which to gauge what I see.

Not long ago I was studying "Safe Streets, Inc.," an anti-drug, anti-crime campaign in Tacoma, Washington. "Safe Streets" focused on "the Hilltop," the inner ring of older housing and slums surrounding the Puget Sound port and downtown of this old West Coast industrial hub. A neighborhood organizer described their efforts to send forth graffiti "paint out" teams, stage block parties, set up telephone trees, mobilize churches, and take back the streets from the gangs and drug dealers. She said something that summed up much of urban America's problems today: *"Nobody's talking over the back fences anymore!"*

In Vienna, or Forsyth, half a century ago or today, such a concern would be unimaginable. A vivid measure of the Tacoma campaign's success—and of what America must learn to restore and preserve—is that a year after "Safe Streets" began introducing neighbors and starting them to "talking over the back fences" again, the Tacoma Police Department's 911 telephone load dropped 21 percent—28,000—in a year. Thus, a mother worried because her daughter had not returned from school reached for the phone to dial 911, but noticed her "Safe Streets telephone tree" chart and called her leader instead. In ten minutes they found the child playing in a yard a couple of blocks away, and didn't bother the police.

What is a small urban miracle in America today was once ordinary life in the Small Town USA that Harold Clarke writes about. America was once a nation of farmers and the small towns that served them, communities like Monroe County and its county seat, Forsyth. Most Americans lived in such places well into the lifetime of those of us now called "the older generation." The 1920 census was the first to count more than half of Americans living in "urban" places, which the Census Bureau defined as towns of 2,500 or more. That year, we became 51.4 percent "urban"—54,314,000 of us—while the other 51,396,000 of us stayed on the farms and in small towns like Forsyth. Georgia was even more rural than the rest of the nation: in 1920 only 727,859 of the 2,895,832 Georgians, one in four, lived in places of 2,500 or more.

We are now an urban nation, with more than half of the 258,000,000 of us living in metropolises of a million or more, and only 35,000,000 in small towns of 2,500 or rural areas. We are "a nation of strangers," fearful of runaway crime, choking in our rush-hour traffic jams, and stressed out by the ordeal of coping with our urban sprawl. Very few Americans today can understand or appreciate what small-town life was like.

That is why Harold Clarke's charming memoir of growing up in Forsyth is important. He depicts a true community, where "everybody knows everybody" and where people minded everybody's business, shared their cares and sorrows, and were there in times of need.

Forsyth in 1930 numbered 2,277 people, 1,315 of them white and 951 black. Monroe County counted 11,606, of whom 6,750—58 percent—were African-Americans. Such rural and small-town settings were the habit for most of mankind through most of recorded history. Railroads and the telegraph changed transportation and communication radically in the latter nineteenth century. But the horses and buggy or wagon were still the chief methods of transportation around town.

Not until 1925 was what was to become U.S. 41 paved inside the Forsyth city limits. This eighteen-foot-wide ribbon of concrete reached the Lamar County line, over toward Barnsville and Atlanta, in 1926, and in 1927—the year Harold was born—it stretched as far as Bolingbroke, about halfway to Macon. Mr. Henry Ford was selling his wonderful Model T for $750, and the Republicans were campaigning on a slogan of "a chicken in every pot, and two cars in every garage." By the decade's end, U.S. 41 connected Milwaukee and Chicago to Miami, and Forsyth and Vienna were bisected by "America's Main Street," which throbbed day and night with trucks and tourists and migrating people. Newfangled "motels" and "cozy cabins" began to spring up as Americans took to the highways. Somewhere along the way, we left community behind.

In 1960, Monroe County was down to 10,495 people, and the black population had dwindled to 48 percent—5,080. The postwar "Tractor Revolution" forced huge numbers of blacks—and whites too—out of the rural South and into distant cities such as Newark, Cleveland, Detroit, and Chicago. The 1960 census was the first to count more than half of the blacks in the United States outside the eleven former Confederate states.

Then Interstate 75 came roaring through, and by 1990 Monroe County had grown to 17,113. The African-American component had stabilized at 5,406 but now only 31.5 percent of the population. Forsyth itself grew to 4,168, still small enough that "everybody knew everybody." And Harold and Nora Clarke had the good sense to move back from Atlanta.

As I read this book, I chuckled to discover that Harold's older sister, who moved to my hometown in the early 1930s, lived first in the house where in 1934 I was born—on the kitchen table hardly 150 feet from U.S. 41. And when I came to Harold's description of his billy goat and cart, I had a startling flashback across more than half a century. I remember that goat! Once, when Harold came to visit his sister's family in Vienna, he brought the obstreperous critter with his cart along and created a sensation among "our gang" in the neighborhood.

Now that's community.

# North Lee Street

Not long ago, I stood on North Lee Street in Forsyth, Georgia, just across Johnston Street from the Confederate monument. Looking away from the courthouse square, I saw the signs on Interstate Highway 75 at the bottom of the hill some half mile to the north. Countless cars from countless places moved along the highway's eight lanes of concrete, most of them hurrying unnecessarily to reach unnecessary destinations to do unnecessary things. On North Lee Street itself, a steady stream of impatient drivers moved their cars in either direction along the busy avenue of commerce and trade.

As my eyes scanned Lee Street, its present character created a mood of movement, of enterprise . . . of business. Activity flowed nervously from the drug stores, financial institutions, offices, shopping centers, and congested strip of gas stations, motels, and fast-food spots.

Then my eyes fell upon a building sitting above North Lee Street two blocks from the courthouse. The old, but well-kept, frame structure with a Victorian appearance looked down on the newer masonry buildings as if to say, "You can't run me out of the neighborhood." Now an office building, this house began as a pioneer four-room dwelling in 1827. In the 1890s, its owners made additions and changed the house into what seemed modern for that day.

Now she stands looking like a stern old woman with a warm and loving inner spirit understood only by those who know and love her. I know and love this old lady on North Lee Street. I was born in one of her rooms and lived within her confines from then until love and marriage carried me to different surroundings. My continued gaze at the old house where I lived so long somehow erased from my view the hustle and bustle of today's North Lee Street.

So again I looked along the street, and this time through memory's eye. I saw things most people in Forsyth have never seen. I saw again the North Lee Street of the 1930s.

Both the pavement and the business life of the street ended one block north of the courthouse square. The last two businesses typified an earlier America. One of them was James Tribble's Stable with a blacksmith shop and the other was Oscar McCommon's Buggy and Wagon Shop, also containing a blacksmith shop. Past their shops the narrow, dirt street accommodated homes, except for the city hall near Mr. McCommon's place. You could not see to the bottom of the hill then. The limbs of the large oak trees lining the sides of the street reached for one another, sometimes intertwining their fingers over the street, forming a tunnel of greenery. My old house did not sit above North Lee Street then because the level of the street had not yet been graded down.

Little boys played baseball in the street without worrying about being run over, and families sat in rocking chairs or a swing on the front porches after supper. As that street has changed, so has the town changed and so have its people.

Then I realized that my children never knew the street or the town as it was back then. Even though they were all born Forsythians, the flavor and spirit of Forsyth of the 1930s rested long dead outside their knowledge or understanding. That is true unless . . . unless somebody recreates it for them in words. Why should not I be that somebody?

After all, they ought to know.

They ought to know that you could keep up with affairs of the community if you sat on your front porch often enough.

We knew when new construction was going on in town because the boardinghouse across the street would be busier than usual. We knew when a new picture show was showing in town because Gladys, the girl next door, was picked up by her boyfriend Lyle earlier than on other evenings. We knew when it was time for Wednesday night prayer meeting because we heard the church bell. We knew when there was a fire because we heard the fire whistle. The front porch sitters of that era observed the news of the community firsthand rather than by remote control.

They ought to know that during the dry periods of October the edge of the street would be littered with wuffs of white fiber clinging to the shrubbery and grass. This was not the result of careless littering. This was the spillage from the passing of wagons loaded high with fluffy cotton on its way to the gin.

I do not imply that this was a glorious time for cotton, or that it was still king. This is not true at all. The boll weevil had hit more than ten years earlier, and, as if this was not enough, the Depression had driven the price of cotton to the vicinity of five cents a pound.

Even before this, not many people had been what we would call rich or wealthy, but quite a few had earned the reputation of being "well off" or "comfortably situated." Many of those saw their wealth slip away from them. The more fortunate ones somehow maintained their dignity by assuming a state which Mama always called "genteel poverty."

Even without losing their gentility, many people felt the devastation resulting from the Great Depression. One fine lady of social eminence suddenly dropped out of sight. Her husband had lost everything, and, as Mama described it, the lady "took to the bed." For the rest of her life she remained a recluse—a casualty of the Depression.

A great exodus resulted. This exodus was a painful one which removed from the community many of its brightest young people as they sought greater opportunity in more sophisticated and cosmopolitan places. The exodus also removed those of few skills who had eked out a meager living by chopping and picking cotton or trying to maintain a tenant farm while living in the shabbiest of shanties. These were the blacks who left Middle Georgia for Detroit and Cleveland and other places seeking something better.

My children also ought to know that even as there were those who did not leave "the loveliest village of the plain" during the land buy-outs in Ireland, there were those who did not leave small town America during the ravishing years of the Depression. They stayed and lived a better life than seemed possible at the time.

My children ought to know about the children of the '30s. Born in the more optimistic 1920s, these citizens felt the molding influence of forceful times. The doubts and pessimism of the Depression-ridden 1930s gave them the capacity to tough-out hard times and instilled in them a belief that it could happen again.

Fear and excitement mingled together during the war of their teen years and early adulthood, setting them apart from most generations. Some never came back from World War II. Some came back wounded. All came back different. Most came back believing that any battle could be won. They came back looking not for normalcy but for a better life in a better world.

For the most part, they hit the ground of the postwar world running. They held an almost funny conviction that they had better get into the swirl quickly or the great new life would run off and leave them.

They possessed a strange mixture of the stoicism of their parents and the epicurean ways of the "Me Generation." They could not quite cast off the low expectations of earlier generations. Nor could they fully resist the "live for today" philosophy which later typified the Yuppies. Most of all they stand convinced that no generation has received blessings of experience compared to theirs. Accidents of history conspired to allow them to see firsthand some of the most fascinating of eras. All this shaped their lives.

My children ought to know what shaped me and my fellows and, by extension, what shaped our children.

If they ought to know these things, so should others of their generation. For that matter, those of my generation who do know these things ought to be reminded of them.

"It's a poor sort of memory that only works backwards."

The Queen in *Alice in Wonderland* said that, sounding wonderfully nonsensical. But it takes on a cloak of rationality if my backward-working memory can acquaint others with the experiences and human values of another time. Perhaps by doing that, some unknown reader may be better capable of coping with his or her own time. So I make the effort in the pages that follow to cause my backward memory to work forward.

Because they ought to know.

In the following pages, I make no effort to present a document with the technical accuracy of a seriously researched historical work. I aim at recapturing the feel and spirit of an earlier time by relating some events of that time as I remember them.

My memory could depart from accuracy at some point. That possibility, or even likelihood, does not distress me. After all, the significant effect of past events on the present often depends not so much on what really happened as on how it is remembered.

What you are about to read is simply the impressions of one who lived as a youngster in a small Georgia town in the years just before World War II.

I hope it gives you a better insight into that era. I also hope it gives you a chuckle or two, and maybe a little tear.

# CHAPTER 1

# Finding their Place

I do not know when Daddy felt the call to the ministry, but I suspect that he resisted it initially. Comments about his youth led me to think he tended toward the wilder life then. His youthful rambunctiousness and his later turn to spiritual devotion fit the pattern of the difference between his parents.

My grandfather, Lee Clarke, traveled the fast road, and my grandmother, Rosa Gravely, out-Calvined Calvin in her blue stocking lifestyle. After the birth of my father Jack Clarke and his two sisters, his mother took the girls and left Virginia for Clinton, South Carolina, where she taught at Thornwell Orphanage. Daddy stayed behind with his Gravely grandparents. After attending a military school, he joined his mother and sisters in Clinton and entered Presbyterian College and graduated valedictorian of his class in 1905.

Years later, he reflected on his youth, "I left those foothills of the Blue Ridge in my youth, but with the traditional love of a native of the Old Dominion, I always remember the tenderness 'the mountains clothed with mist, the sunset skies of amethyst and the groves of oak, sunkissed in Old Virginia.' "

The divine call came to Daddy with a substantial push from his mother. He entered Union Seminary in Richmond, Virginia. Recalling his three years of study there, Daddy later wrote:

On Sunday afternoons I exhorted before the unfortunates at the State Penitentiary. This brought about a decided decrease in crime in Virginia since it got noised abroad in the underworld that those who were convicted and sent to the pen would have to listen to the exhortations. Virginia at that time became noted also for the strict imposition of the death penalty. Perhaps with a view to give a lighter sentence than a series of Sunday services at the penitentiary.

While finishing his seminary education, tragedies befell Daddy quickly. His fourteen-year-old sister Sally died while he was still in Virginia. Then, during his last year in the seminary, his mother's health began to fade. She wrote him a heartrending letter hinting strongly that she was dying. She stated her love for and pride in him and suggested the care that he should provide for his other sister, Julia. She asked to be buried in Clinton rather than Virginia so little Sally would not be left alone in her grave in South Carolina.

Shortly afterwards, five months before Daddy's graduation, his mother died. After Daddy's death, I found the letter from his mother. At the bottom he had written, "She hath done what she could."

Not long after his mother's death, young Julia died. She was only twenty-one years old. So in his twenties, Daddy found himself alone, looking for a life to live and service to render.

Despite the melancholy of the time, an event portending years of joy occurred unbeknownst to either of the principals involved. Mama lived in Lafayette, Georgia, where her father, Hugh Lumpkin, practiced law, but she had cousins in Richmond. During the June of her seventeenth year she visited them. Someone suggested that they attend the Union Seminary commencement exercises, and they did. Without either of them knowing it, two people who would marry three years later and spend fifty-six years sharing joys and sorrows, successes and failures, shared their first joy together.

The handsome young man that Mama had seen graduate from Union came to her hometown in a few weeks as pastor of the Presbyterian church. Mama soon left to go back to school at Brenau College in Gainesville, but, three years later, they married.

Their marriage followed a fairly usual courtship but an unusually romantic proposal. The young couple attended a party together where Daddy slipped a little piece of paper in Mama's hand. He had borrowed the words of Robert Browning:

Grow old along with me!
The best is yet to be,
The last of life, for which the first was made.

Mama understood the intent. She wrote back: "I accept your proposal."

After living in Lafayette for nearly two years, restlessness and a need for academic fulfillment pulled Daddy away. This time a fellowship for graduate work at Johns Hopkins University sent them and their baby girl to Baltimore. For two years, they lived in Baltimore with some of the summers spent in the little town of New Market, Maryland. During that time, Mama looked after Rosa Emiline and gave birth to Jack Jr. Daddy studied, and also preached when he could.

About graduate school, Daddy recorded:

Here I majored in Philosophy and thereby hit upon the hardest course in captivity. I was the first to receive a graduate degree in Philosophy there in sixteen years thereby denoting a softening of the brain or heart on the part of some of the faculty. I found a higher institution of learning a most efficient means of dispelling conceit and convincing one that nearly everybody knows more than he does. After tying bow knots in my cerebral convolutions for a couple of years, I turned from the abstract to more practical phases of life.

Daddy sometimes demonstrated his impatience with academic stuffed shirts in quiz answers. One test instructed, "Discuss some of the societal similarities between humans and ants."

"To begin with," Daddy answered, "they go to picnics together."

The fact that the rest of the answer was scholarly failed to impress the professor. Maybe anthropologists don't go to picnics.

Memories of his preaching in Maryland sometimes evoked smiles and laughter—which can follow moments of gravest embarrassment. Daddy went by train to a small town to preach one Sunday. His trouble started with the lateness of the train and continued with poor directions to the church. Rushing in the church, Daddy saw a man sitting in one of the three chairs behind the pulpit. Thinking the man was an elder waiting to introduce him, Daddy hurried down the aisle and sat in one of the other chairs. He bowed his head both to utter a prayer and catch his breath, then looking up he saw the other man peering down at him.

"Can I help you?" came the question.

"I'm Jack Clarke, here to preach for you Presbyterians today."

"I'm afraid this is the Methodist church," the man smiled curiously, "but we would be happy to hear your sermon."

Daddy thanked him, declined, and finally found the Presbyterian flock waiting in need of spiritual exhortation. He gave it to them albeit not without the kind of distraction which follows humiliation.


Mama and Daddy finally made their way back to Georgia. He taught German, English, and history at Tech High in Atlanta for a time. The great golfer Bobby Jones was one of his students. Daddy always had nice things to say about Mr. Jones, but he did not say much nice about the business of teaching.

"I hardly know which got the worse of it," he wrote later, "I or the school. I did not have enough experience or police qualifications for the task and have since turned to less exacting channels of toil."

The less exacting toil which he picked was the ownership and editing of a country newspaper. This brought Mama and Daddy to Forsyth. With them came another daughter, Rachel, who had been born in Atlanta. The spring of 1917 not only began America's involvement in World War I, it began the Clarke family's involvement with that little Middle Georgia paradise, Forsyth.

## CHAPTER 2
# The Wonderland

Forsyth's courthouse square and the business section around it was a wonderland in the time of my youth. Though we had no Mad Hatter or March Hare, Alice might have found some characters to attract her wonder.

Lifelong familiarity tends to veil the sharpness of unusual images. For this reason, I failed to understand all the fascinating characteristics of Forsyth's folks and even missed for many years the significance of the name of the streets bounding the public square. Almost every town has a Main Street, but the other streets bear names reserved for Southern towns: Lee Street, Johnston Street, and Jackson Street, as in Robert E., Joseph E., and Stonewall.

Let us turn now to the happenings and people around town. My sister Rachel's boyfriends gave her funny presents sometimes, and I mean "funny" like strange, not "ha ha" funny. One boyfriend gave her a real greyhound, and another one gave her a stuffed raccoon. Now this was not one of those stuffed animals made of fuzzy fabric and filled with cotton or foam rubber. This was a real raccoon that he had stuffed in the taxidermy class. After thanking the boy graciously for the gift, Baby (that is what we called Rachel) came home almost stomping as she walked.

"This is ridiculous, disgusting. Why would he think I want something like this?"

As she flung it on the seat of the big coatrack next to the telephone in the hall, I jumped at the chance to gain ownership.

"Can I have it?"

"With my blessings," Baby sneered, tripping up the stairs.

Delighted at the prospect of fun with the raccoon, I ran into the backyard, my head fairly swimming with ideas of what to do with the deceased, but preserved, animal. Before I could set out on an errand of mischief, Mama called on me for one of constructiveness.

"Harold, run up to Penny Profit and get a loaf of light bread."

The Pippin family operated the Penny Profit store on Johnston Street two and a half blocks from our house. It occupied two adjacent buildings connected by an opening in the wall about halfway back. They sold groceries on one side of the opening and furniture on the other.

Like the other grocery stores in Forsyth, Penny Profit delivered in response to phone calls and gave credit when the customer said simply, "Charge it." Mama did not call for the loaf of bread because she hated to trouble them for one item, and I could go after it quicker.

When I walked in the store the usual staff (all Pippins) moved around doing the usual things. Mr. Joe Frank sat with his coffee by the potbellied stove. Frank Jr. (called Baby by his sisters) stood behind the meat counter. Doris dusted the canned goods with a feather duster while Minnette talked to a customer and Maude sat on a stool by the cash register.

"What can I get for you, honey . . ." Doris began when I entered the store, but she stopped short of her usual greeting when she saw the raccoon under my arm.

Her voice fell to a whisper as she pulled me over to the corner.

"Let me have that for a minute."

Without being noticed by Frank, she took the raccoon and tip-toed to the counter under which they kept the brown paper sacks. There she put the raccoon. She walked over to the bread rack and called to Frank.

"Baby, get me a sack for Harold."

Nonchalantly, Frank walked over and reached under the counter. His hand touched not a sack but a strange furry thing. At the same time his eyes met those of the raccoon. With something between a howl and a screech, Frank leaped almost flat-footed over the counter. The sisters, the father, and the customers doubled over with laughter.

"Lawdy, I liked to jumped outta my skin," Frank panted, leaning breathless against the wall.

After regaining his composure and good nature, he looked at me and Doris with a twinkle in his eyes.

"I'm a good mind to jerk a knot in both of you."

As I took my bread and started home, my thoughts centered around how the raccoon offered a chance for lots of fun around the square in Forsyth playing tricks on the folks who worked at those businesses.

A few doors up Johnston Street from Penny Profit and across from the courthouse sat the building which housed Bramblett Hardware since 1873. Through the years this business gained a position of prominence in the economic and political and civic life of the town. Its owners nurtured that standing by drawing opinions from the populace and dispensing advice. Mr. Walter Bramblett excelled in testing attitudes.

In the late thirties, Mr. Bramblett talked to a farmer who had survived the Depression.

"Thinking back," Mr. Bramblett queried, "how did the Depression affect you?"

"Those times were hell," the gnarled fellow said, "I might near perished to death, and I did a little of everything to keep body and soul together." Then, about to walk out, he turned around. "I even went to preaching one time," and then sort of as an afterthought he continued. "I'll tell you something else, Walter. I ain't none too good to do it again if times get hard enough."

Having confessed his misspent past, he left. A few years before that, another Depression sufferer engaged Mr. Walter in a conversation at the store. This fellow had become convinced that Huey Long had the right idea with his share-the-wealth program.

"When the Kingfish gets to be president," the visitor said, "I'm gonna share my wealth with Hugh Hardin."

Knowing that Mr. Hardin was Forsyth's richest man, and understanding the fallacy of the visitor's reasoning, Mr. Bramblett had another suggestion.

"Maybe Huey would decide he would rather you share your wealth with Rufus Davis."

"No siree. Rufus is as lazy as a hound dog in July and ain't got nothing to share," said the man, whom Mr. Bramblett had reconverted to capitalism after his flirtation with cajun-flavored socialism.

Next to Bramblett's, Mr. Charner Hill ran Monroe County Bank. A gentleman, with gentle ways, Mr. Hill found the hard truth that bankers often do a prospective customer the best favor by just saying, "No." Not all folks, however, appreciate the favors that you do them. Demonstrating such ingratitude, an old man came out of the bank door mumbling.

"What's wrong?" asked another man, moving in the other direction.

"Damn a bank that won't bank," answered the first.

Mr. Hill understood what most unsuccessful loan applicants miss. "Making a loan the lender can't pay is no favor and declining such a loan is no disservice."

Next to Monroe County Bank, Forsyth Mercantile Company looked to me like the picture of permanence and stability, but it is gone now. For more than sixty years, it prospered, and for much of that time it had a men's department, a women's department, and a grocery department with some tools for sale. Mr. Ed Rudisill ran the men's department. Mr. Beeler Urban Rumble ran the women's department, and his son Mallory (known as Bubba) ran the grocery store.

The dry goods store was all in one building with the groceries next door, but again an opening in the wall connected them. The wall opening held the telephone for the whole store, and sometimes the phone worked well. Sometimes not so well.

The eccentric telephone particularly irritated Mr. Rudisill and caused him to stomp and stammer. One day it went totally bad. At first he could not get the central (operator) no matter how much he turned the crank. When he finally got her, she connected him with three straight wrong numbers. That did it.

This time Mr. Rudisill did not stomp and did not stammer. He calmly went over the rack holding the axes and removed one. With one sweeping blow, he chopped the errant phone from the wall.

Mr. Rudisill proved he was not out of control, though. After destroying the telephone, he went out the door and whistled softly for his big German shepherd, Prince, which always followed him, and went home for his midday dinner.

Mr. Beeler Rumble became a legend too. Although he succeeded in business handsomely, he never owned or even wanted an automobile— thus showing a wisdom signally absent today. His salesmanship relied more upon persistence than tact. A lady looking for galoshes tried on the pair that he brought her.

"These are too little," she complained.

Without any change of facial expression or voice inflection, he answered her, "They're not too little. Your feet are too big."

Toward the late '30s, they closed the Mercantile Grocery Store and a bowling alley operated there for awhile. Then it became a restaurant called the Dine-A-Mite and next a movie theater. Finally, the roof was removed and an open-air cabaret and bar opened. I wonder if the ghosts of the Rumbles and Mr. Rudisill and his handsome dog tap their feet to the music played by Buck Wilder and his band called Fox City. (Buck is related to the Rumbles.)

On the corner, Mr. Ashley Phinazee had City Drug Store, a hangout for young folks. The slow-moving and slow-talking Mr. Ashley looked for the world like the movie actor Edward Everett Horton and sometimes acted even funnier in a low-key way. He masterfully made himself the butt of his own jokes.

After Congress passed the Social Security Act, Mr. Ashley's barber friend, Jim Weldon, dropped by the drug store. No man in Monroe County moved more slowly than these two.

"You fixin' to go over to the courthouse to sign up for your old age pension, Ashley," drawled Jim.

"No-o-o-o," replied Mr. Ashley in a syrup-like voice, "I'm not that old yet."

"You're liable to be by the time you get across the street to the courthouse," explained Jim.

Jim doubled as coroner for the county and of his service he liked to boast, "I've got the best record of any judge this county ever had. Never been reversed. When I say they're dead, they're dead."

Dr. Cullen Goolsby owned the drug store building and had his office behind City Drug Store. But because of his old age and near retirement, he spent most of his time in the drug store visiting with customers. He liked to tell us youngsters about his youth in adjoining Jasper County.

"Bloody Jasper, we called it," he always told us. "When I lived there, I wore my pistol as regular as I wore my hat whenever I left my district." Dr. Goolsby played checkers expertly and played the fiddle not so expertly. But he played them both in the drug store, checkers more often than the fiddle. What he liked most was sitting and talking to his old friend, Major Tom Boulware, the grandfather of my friend Barrett Sutton. The old men understood each other, and I wish that I had listened more to their conversations. I appreciated Dr. Goolsby for another reason. Mama and Daddy suffered through the flu in 1918, and he pretty near saved their lives.

Across Jackson Street, Alexander's Pharmacy sold Rexall products. Two bus lines served Forsyth then, but we had no bus station. So the Greyhound busses stopped at Alexander's, and the Colonial busses stopped at City Drug. Sometimes the drivers became mixed up, and the competitive spirit of the drug store exploded. I have heard that at least one time Dr. Goolsby used his pistol to chase off a Greyhound bus which stopped erroneously at City Drug.

Forest Alexander dispatched busses, recorded community events with his camera, and ran Alexander Pharmacy. He also commented quickly on all events, penetrating the issue with often caustic words. I heard him talk about one man having his heart on his left hip and another being self-estimated. He described one fellow as being born in the objective case. He told me that hate destroys people and explained that no person has a greater chance to set the tone of a community than a superior court judge. He hit the target on all of these issues.

He liked to tell about the customer who called about four o'clock one morning.

"Did I wake you up?" the customer asked.

"No," snapped Forest, with a sleepy voice, "I was just sitting here waiting for you to call."

The Alexanders employed a man called Deefy. His family named him Willie Jossey at birth, but few people in Forsyth ever knew that. Born deaf, Deefy never learned to hear or talk. However, he did attend school and learned sign language and a little writing. He gave a comic appearance always wearing a porkpie hat with the brim turned up all the way around, and his knee-high rubber boots emphasized his Charlie Chaplinlike slew feet. His silent movie comedy looks only thinly disguised the brightness of his mind and the friendliness of his spirit. The omnipresent black man seemed never to sleep and to know everything that happened in town. If you learned to understand his pantomime gestures, you could learn a lot about the community.

I learned enough to know that when he waved me down, held up three fingers, moved his hands to form the shape of an hourglass and pointed toward City Drug Store, that meant three girls were over at Mr. Ashley's.

The Farmer's Bank stood at the other corner of Jackson and Johnston Streets, and Mr. Bob Persons was the Farmer's Bank. Small in stature but mighty big in assertiveness, he never hesitated to take a stand. He gained national fame by standing up to Franklin D. Roosevelt when the president ordered a bank holiday to relieve runs on deposits. Mr. Bob said, "No." Refusing to close his bank, he invited depositors to come by and get their money if they wanted it. Few, if any, came.

Some years later, my friend Banks Worsham and I walked toward the Farmer's Bank where Mr. Bob sat on a sort of curb between the bank and the sidewalk. Motioning us toward him, he asked a question.

"What you boys plan to do when you finish school?"

"I want to be a lawyer," I told him.

"That's all right. My brother Ogden and I practiced law for a long time and had lots of fun until I decided time had come to start making some money."

That statement gained Banks's attention.

"That's what I want to do, Mr. Bob. How you go about making money?"

Mr. Bob sprang to his feet and arms waving said, "You just got to git out and git it." That may have constituted the best lesson in personal economics that I have ever heard.

"Forsyth's best store"—that slogan always appeared after the tradename E. W. Banks Company, the dry goods store on Jackson Street next to the Farmer's Bank. The store carried the name of Elbert Banks who moved in from the country as a young man to work for Mr. Luntz in his store, later becoming a partner and, at the death of Mr. Luntz, the owner.

People liked to call the merchant Mr. Baptist as well as Mr. Elbert, and he developed a reputation as the unofficial welcomer of all newcomers to town. This accrued to the benefit of both his store and his church.

Among the clerks, one stood out in my childhood memory. Lyle Hollis had worked at the Mercantile and even became police chief for awhile, but settled in at E. W. Banks Company. He seldom walked when he could run, and he seldom spoke normally when he could utter words with a combination of speech, laughter, and song. He also learned to walk great distances on his hands. As a little boy, I always wanted Lyle to wait on me when we went to the store.

The Hardin offices on Jackson Street housed a myriad of activities. Mr. Hugh Hardin's business fingers reached into everything from the oil business to textiles, banking, lumber, and who knows what else. He impressed me with his unshakable coolness.

During the '30s, the dozen or so drivers for Mr. Hardin's trucks decided to unite their demand for a pay raise. They designated a driver named George as the spokesman. They lined up in front of Mr. Hugh's desk waiting for the spokesman to speak. After a time of uneasy quiet, George spit out the words.

"We want a raise or else."

More silence while Mr. Hugh looked into each eye individually.

"Or else what?" the boss asked.

More silence.

"Or else we'll just keep on driving for the same ole pay," answered George.

The drivers filed out of the office with more silence.

In contrast to the orderly operation on the ground floor of Mr. Hardin's building, was the little telephone exchange upstairs. Every call, whether local or long distance, went through Miss Mary Hough or Miss Mabel Alexander who acted as centrals, not operators. If Deefy knew most things happening in Forsyth, these two women knew everything.

As my sister talked to one of her friends by telephone, she suggested that they contact another friend, Lela, about some plans for that night. Suddenly a voice broke in.

"Lela can't go. She just accepted a date with Joe."

Most anybody could remember the telephone numbers. The number at Daddy's office was 9, and our number at home was 9OJ.

A. Bloom Department Store held a special place for me because that is where I bought my farmer-like straw hat every summer, and it is difficult to realize what an important event that was to me back then. Besides that, Mr. Bloom's son, David, worked there. David was my Boy Scoutmaster and set the kind of example boys in any generation need.

Mr. Bloom came to Forsyth about two years before Mama and Daddy and opened a ten-cent store. He built this into a department store.

Beyond Bloom's on Jackson Street was Banks and Hill Grocery Store which served the local carriage trade.

On the corner of Main and Jackson, Charlie Antonio ran the only restaurant in town with a hotel on the second floor. Today Forsyth boasts two Chinese restaurants, a Mexican restaurant, a pizza place, and a taco stand together with a great number of other eating places, but we have no Greek restaurant. Charlie Antonio came from Greece, so I guess we had a Greek restaurant in the thirties—but not really. The food at the Royal Palm Cafe fit the taste of Middle Georgia folk rather than those of Athens, Greece. They cooked the vegetables well done with a heavy amount of pork fat meat. All the meat had gravy.

During the mid-thirties, Charlie Aycock opened a Plymouth-DeSoto dealership. A daring businessman and sportsman, he came to Forsyth boasting that he brought with him five dollars and the best looking red-headed wife in Georgia. I do not know about the five dollars, but Nell Aycock certainly fit the description he gave her.

Charlie excited local young men by hiring them to go to Detroit to drive new cars to Forsyth. This kind of cosmopolitan experience came rarely back then.

At the Main and Lee Streets corner, Mr. Lee McGee operated Forsyth's other hardware store. For some period of time, Mr. Hugh Worsham had a connection with that business. He built some houses, but business was slow in the 1930s. Later he left Georgia Hardware entirely to engage in a successful lumber business. I never really understood the association of Mr. McGee and Mr. Worsham because of the stark contrast in their personalities and business styles.

Mr. McGee epitomized quiet conservatism in everything he did. On the other hand, Mr. Worsham, who was known to his friends as Pink and to his son Banks's friends as Mr. Pink, moved constantly with a flare for action. Where Mr. McGee was quiet, Mr. Pink was outspoken. Where Mr. McGee preferred caution in all things, Mr. Pink loved to take a risk.

"If you don't take a chance every now and then," Mr. Pink used to say, "You're liable to end up wearing a linen duster at Christmas time."

To the uninitiated, linen dusters fit neither weather nor fashion of the Christmas season.

Across Lee Street, Mr. A. L. Willingham sold Chevrolets. Perhaps his most unusual sale was to Julia Simmons. Aunt Simmons gained fame as the local fortune teller and spiritualist. The mention of her name scared me and my friends; we were convinced that she might turn us into a frog or something.

When she bought a truck, she brought a fertilizer sack full of loose change to pay for it. For many years, a picture hung at Willingham's Garage showing the money piled high on a table and being counted by the people who worked there.

Beyond Willingham's, the Ford place furnished competition. L. C. Bittick owned and ran it while doubling as county sheriff. His ability to carry out both duties testifies to the law-abiding character of the county and the competence of Mr. Bittick, I suppose.

Mr. Jim Roquemore did well across the street with a small grocery store. One statement may explain that. Somebody warned Mr. Jim about giving credit to a local resident, saying, "He won't pay anybody."

"No," said Mr. Jim, "Everybody pays somebody. I just make sure I'm the one who gets paid."

Lee Street had two barber shops, John Bland's and John Dorner's. Mr. Dorner came from Austria and said he settled in Forsyth by mistake. Speaking and understanding little English, at the time, the young man got off the train in Forsyth thinking it was Macon. He liked Forsyth, and it liked him so he stayed for the rest of his days. I counted his children as my very good friends.

Jep Castleberry's drug store also faced Lee Street. Along with his son, Edgar, Mr. Jep had a knack for training wild animals. They had raccoons, monkeys, and others. He even had a squirrel in his yard which ran out to greet him every time he came home, partly because he liked Mr. Jep, but mostly because Mr. Jep usually brought him an ice cream cone.

When Mr. Jep came home late, the squirrel got restless. So much so that he raced out to meet his benefactor leaping onto his lower leg and climbing up Mr. Jep's body following a circular course. So fast and so many times the animal circled the druggist that he turned Mr. Jep's pants completely around. So he walked in his house wearing his pants hind part before.

The Citizens Bank of Forsyth sat at the corner of Lee and Johnston Streets. Mr. Hugh Hardin was its president, but John Stephens presided as the full-time executive vice president. An affable fellow, Mr. John enjoyed an occasional mild dissipation while his wife, Miss Pete, would have grandly qualified to head anybody's temperance organization.

Because of this conflict of interest, Mr. John looked forward to his fishing trips like the discovery of the treasure at the end of the rainbow.

"The only thing wrong with a fishing trip," Mr. John commented, "is that some fool may want to fish."

Mama met with Miss Pete and several other ladies for their regular Coca-Cola session at Alexander's one morning while Mr. John and some of his friends were in Florida on a fishing trip.

"I heard from John this morning," said Miss Pete, displaying a colorful postcard, "He says, 'I'm visiting regularly with my good friend Jack Daniels.' "

Miss Pete smiled broadly and concluded, "Some old fishing friend of his no doubt."


Louis Joseph came from Lebanon to settle in Forsyth where he started a clothing store and raised his family. Custom called for a big blackboard to be placed in front of Mr. Ed Williams's pool hall on election nights and huge crowds gathered to watch the posting of the returns and argue about politics. Sometimes alcohol intensified the arguments, and fights ensued. During one such fight a shirt was torn off. Mr. Joseph ran from his store giving the bare-backed fighter a new shirt. When word got around, shirt-tearing spread up and down the street. After giving away more shirts than he should, Mr. Joseph caught on and ended his generosity.

Then the courthouse clock began striking . . . and it kept on striking. Thirteen strikes.

"I gotta go home," mumbled one of the imbibers, "it's later than it ever has been."

Election nights were not the only times stores stayed open late. It happened every Saturday when people just hung around. Some bought things, but others just talked or looked at haircuts. The later the night became, the cheaper the price became on some items. During a criminal trial for an offense committed on a Saturday night, the prosecutor asked a witness what time the event happened.

"About two minutes after nine," responded the witness.

"How can you be so exact?"

"Because Mr. Pippin had just marked the popeyed mullet down to a nickel a bunch, and that always happens at nine o'clock."

I heard that story as a Forsyth occurrence all my life. Later I read a similar yarn in Judge Arthur Powell's book, *I Can Go Home Again*. This may be apocryphal as to most small Southern towns.

That brings to mind Judge Ponder Carson. He held the office of Justice of the Peace and sometimes practiced a little law. He wore a funny-looking goatee and a fedora hat with the crown standing high and uncreased and the brim turned up all the way around. In other words, he wore it just as it came off the shelf. He also carried a cane. He found great pleasure in catching little boys by the neck with the crook of his cane and thumping them on the head. It hurt. So I avoided him.

After I complained at home about the judge's antics, Daddy tried to pass it off saying, "Well, it's just his way."

"Maybe so," Mama said, "But it's a mighty poor way."

During a court week, the superior court judge asked a poor man accused of a crime, "Do you have a lawyer?"

"No, sir."

"Do you have any money to hire a lawyer?"

"No, sir."

"Well," said the Judge, pointing at the Justice of the Peace, "go over and talk to Judge Carson. He'll defend you."

The prisoner looked at the funny-looking man for awhile and turned to the judge on the bench.

"If it's all the same with you, Your Honor, I'd just as soon plead guilty," said the defendant, resigned to his fate.

Indeed all these people and others turned the square into a wonderland. And, as years go by, memory causes that wonderland, like Alice's, to become "curiouser and curiouser!"

## CHAPTER 3
# The Memory Search

I tried to identify my earliest recollections and totally failed. Then I tried to identify my earliest recollection of a crisis and succeeded. The days of my very beginnings saw two crises of enormous dimensions. One personal to our family and the other affecting all of society. But I do not remember the first and did not understand the second.

The first family crisis came about six weeks after my birth. My two-year-old sister died of pneumonia. Although I do not recall the event, its effect on my family also affected me. My father had a complex personality. He was perhaps the most scholarly person I ever knew and at the same time one of the most unassuming. He was among the wittiest persons I ever knew and at the same time one of the most private. He was a person with deep-seated emotional feelings and at the same time one who was singularly undemonstrative. As an example, I only remember him hugging me one time. That happened when I came home from the Army, and I was twenty years old.

His parents separated during his childhood, so he lived with grandparents and attended military school while his mother taught in another state. This undoubtedly contributed to his paradoxical nature, as did the death of his mother and only two sisters just as he was reaching adulthood. I believe that the death of my sister Essie Black left an even deeper mark. I suspect that I never knew the Jack Clarke of an earlier time and that much of his reserve during my lifetime flowed from this sad experience.

If Daddy responded to Essie Black's death with an armor of reserve, Mama did the opposite. She immersed herself in outgoing activism, a big part of which was directed toward me. According to my theory, she turned to her surviving infant with all the attention both children would have received. I became the object of a double dose of affection, protection, praise (most often undeserved), and encouragement. Despite the loss of her youngest daughter at two, her oldest daughter at thirty-five, and several other tragedies, she remained an incurable optimist. She repeatedly quoted the scripture passage: "All things work together for good to them that love God," and she truly believed it. So I did feel the effects of the loss of my sister, but I do not remember when it came about.

I often speculated privately on what it would have been like to have a sibling near my age. Even though I had two sisters and a brother, years separated many of our interests. My eldest sister, Rosa Emiline, was fifteen years my senior. My brother, Jack Jr. (Bubba to me), was thirteen years old at my birth, and my other sister, Rachel (Baby), was eleven years older than me. Bubba and I never had close ties in my childhood because he was away most of the time.

Bubba's escapades grabbed wide notice early. During his first high school year, a new and different teacher came to Forsyth to teach Bubba and his classmates. The teacher's difference lay not only in his gender (male), but also in his picky ways and small stature. The picky ways irritated Bubba and his friends, and their irritation eventually led to action. After hearing a shrill rebuke from the "Professor," Sumpter Boatwright and Tyson Brown joined Bubba in going after him. While the rest of the class looked on amazed, the rebellious trio grabbed the little teacher. They sat him firmly on the steaming radiator under the window. As the boys held the teacher in the hot seat with his stubby legs dangling short of the floor, he bellowed more from indignation than from pain. The class answered with cheers.

The commotion sent a signal to the principal. The principal sent a signal to the three "bad boys." As a result, Bubba and Tyson Brown finished their high school careers at Georgia Military College in Milledgeville, and Sumpter went to Gordon Military College in Barnesville.

The teacher moved on too. He went to Atlanta where he became a lawyer and perpetual political candidate. Some still remember him as the man who ran often but not well—Wyman C. Lowe.

The stock market crash and the onset of the Depression came when I was two. The market escaped the attention of a small child, but I remember enough of the Depression to know that unemployment and suffering ranged far and wide and that risk faced us all. Even so I cannot claim it as a personal crisis in my own life.

The first real personal crisis that I recall took place when I was four years old. That is when my oldest sister got married and left home when she was barely nineteen. She had been away before having spent a year at Agnes Scott College in Decatur, but that lacked permanency. Marriage seemed to me like forever.

I did not like the prospective husband. This started I think when I was invited to go to ride with him and my sister, Rosa Emiline, in Bill's roadster. The initial thrill was all right because for the first time I was riding in a rumble seat, which sounds sort of exciting even today. But the thrill turned into a mixture of fear and anger when Bill decided that they wanted some privacy and accomplished it by closing the cover of the rumble seat while I was still in it. So our relationship began on a bad foot. He was also a Georgia Tech graduate which, even at my tender age of four, I did not view as a positive characteristic.

My feelings about my brother-in-law never improved much. The next step backwards occurred after the marriage when I rode with him from Forsyth to Sparta where they lived for a time. I apparently misbehaved in a fashion befitting a spoiled brat just as we were about to reach the town of Milledgeville. The reform school for juvenile delinquents was located in that area, so Bill pulled off the side of the road. He turned to me in the back seat and without a smile said, "If you are gonna act that way, I'll just drop you off at the reform school." The fright of being closed up in a rumble seat was small potatoes compared to the thought of being put in that prison. This was strike two in the relationship between Bill and me.

Strike three took place when Rosa Emiline and Bill came to visit us not long afterwards. I looked forward to my sister's visit, but that pleasant prospect was overshadowed by Bill's coming. Past experience convinced me that he intended to carry me to the reform school, and I did not intend to go. To avoid this fate, I tried to think up a way to run him off just as quickly as he arrived.

I hid in the coal house, awaiting his arrival. At first my plan worked pretty well. My sister came through the backyard alone and into the house. Then Bill came through the gate carrying a couple of suitcases. I charged out of the coal house and, with all my might, threw the ax at Bill. Because of my lack of strength and aim, my intended assault and battery was only an assault. But I did not wait around to see. I ran as hard as I could to my Aunt Rachel Wyly's house where I confessed my misdeed. Just what sort of punishment I received I do not remember. But I do recall Bill mumbling something to the effect that he should have left me at the reform school when he had a chance.

But to return to the wedding. I was against it because Rosa Emiline, whom I called Sister, held a special place with me. Every afternoon she read to me the Uncle Wiggly story from the newspaper. While it was not so terribly important, it seemed so at the time. I think though it was more symbolic of our overall relationship with her being the oldest of five children and me being the youngest with the age span ranging from nineteen to four.

The closer the wedding day came the more upset I became, and Mama and Daddy noticed. To keep me pacified, they bought me my very first baseball glove, and Daddy explained how I might be the next Carl Hubble. Hubble was the star pitcher for the New York Giants.

When the day of the wedding came, excitement ran through the house, and I was caught up in it. Sister looked beautiful and even Bill did not look too bad. Daddy performed the wedding ceremony, Mama cried, and I showed my Southern heritage by asking for some grits to throw at the bride and groom. I did not understand all of the laughter from the others as they threw their rice.

I think the wedding took place about noon and when late afternoon rolled around, it all hit me. It is Uncle Wiggly time, and Sister is not here. About that time, my other sister, Baby, came in with the newspaper. She offered to read Uncle Wiggly, and I hurt her feelings by saying no.

If Sister could not read to me, I did not want to be read to. I just wanted to cry and be left alone. Supper time came and went, and the sadness grew as bedtime approached. Mama tucked me in bed and sat there while I said my prayers. She kissed me on the cheek and left me lying there holding my new baseball glove. I tried to think about Carl

Hubble and the Giants, but all I could think about was Sister and Uncle Wiggly. So I pushed the baseball glove on the floor, sobbed twice, then once more, wiped my tears on the pillowcase and . . . went to sleep.

# CHAPTER 4
# Another Pulpit for Daddy

When Mama and Daddy stepped off the train in Forsyth in 1917, they set foot on the soil of the last hometown they ever knew. Daddy lived there for the last fifty years of his life, and Mama spent her last fifty-four years there.

My folks arrived in Forsyth just ahead of the boll weevil and before the politicians carved off much of the best farm land in Monroe County to make a part of Lamar County. By the standards of the time, Monroe County and its seat, Forsyth, were prosperous—their prosperity based almost entirely on the cotton economy.

The county produced 40,000 bales of cotton a year. In those days cotton ginners and warehousemen held leadership places in the business of the town. Cotton warehouse receipts counted as the most important collateral for bank loans. Nobody dreamed that cotton prices would drop to five cents a pound by the early thirties. Certainly nobody had the nightmare that a little bug was marching from Mexico hell-bent on destroying much of the cotton before picking time every year. Even with World War I going on, in 1917, Forsyth was well satisfied with its lot.

The town looked good for other reasons. Its tree-lined dirt streets flanked by handsome well-kept houses—some antebellum but the newer ones also—told the passersby that the owners "did well" and showed that fact proudly. The town treasured cultural things too, partly because of Bessie Tift College, partly because of the nature of the people.

In addition to these assets, Forsyth stationed its churches as center-pieces of the community. In the 1820s a little group of Presbyterians formed a church in Forsyth. Suffering through ups and downs resulting from everything from the Civil War to economic panics (as they called Depressions in those days), they survived. By 1917, the Presbyterians had moved their picturesque little two-steepled church to the corner of Jackson and Adams Streets, a block north of the courthouse and just behind the city hall. The few members of the church descended mainly from its pioneer beginnings. Names like Anderson, Sneed, and Gamble appeared on the earliest records and remained on the church roles through the generations.

Daddy looked forward to working as the county editor and as a devoted church member. Pastoral service was not part of his plan. But just as he faced the call to the ministry more than ten years earlier, he faced the call of this little church a year or two after coming to Forsyth. They needed a preacher, and his resistance to spiritual demand collapsed again. He became pastor of the Forsyth Presbyterian Church; he considered it a temporary arrangement. More than thirty years later, he finally retired from the pulpit.

Daddy served the smallest of the three main pastorates in Forsyth, much the smallest. The Presbyterians held services only two Sundays a month, and Daddy's living came from the newspaper. Nevertheless he played a major role in church life in Forsyth.

The Baptist and Methodist churches dominated the town, and in this very fact lay the foundation for disagreements between the preachers. Occasionally, there was the need for almost invisible mediation. Daddy met that need because his small church posed no threat to the others and because he had developed seniority in the clerical community.

Pastoral duties of visiting and counseling did not appeal to Daddy, and he did not perform them well. He solved this by not visiting and doing little counseling. But what he lacked in those areas, he tried to make up for with good preaching. He had a gift for conveying profound thoughts in simple words in a brief time. His voice was not powerful, but he disliked histrionics anyway. With remarks of subtle humor scattered through the sermon, he finished church by 11:45—a much appreciated achievement.

Living in the home of a preacher presented interesting happenings for a young boy. Couples would come by unexpectedly wanting to get married. Daddy usually accommodated by ushering them into the parlor where Mama dutifully played "Oh Promise Me" on the piano and Daddy solemnized the vows.

I thought all this wonderfully fascinating and watched by peeping through the French doors separating the library from the parlor. Some of the ceremonies did not follow the usual routine. In fact, one of them did not take place in the parlor at all. Somebody knocked at the front door one Saturday night, and Mama answered.

"Can I see the preacher, please ma'am?"

"Certainly," Mama replied courteously.

"What can I do for you?" Daddy said, as he walked up the hall from the bedroom.

"Me and my sweetheart want to get married, if you can do it for us, Preacher."

"I'll be happy to do that, Jim," Daddy said, obviously knowing the young man.

"Well, there's just one little troublesome thing about it, Preacher," said Jim, shuffling from one foot to the other and kind of looking at the floor. "Lucy Ann's awful timid and she won't come in the house. We were just wondering if you would mind coming out to the car and doing the wedding out there."

"Well, this is not the most ordinary situation I ever ran into," Daddy said, as he smiled, "but, I don't know that there's anything wrong with it. So let's go on out front."

I did not get to really hear or see close up what went on out in the car, but Daddy said that it was a nice wedding. I have often wondered whatever happened to that couple. I bet they had a pretty good life together.

In those tender years, I wondered why in the world a boy wanted to give up his freedom to do something like that. Happily, time, maturity, and love taught me the marvelous answer to that question.

As a little fellow, I found no such fascination with church itself. I went because it never occurred to me that anyone could do otherwise. When I got to Sunday school, Mr. Gamble usually sat on the steps waiting for everybody. Mr. Roland Anderson stood inside ready to take over the opening part in his role as Sunday school superintendent. Lareeta Cater and I were the only full-time young Sunday school scholars, as Mr. Anderson called people who went to Sunday school. (We still sit in the same Sunday school class together.) But in those days our class consisted of us together with children from Miss Annie Rowland's school and various short-term members.

In the winter a coal-burning stove warmed the right front corner so most of the congregation gravitated to that side. In the summer we sat close to the open windows and rhythmically swished the cardboard funeral home fans back and forth for cooling. But I do not remember feeling too hot or too cold.

Mama played the piano to singing that sounded neither enthusiastic or particularly good. I took the absence of a choir for granted, and I do not think that it bothered Daddy too much. He liked to say that he was scared of only two things, a mad dog and a church choir.

Church took on a greater interest for me during a revival when I was seven. As Dr. William Huck preached, I decided the time had come to profess my faith and join the church. I professed, and the joining procedure followed. Surprisingly, I had not been baptized as an infant so a sprinkling lay in store for me. But we had no plumbing in the church and no baptismal fount. To solve the problem, Mama quickly fetched the sugar bowl from our silver service, and I ran down the street to fill the bowl at the fountain on the city hall wall. Following that, Dr. Huck sprinkled me, put his hand on my head, and said the appropriate things. I looked down sort of embarrassed as the old people came by and extended the "right hand of fellowship." I think and pray all that stuck. Presbyterian doctrine says it must.

The coming of a new preacher to one church or the leaving of an old preacher always inspired a union service. At these gatherings, the three ministers spent most of their time poking good-natured fun at one another. Such a gathering was called to say farewell to Harry Smith, the Baptist pastor, who was leaving to take a post of rank at Mercer University in Macon. During this service, Daddy directed his verbal darts at the Methodist belief in "falling from grace."

To my way of thinking, Baptist and Presbyterian pastors are called to easier tasks than are Methodist pastors. Baptists and Presbyterians were foreordained before the foundation of the world and according to my erratic reasoning it would appear that the main task of their pastors is to keep them from falling from the high estate in which they were created by drifting into the Methodist fold. I do not know how often a Methodist is saved, but I would judge, in a blundering sort of way, that the average is about once a year. That complicates the task of the Methodist pastor and one might reach the groundless conclusion that the Lord foreordained the rest of us in order to have more time for the Methodist.

Daddy ended his comments with an expression of admiration for Mr. Smith saying, "It is needless that I take up your time to tell you how supremely Harry Smith has served this church and community. As the years go on, we will cherish with gratitude the memory of how he abounded in the work of the Lord, constantly, ably and in the beauty of holiness."

Mr. Smith's son, Dr. Pat Smith, has been my neighbor and good friend for many years, and Mr. Harry himself has now returned to Forsyth to live.

Early every summer I began looking forward to the annual Sunday school picnic at Indian Springs. The looking forward process involved a bunch of worry—worry about rain. The road from Forsyth to Indian Springs was dirt and about impassable when it rained. I do not remember rain ever canceling the picnic, I just remember worrying that it might.

The most fun at the picnic was playing on the rocks over which a creek flowed. The slipperiness of the rocks caused many a fall into the water. So certain was Mama of my impending fall she always brought along an extra set of clothes for me. I rarely disappointed her expectations.

On the way home from one of the picnics, I rode in the car with some of the boys from Miss Annie's school.

"I sure will be glad to get home," I sighed, exhausted from a long day.

"Why," said one of Miss Annie's boys, "this is so good, I don't want it to ever end."

I said nothing else. I just sat quietly ashamed of my failure to appreciate kindness, fun, simple joy, and love like I ought to have. I do not remember the little boy's name, but I hope that I never forget the lesson of his poignant exclamation. What we take for granted may seem like a treasure to so many.

A boyfriend gave my sister Baby a greyhound that had discarded from a race track. Lord knows where the boy got the dog. We all knew Baby did not want it, but she would not dare tell her young swain of her ungratefulness.

The poor animal, Prinz, suffered from some sort of rheumatic condition which virtually crippled him in wet weather. Other times he ran like the wind. His main characteristic though was that he was painfully shy or, as they say, cowed.

We speculated that somebody beat the unfortunate dog when he could not run on a damp day. Prinz refused to let any of us get close to him for a long time. Daddy secretly took this as a challenge. He began his effort to win Prinz's friendship by leaving food at the back door.

Within a week or so, Daddy had won enough of the dog's confidence that he was feeding him from a can with a fork. From then on, Prinz followed Daddy just as my dog Duke would follow me. One difference emerged. The picture show people let Prinz remain under Daddy's seat while I had no such influence with them.

About to doze off in church one warm morning, I felt Mama elbow me gently. There came Prinz slowly walking up the aisle to the pulpit. Mama's nod told me that I should get the dog out. I went to the pulpit and pulled him by the collar down the aisle to the outside. In a few minutes, here he came again. Again, I took him out. On the dog's third entrance, I again rose to do my duty but this time Daddy shook his head slightly and with an easy movement of his hand waved me to sit down. For some time, a man and his dog occupied the Forsyth Presbyterian Church pulpit together.

In the ripeness of time, that church filled when friends of my parents gathered there for Daddy's funeral and then later for Mama's funeral. It seemed a sad finality to relationships going back to 1917. But it dawned on me that no final separation between them and that church could occur because their influence survives.

I expect one day my own funeral will be conducted there. I hope that I may leave some influence worthy of survival—knowing full well it could not come close to theirs.

# CHAPTER 5
# Friends that Last

So pervasive was Calvinism at my house that I just accepted some things and some relationships as part of our preordained lives. My friendship with Barrett Sutton fit that pattern. Barrett's mother and my mother enjoyed almost sisterly bonds, and, when Barrett and I were born a couple of months apart, we began a lifelong association even though geography rations our visits.

I do not remember not knowing Barrett. I do remember us so far back that we were being dragged around by our mothers, but the better memories came later.

Barrett lived on West Johnston Street in what was then the last house on the south side of that street. I liked his neighborhood because lots of boys and girls near my age lived there.

Of all the people in the neighborhood, Barrett's grandfather interested me the most. Major Boulware looked more like an old southern gentlemen than did Colonel Sanders of the fried chicken fame. A retired civil engineer, the Major had been everywhere, seen everything, and built plenty of interesting things. Years before he built the dam at High Falls near Forsyth and during his stay here came to know James Phinazee Sutton, known to his friends as Jim Bob.

Jim Bob Sutton impressed Major Boulware so much that the Major commented to a friend, "If Jim Bob weren't married, I would claim him for my daughter Katherine."

A long time later, after Major Boulware did numerous other projects in other places, he received word that Mr. Jim Bob's wife had died. He proved himself as good at matchmaking as at engineering. In due time, Miss Katherine Boulware and Mr. Jim Bob became Mr. and Mrs. James P. Sutton. My friend Barrett was the second of two sons of that union.

By the time I knew Major Boulware, he was very old and living with the Suttons. He lived in a room at the back of the house which afforded him privacy and independence. But he never seemed to mind the way Barrett and I often invaded his privacy. Sitting there by the coal fire in an open grate, he would tell us of great wonders. Sometimes he revealed the mysteries of how things were built, sometimes he explained the dangers of that funny-looking little man who had just gained power in Germany, even though few of us took Hitler seriously at that time. Other times he tried to teach us to play chess—without much success.

He appreciated everyday things too, like sports. It must have been a picturesque site—two snaggletoothed little boys huddled by a primitive radio listening to a World Series game or a Georgia-Georgia Tech football game with an old gentlemen of quiet dignity and ample white hair and a neat goatee.

Perhaps the most surprising thing about the scene was the older man's detailed knowledge of sports. With calm and patience, he led us to a clearer understanding of what the man in the box called radio was trying to convey. From a man whose productive life reached far back into another century, I learned the difference between a wild pitch and a passed ball and a fumble and an incomplete pass.

Not knowing we would try to follow the instructions, Major Boulware told us about how people used to make wine from wild cherries. This perked our attention.

"There's a wild cherry tree in the Cabaniss grove," Barrett whispered with a twinkle in his eye.

Without a word between us, we headed one block down to the grove. We quickly filled two paper sacks with cherries and followed the wine-making instructions the best we could remember. But our memories were not good enough. After we put our squeezings in jars, we hid them on a shelf in the Sutton's pantry. Nobody noticed the jars until they forced attention upon themselves. They fermented all right. In fact, they exploded all over everything in the pantry. The two little boys never got a sip of their cherry wine, and Barrett's mother never knew what caused the mess. Major Boulware knew, but, typical of him, he held his peace.

A bunch of boys gathered in Barrett's backyard one afternoon for a makeshift baseball game. As we pitched, hit, caught, and ran, Barrett's little black and brown shaggy dog bounced around with us. He liked baseball at least as much as we did. He jumped around the batter and then ran with him. The fun ended when a batter swung at a low pitch, missing the ball but hitting the little dog's head.

The pitiful pup fell to the ground and lay motionless. The other boys left, but I stayed with Barrett who took it hard. We knew Major Boulware was on the front porch (he called it the piazza) in his favorite rocker. Barrett carefully picked up his pet and carried it to his grandfather who always had the answer for everything.

"My, the little fella's hurt. Let's see what we can do," said the gentle old man in the kindest of voices.

He stooped beside the dog, examining him carefully.

"How bad is it, Grampa?" asked Barrett, not really wanting to know.

"Can't tell for sure, son."

"What's his chances?"

"Maybe 50/50."

I listened to this exchange, feeling sorry for Barrett, but convinced that Major Boulware could make anything all right.

We stayed on the porch a long time. Major Boulware just rocked. Barrett softly patted his injured dog. I did not know what to do. Finally, Barrett said the dreaded words.

"Grampa, he's not breathing."

The old man went to Barrett and the dog. He put one hand on the dog and the other one on Barrett's shoulder in a kind of embrace. Then he put his arm around Barrett.

"We'll have to bury him," he said, leading Barrett into the house.

That day I realized that there were some things even Major Boulware could not do. But in the face of the impossible, he made the inevitable easier.

Barrett's mother always reminded me of Spring Byington who played Mickey Rooney's mother in the Andy Hardy movies. Her sweet flighty appearance and actions disguised a mind of purest logic. She demonstrated logic in its purest form in an encounter with Mama.

Although called Bubba, my brother's real name was Jack Clarke Jr. He was something of a rounder. By contrast, my father, Jack Sr., was dignified and a picture of propriety. When Bubba was about seventeen or eighteen, he and a Bessie Tift College girl sneaked off and married. This dashed Mama's hopes for Bubba, leaving her in tears. After turning the crank on the telephone, she called out the Sutton number to the central.

When Miss Katherine answered, Mama sobbed, "Please come over here. I need you."

Without bothering to reply, Miss Katherine headed out the door and toward our house. When she came through the side door directly into Mama's bedroom, they embraced.

"Jack ran off with a college girl," Mama said, through her tears.

"Jack Jr., or Jack Sr.?" Miss Katherine said, with the best analytical look on her face.

Suddenly, Mama's tears stopped. Then a smile broke through, because of two reactions. First, the very idea of Daddy and a college girl running off was funny. Besides that the question put the event in perspective. The failure to jump at an obvious conclusion may sound flighty when it is in fact logical.

An accomplished educator who led our school system as county school superintendent, Miss Katherine dealt everyday with logic. But sometimes logic escaped her entirely. One afternoon she drove Barrett and me to the Indian Springs swimming pool in her 1933 Ford we called "Leaping Lena." As we started on the seventeen-mile drive home, we noticed she never shifted beyond second gear. All the way home, we laughed while she poured out continuous conversation.

Sometimes she failed to grasp unwanted reality. Mama loved to tell me of one of those times. She and Miss Katherine were riding in the front seat with Barrett and me in the back making undue noise.

Without looking back, Miss Katherine beamed, "Isn't it wonderful how our boys get along. Listen to their happy play."

Mama looked to the backseat to see us fighting like cats and dogs. She did not bother to tell Miss Katherine of her mistaken impression.

Barrett and I were two of four boys who started the first grade together whose mothers shared close friendships. The other two were Banks Worsham and Sonny Ensign who bore the real name Charles Joseph Ensign.

On the first day of school, Sonny rose in a poised and precise manner announcing, "My mother requested I ask you to call me Charles and not Sonny."

"Thank you," said Miss Merle, our teacher, "Now you all heard that, so let's all call him Charles."

The second day Sonny rose again. "Miss Merle, I made a mistake yesterday," he explained, "My mother doesn't want you to call me Charles. She wants you to call me Joseph."

Again Miss Merle gave the appropriate instructions.

A few days later, Sonny told the class he was wrong again and that Joe was the preferred name. Even though Barrett and I always had trouble thinking of Sonny as anybody but Sonny, his adult name became Charles.

We liked Sonny and Banks, but neither of them liked the team games that we enjoyed. Sonny's interest ran toward music and art, while Banks mainly hunted and fished. That left us two to find interesting things.

When the outstanding trial lawyer, Abit Nix taught me in law school, he once said, "Whatever you do, don't be average. Be smarter than the average, be taller than the average. Just don't be average."

The advice seemed sound, and Barrett followed it without ever hearing it. He was certainly taller than average and beyond that Barrett was smarter than just about anybody. Lots of Sunday afternoons boys and girls (some two years older) would gather at someone's house. While the rest of us played, Barrett did the homework for the whole crowd. I still marvel that he possessed all this intellect without losing normalcy or becoming that most insufferable of all beings, an intellectual snob.

A friend of mine says, "When you can do it, it ain't bragging."

Knowing Barrett, I say, "When you can do it, you don't have to brag." By nature he is totally unassuming.

Do not think that Barrett was perfect though. I sure did not think so and our continuous little-boy fighting testifies to that. He fought other folks too.

At Barrett's invitation, I went to his neighborhood to take part in a gang war. Our gang wars were make believe or as we said back then, "play like." Our weapons were no more dangerous than the wooden Tom Mix revolver you could get with Ralston cereal boxtops. One afternoon the war grew a little out of hand. One of the Strickland boys committed an act of violence which set Barrett off, and his temper rivaled his quiet reserve as a dominant trait. It happened in the Sutton yard, so Barrett disappeared into the house. "We scared him off, didn't we," Junior Strickland sneered.

The answer to the rhetorical question became clear in a moment. The front screen door of the Sutton house flew open with Barrett charging out hotly pursued by Major Boulware. In his arms Barrett carried a five foot long muzzle-loading musket handed down from an ancestor. To us in the yard, this looked more terrible than the German Big Bertha of World War I. The retreat from the Sutton yard looked like a covey of quail flushed by a poorly trained pointer.


Although we had a succession of dogs, I counted only one as mine alone. We loved one another, me and that big shepherd named Duke, but he never gained community-wide popularity. Even Barrett was one of his enemies.

I could not go anywhere without Duke. He became a regular at school. First lying around the school yard waiting for me and sometimes getting into the hall and lying at the door of the classroom.

Old Duke had decided to appoint himself as my personal protector. At first this was fun because when a boy hit me jokingly, Duke would go after him until I called him off. That is where Barrett comes in.

On my eleventh birthday I went to school, and, as usual, Duke followed. He stationed himself at the school steps, waiting for recess when we could play. He did not know what play would involve that day. Custom was that the birthday boy received from his friends blows to his backsides in a number equal to his young age. The birthday boy attempted to avoid this by running, and if this failed he fought.

When I left the schoolhouse, Barrett came after me, and I ran. He caught me, and we fought. But not for long because Duke intervened. The big shaggy dog went after Barrett's shoulder and while the injury was not so great, he pretty well totalled the boy's shirt. This time calling Duke off did not help. Only by pulling at him with all my might was I able to free Barrett. Duke gained Barrett's respect, but not his friendship.

Two years earlier, during 1936, Barrett and I went to a night program at the high school. He hurt his foot that day and was limping badly. Someways into the program, a lady came to Barrett. "You need to come with me," she whispered.

I had no idea why Barrett had to leave until I got home. My mother called me in and explained it to me.

"Poor Barrett. His father died tonight."

Barrett has been my friend in good times and bad times. Those are the best kind of friends.

CHAPTER 6
# Everybody Is Mortal

Old folks die. They need to. They're old. Young folks live. They don't die. They don't think about it. That is the way children see mortality.

I innocently believed these propositions. I remember when my grandmother died, and I do not remember feeling sad about it because she was old and I was five. A great uncle died when I was six, and I still had no deep feelings because he was even older than my grandmother.

To a child, everything needs to fit. Old age and death, they fit. Childhood and life, they fit. That is the way the world works. My two-year-old sister died when I was six weeks old but that was beyond my emotional reach, and at seven I still connected the old with death and put the young beyond its reach.

Then it happened.

After supper on summer nights, I sometimes was allowed to "play out." This meant playing with other children after dark; it gave a little boy or little girl a special feeling of privilege. Adults seemed to reserve nighttime for their playing and insisted that children be in the house after dark. When I had a chance to "play out" after dark, I was reaching into the world of vast mysteries.

The shadows cast by a tree or shrub standing between me and a streetlight covered ground with which I might have detailed familiarity. Yet, because of the darkness, an exciting unknown lay waiting for my discovery.

Mama allowed me to play out that night because Billy Hill and his two cousins Shirley and Jane were visiting their grandparents, Mr. and Mrs. Willingham, across the street from us.

I hurried over to the Willingham's yard where I found Billy, Shirley, Jane, and another neighbor Norris Sikes waiting and ready to get started with the nighttime games. When I arrived most of them were just bounding about catching lightning bugs, while Shirley played with a June bug on a string. I always liked that because the beetle-like bug zoomed around your head making a nice buzzing sound. All you had to do was tie a piece of sewing thread to one of his legs.

But I knew something better would be played. The best of all the games for people of our age was known as "Ain't no boogers out tonight." Like so many other games, one of the players would be "it" and would hide. The other players would then skip and dance around the yard singing a little ditty going like this, "Ain't no boogers out tonight 'cause Daddy killed 'em all last night." About that time the "it," who played the part of the booger, burst out of its shadowy hiding place and screamed in a blood-curdling way. This scared all of us even though we fully expected it to happen. The lack of surprise did not prevent the raising of goose pimples. There was lots of running, lots of laughing, and lots of fun; but, when it ended, you only had that dreadful fate to look forward to—the obligatory pre-bedtime bath.

The game did end, and the bath did come. As I sat in the tub happily remembering the boogers, my mother rapped at the door saying that she needed to talk to me. I put on my pajamas and went to my parents' bedroom.

"James and Lawton English," she began, "went to the beach at St. Simons for a vacation. Something happened while they were playing in the ocean and they both drowned."

I sat there stunned because Lawton was a year older than I, and James only three years older. They could not die. They were little boys like me. Little boys do not die. They live. This does not fit. The world does not work this way. Something is wrong. All these thoughts and others swam through my young head so confusing me that I did not realize that for the first time I was facing reality.

I thought a lot about James and Lawton that night. About how they had played at my house and I at theirs and about how that could not happen anymore. Some of the comfortable innocence of childhood evaporated and would never materialize again.

I occasionally drive by their graves. Miniature tinted photographs of each of the boys appears on his grave. They look quaint and almost ancient. Their headstone bears the simple inscription, "Both Drowned While Playing on Beach."

I find myself wondering what sort of life these two boys might have lived. Would they have been successful lives? Happy lives? Sad lives? Would those lives have contributed to a better town? A better state? A better country? No one knows. Only a few of us even remember they were here at all.

CHAPTER 7

# First Grade Dropout

I may have set a record as being the world's only first grade dropout. But I was not even successful at that, because every time I dropped out my mother pushed me back.

Early September 1933 found me just short of six years old, timid, and big for my age. Being the youngest of five children, I had developed little in the way of independence. Then suddenly the time came to go to school. My school was Banks Stephens Institute, a massive, solemn-looking brick building about four blocks from my house. Even though it was built only some twenty years earlier, it appeared old and ominous to me. I remember the walls as seeming black, the windows too high to see out, and the floors having the dirty-looking oily finish that came from long use of sweeping compound. Even the smell of the place was bad. I thought all of this just went with the grim business of growing up, an idea that I did not much like but for which I knew no alternative.

My teacher, Miss Merle Smith, was bright, pretty, and kind. The other first graders, for the most part, acted nice enough, so the first couple of days turned out better than expected, except for two things. Nobody told me there was a restroom at the school, and one of the other little boys bugged me for some reason.

The restroom problem headed the list. Although school let out at noon for first graders, a full morning without the use of plumbing facilities was painful. But again I just figured that is how life is when you get old enough to be away from home. The other problem, Walter Culver-house, amounted to little more than a minor irritant, or gnat bite. Walter seemed to know things I did not know, yet he was littler than me.

The Culverhouse irritation and the restroom discomfort converged on the third day of my first grade life. Walter turned good guy, I thought, when he explained to me that the school did indeed have a restroom. He pointed me to the portion of the basement located at the southeastern corner of the school.

My appreciation of Walter turned to horrible embarrassment when my entry to the basement was greeted with a mixture of young feminine screams and giggles. I knew what had happened. That rascal had sent me to the girls restroom. That is when rage took over.

I charged up the steps and into Walter with my fists flying and landing squarely on him. When my tormentor retreated into the school house crying mightily, I felt deeply satisfied. It became even better. The other little boys clapped their hands and patted my back because of my manly act. But this moment of pride and joy quickly passed, and I suddenly faced the very darkest moment of my young life. My neighbor Eva Grant walked up to me.

"I just saw Walter walking down the hall of the school with Miss Florrie Childs [the school principal]. He was crying but she told him not to worry that she was going to put Harold on the electric spanking machine."

Nothing more needed be said. I immediately found the alternative to first grade life. I left and in a hurry. It never occurred to me that I could not spend the rest of my life in hiding, so I sought out the most secret place I knew.

Our house contained an upstairs room we called the sleeping porch. No one occupied it at that time, so it offered a good opportunity as a long-term hideout. Furthermore, a large steamer trunk sat in the corner of the room empty. This became my hiding place.

Proving her concern for her pupils, my teacher, Miss Merle, came to my house not just to tell my mother about my escape but to help look for me. I can still feel the fear that I experienced as I heard them going from room to room like a posse tracking a fugitive. I did not know they were worried about my safety and wanted me to reassure me. I only thought they aimed to put me on the electric spanking machine.

The passage of time erases any possibility of remembering how long I stayed in the trunk or just what happened when I got out. It seems I was there for weeks or perhaps months. I now doubt that it was even an hour, and I expect that my treatment was more like that received by the prodigal son than that of a dangerous fugitive. But that did not matter. The tone had been set. School was bad, and I did not intend to go back.

On the days that followed, my mother would carry me to the school and stay so that I would not run away. I was put on the second row and my mother sat in a corner seat on the back row.

The schoolroom had two doors, one near the front of the room which went out into the hall and another at the back which went through a cloakroom into the hall. As the school day progressed, I kept a wary eye on my mother who undoubtedly had plans of sneaking out through the back door. When she executed this plan, I would put my plan in motion.

My plan involved bolting out the front door and running as hard as I could until I could find another hiding place. Most often, I picked the woods near Blue Hole or the lumber stacks at Hooks's Lumber Yard. I do not know for how many days this went on, but I think that it was for the major part of the school year. At least it was enough to cause me to fall far behind in the complex subjects of the first grade.

Because of this I spent most of what would have been my summer vacation at Miss Merle Smith's house making up all of those things I should have but did not learn during the school year. During these days, I came to appreciate and like her, but neither school nor being deprived of playing outside seemed right. For a long time, I did what most people do and tried to blame my first grade problems on somebody other than myself. Walter Culverhouse, who undoubtedly was then and is now a nice person, was the object of my misplaced blame.

Looking back, it becomes fairly clear that the problems of the first grade really did not have much to do with Walter nor with the embarrassment of going into the little girls room. It actually had to do with my inability to learn some things that the other children found easy to learn. Reading came quickly to most of the other first graders, but I just could not get the hang of it. Try as I might, the letters and the words just did not fit or come across to me.

As a matter of fact, I still read slowly. I still have a tendency to transpose parts of telephone numbers. I know now what nobody knew then. My problem was not Walter Culverhouse or the little girls restroom.

My problem was dyslexia of some degree or another. I know one other thing. Somebody ought to shoot the fool who says your school days are the happiest days of your life.

# CHAPTER 8

# The Rest of Grammar School

Even after the first grade ended, the downside of school lingered. I still could not read very well, and school was no less confining. But as the years went on, the positives began to outweigh the negatives.

Miss Florrie Childs was the principal that I expected to put me on the electric spanking machine. Miss Florie was married, but, in that era and that area, we referred to school teachers as "Miss" rather than "Mrs." In fact, it did not matter whether she was a school teacher or not. When the first name of a woman was used with her last name, the prefix was "Miss," single or married. For instance, we would say Miss Florie Childs or Mrs. Charles J. Childs. Nobody had thought of "Ms." at that time, even though we pronounced "Mrs." as "Miz."

Miss Florrie ran a tight ship, and she had all the tools to do it. We believed her when she said she had eyes in the back of her head. If she was filling in for a teacher and writing at the blackboard, she was likely to wheel around and point a finger and say, "Frank, sit up and behave yourself." Poor old Frank might have been behaving, but Miss Florrie knew that it was unlikely. Her high percentage of accuracy convinced us that those other eyes were somewhere under her hair.

There was another powerful tool to keep us in line—the black book. If you misbehaved in class, your name was put on the blackboard. If you misbehaved additional times, the teacher placed a check by it. Once you had two checks in one day, the teacher sent you to Miss Florrie's office.

Once there, Miss Florrie issued the stern and horrifying warning, "If I see you in here one more time, you're gonna have to sign your name in the black book."

I do not know what the black book was, and I do not know what it did to you to have your name in it. In those days, I had some sort of notion that it was the opposite to the book of life, a sort of book of death. I was certain that once your name was in the black book, a curse would follow you the rest of your days. I do not know anyone who ever saw Miss Florrie's extra eyes, her electric spanking machine, or, for that matter, the black book. I do know that a whole lot of children were scared into acting halfway decent because they truly believed those things to be real.

Miss Florrie was not an ogre. To the contrary, she was a fine and sweet person who was a good teacher and friend as well as a good school administrator. She was the only person that I knew who had been out West. Miss Florrie had taken a trip through the Southwest to California. This caused her to be in demand as a fill-in teacher in geography class. As pre-TV children, we listened in awe to the stories of the wonders of that far section of our country.

Banks Stephens had other interesting teachers. Miss Annie Parks taught the third grade, but somehow I missed her class. That disturbed me because she always organized a third grade baseball team that could beat almost everybody else.

Miss Helen Craig taught me in the fourth grade when she was a first year teacher. She also taught some of my children, and we all agree that she ranks among the very best. Helen would drill, drill, drill until it sunk in.

I failed to mention the second and third grades. Even today, I seem to block those out of my memory. Not because of my teacher, but because of the continuing struggle to survive the rigors of school. Miss Marguerite Anderson taught me both years and did as well as anyone could have considering my learning problems. If nothing else, I think that she sanded off some of the sharp edges of fear so as to make the drilling exercises of Miss Helen's class easier.

My fifth grade teacher aroused another and new interest. For the first time, I looked at a teacher and found her not just nice and pretty, but beautiful and attractive. Miss Kate Lassiter had long, blond hair and beautiful teeth which made her smile believable. Whatever she said I believed.

Then came the sixth grade, the last at Banks Stephens. All sorts of things happened because for the first time we had a man teacher. Mr. Frank Williams did not fit the stereotypes of Mr. Peepers or the Dickensian hickory-stick-wielding schoolmaster. For one thing, he lived at Juliette, a little community some ten miles to the east on the Ocmulgee River. And everyone who lived at Juliette loved the outdoors and nature.

Frank possessed all sorts of athletic ability as well as an abiding interest in almost every sport. Part of his job was to stay around after school and play various sports with the youngsters who wanted to be a part of it. We did it all. Baseball during the earliest fall, football right after that, basketball during the winter months, and back to baseball in the spring.

He organized a sixth grade basketball team and several of the mothers got together and made uniforms for us. We did our practicing on an outdoor court at Banks Stephens, but we played our games at the Mary Persons High School gym. Although this seemed uptown to us, it was really just a rundown, homemade wooden building with pot-bellied stoves at either end.

The team must have been pretty good though, because we beat the seventh grade—mainly because we had several boys who celebrated their sixteenth birthday during the course of our sixth grade year. Social promotions had not been invented then. One of these bigger boys resisted punishment one day and learned to his sorrow that Mr. Frank was indeed an athlete.

One of my strongest memories of Mr. Frank had to do with an event several years later. By that time, he was teaching in high school, and I was a student there. For some long forgotten reason, I got into a fist fight one day at recess with my classmate, Willie Lee Seymour. The rest of the students egged us on, and, without my knowing it, Frank was on the sidelines watching. He let us continue to fight until both of us started bleeding. Then he stopped us, and I think we were both happy that he did.

By night my busted lip was swollen, sore, and embarrassing to one who was going to a dance. I had a date with a pretty little blonde named Farice Spangler, and I will always have a warm spot in my heart for her because of something she said that night. When some of the other teenagers made fun of my disfigured mouth, Farice stepped up in her assertive way and defended me.

"You ought to see the other fellow."

That made me feel good, even though Willie Lee was probably pretty much unmarked.

I still see Frank Williams occasionally. Some years ago when I was doing legal work for him, he brought one of my old report cards by the office. I was almost afraid to look at it but surprisingly found that my grades were a little better than I had thought.

Miss Julia Searcy taught public school music at Banks Stephens and added considerably to the cultural atmosphere. Singing in the chorus interested me. The interest died quickly though because I fancied myself as a budding Nelson Eddy while Miss Julia wanted the group to sound like the Vienna Boys Choir. She did not think Nelson Eddy fit in just right as a choir boy. I went on independently trying to sing "Maytime" in an imaginary baritone voice to an imaginary Jeannette McDonald.

Some years later, my relationship with Miss Julia deteriorated even more when she directed the production of "HMS Pinafore." Singing in the chorus seemed a pretty good idea to me for a couple of reasons. First, the production needed my fine voice, and, second, the cast included lots of pretty girls. All went well until during one rehearsal Miss Julia began walking back and forth in front of the chorus obviously listening for something special. I noticed this and thought perhaps she was about to recognize my talent and bring me out of the chorus to do a solo.

She waved her hands to stop the singing and then pointed to me and my good friend.

"Harold, you and Barrett just move your mouths, but don't sing."

As soon as we could do so without much notice, we left never to return. The chorus lost what I thought were two golden voices, and Miss Julia temporarily lost at least one friend. I held my grudge against her for a long time. Only the maturing process allowed me to understand and appreciate Miss Julia's abilities and good qualities. For many years, she was a close friend and client. She never knew of my early animosity.

The idea of spring holidays came along after my school days. I remember the period from Christmas to June as seeming interminable and interrupted only by a half holiday for Memorial Day. In the fall, however, they did give us a few days off. This came in October, not for recreation but to allow the farm people free days to pick cotton.

Another "holiday" period came when money for teacher's pay just ran out. I do not know how they solved this problem, but the "vacation" did not last. I suspect some of the teachers ended up working without pay.

Despite the lack of official spring holidays, I always stayed home one day that time of year. This came on the day after Mama gave me my spring dose of calomel. She gave me the horrid stuff because spring had arrived and not because of any illness. I somehow accepted this as necessary to keep me from getting bilious. I never became bilious, so I do not know for sure what it is. I assumed it caused you to feel real bad and look peaked (pronounced peek-id).

That raises the question of defining peaked. I reckon it as a nonpoetic equivalent of "pale and wan." It is a good thing the poetic phrase exists. How far would Sir John Suckling have got writing:

Why so peaked looking, fond lover?
Prithee why so peaked.


Among the Banks Stephens people, several appeared to me as likely candidates for a bad future. At least one of them ended up there, but it seemed to me that he was the least bad of the bunch. Joe was from a poor family, came to our Sunday school occasionally, and I remember him as having a wistful nature. Nevertheless, he struck fear in the hearts of most of the other boys my age. Even though he once stuck a pencil point into my wrist in the fourth grade (which still leaves a visible mark), I never thought of him as a really bad person.

As a young adult, Joe did a bad thing. After the commission of some other crime, he shot the sheriff who was attempting to arrest him. The wound proved not to be fatal but was nearly so. After Joe went off to the state penitentiary at Reidsville, that same sheriff, Cary Bittick Sr., took an interest in him and was instrumental in having him paroled fairly early. Joe came by to visit me at my office after that; he seemed penitent and expressed resolve to do better. No one will ever know what might have been for Joe because he was killed in an automobile accident not too long after that.

Another one of the boys who was older and seemed "bad" to all of us was George. I do not know what happened to George and can only hope that life turned out all right for him. I do know more though about another boy.

He made terrible threats to all of us. One day particularly stands out in my memory. For whatever reason, he threatened my closest friend, Barrett Sutton, by saying that he would be waiting on the sidewalk after school. No one in our grade took this lightly. After some serious planning, we devised a means of smuggling Barrett out of the school and into safety. Barrett survived without a scratch.

Many years later, my daughter Lee Ann, who is a pharmacist, told me, "Daddy, I met the nicest man who said he was a friend of yours when you all were in grammar school. He comes by the store to get prescriptions filled right often. The other day he brought some of his grandchildren by so I could tell you about them."

It made me ashamed of my bad thoughts. He is doing just fine, and I'm glad.

## CHAPTER 9
# Goat Fever

During the harshest part of the winter of 1935, I caught an acute case of goat fever. Goat fever has nothing to do with body temperature or with being sick. It is a sudden deep devotion to billy goats and an overwhelming desire to own one.

This started because of the wonderful billy goat owned by my neighbor, Tubby Boatright. Everybody in the neighborhood admired the animal and envied Tubby's ownership of it, but the possibility of having a goat of my own lay far beyond what I perceived as the realm of possibility. I did not have the money to buy one, and I never thought that my parents would let me keep it if I bought it.

In the midst of all this, I somehow gained possession of a dollar.

Even more amazing than my great wealth was my parents' agreement that I could squander this fortune on the purchase of a goat.

I first contacted Frank Wilson at Collier Station knowing that he had a whole bunch of goats on his farm. I liked Frank because he had spent time telling me stories about World War I and showing me the mementos he brought back from France. Frank suffered from being gassed during the war. So when I went out to his farm, the conversation came easy.

"Sure, Harold, I'll sell you a goat for a dollar, but you got to catch him yourself."

"Yes sir."

What seemed like a good deal developed into no deal at all when I discovered the difficulty of catching a wild goat. The goats did not scare me, but I must have scared them. When a goat doesn't want to get caught by a young boy, a goat doesn't get caught by a young boy. The result—I came away from Frank's farm goatless.

Next I heard that Dr. Thurmond who lived near Brent also had goats for sale, but my experience there was almost identical to the previous one at Frank's farm. But my hopes began to rise when I found that a neighbor, Mack Frazier, wanted to sell his goat. The goat was domesticated, and he was the most handsome animal I had ever seen. He was big, very big. The long hair from his chest and midsection hung almost to the ground. His massive horns twisted upward and outward with dignity and fierceness.

Just looking at this goat convinced me that this was the animal they had in mind when somebody made up the story of Billy Goat Gruff. I could just see him protecting the other goats as they crossed the bridge, and I had no doubt that he could keep trolls away. In fact, ever since Mack had this goat, no one had seen a single troll in the neighborhood.

I still flush with excitement when I remember the way I coveted him. However, my hopes were shattered when I talked to Mack.

"Nope, I can't take less than a $1.25," he said, without a hint of compromise in his voice.

I fingered my dollar; the extra twenty-five cents seemed out of reach. I must have looked about as pathetic as any eight-year-old boy could when I walked into my mother's bedroom to tell her my disappointment. It made her sympathetic enough to give me the quarter which would make my dreams come true. I bought the goat, and I loved him.

Tyson Brown, a friend of my older brother, gave me an old half-rotten goat harness and a nearly worn-out goat wagon. This equipment would not have been much good to me except for the friendship I had developed with George Tanner, a local blacksmith. I spent many childhood afternoons watching in fascination the deft and powerful hands and arms of Mr. Tanner as he shaped horseshoes and other metal objects on his anvil. That black man of long ago practiced his craft with real artistry and extended friendships equally well.

When I asked him for advice about my harness and wagon, Mr. Tanner gave me something more than advice—help. He made me feel that I was having a part in the restoration of these things and from that

I gained a sense of achievement. I know now that he really did all the work.

Once I got the wagon and harness in order, it was a simple matter to hitch up the goat and set out for the building of a great fortune. In this process, I learned some lessons about free enterprise. Forsyth had a junk dealer named Frank Harp, who had a witty, outgoing, and warm manner. Nevertheless, he drove hard bargains when he bought scrap iron from young boys. My enterprise was to walk around town with my goat pulling the wagon and pick up articles of scrap iron which had been thrown away. When the wagon was full, I would carry it to Frank Harp's place and attempt to negotiate a reasonable price. I always failed.

"Four cents a load is the limit," was Frank's constant announcement.

This disappointed me because an ice cream cone (two dips) cost a nickel. Four cents would only get you a 3-Center and a penny package of peanuts. A 3-Center was a cola drink which cost three cents.

This practice continued for sometime until I woke up to the idea that the price was the same regardless of the amount of scrap iron on the wagon. So I shortened the loads and came to Frank's place two times. As a consequence, Frank paid four cents two times. I could buy the ice cream cone and a three-penny package of peanuts as a bonus.

I walked through town so often leading my goat and the wagon loaded with scrap iron that one of the local businessmen, Tharpe Hill, gave me the nickname "Scrap Iron." He called me that until his death some years ago.

Goat ownership taught me about both human nature and goat nature. Coming down the sidewalk near the courthouse in Forsyth one day leading my goat, I met Frank Willingham. Frank was a lawyer and later served as a superior court judge.

"If you touch the goat's nose to the ground, I'll give you a quarter," Frank offered.

I thought that would be just about the easiest money I ever made until I discovered that goats do not take lightly to having their nose touched to the ground.

I grabbed the goat by the horns and started pulling his head toward the ground. He was a big goat. He was also strong. I never got the animal's nose to the ground. Frank knew something about goats I had not known.

I must have looked terribly disappointed. Frank reached in his pocket and handed me two nickels saying, "Harold, go over to the drug store and get each of us an ice cream cone."

So I learned that goats are strong and do not like their nose on the ground, and I learned that Frank Willingham was a good man who taught me something about goats and treated me to an ice cream cone. He also taught me that jobs that look easy may be harder than you think.

Without any apparent reason, the goat would sometimes decide he just was not going to pull the wagon, so he would just stand there, in harness, with a determined look on his face. For the longest sort of time I tried to correct this by either pushing or pulling the goat, but this effort ended up in total failure. Eventually, I found the real throttle which makes a stubborn goat get up and go. All you have to do is grab the tip of his tail and twirl it around in a circular motion. This makes the goat take off at a full gallop.

One day my oldest sister came to visit with her little son Billy who was less than three at the time. It seemed to me that a little boy of this age really ought to have the opportunity to ride in a goat wagon, so I convinced Sister to put Billy in the wagon for a ride. Trouble arose when the goat adopted his stubborn attitude. I had dealt with that many times, so I just reached up and cranked the tail round and round. Off went the goat at breakneck speed and out of the back of the wagon fell Billy on the back of his head.

While all of this was going on, the goat business failed to gain much favor at home. Someone left a ladder leaning against the roof of the goat's shed. I looked out the back window one morning, and, lo and behold, the goat was climbing the ladder. He tapped each rung before he put his weight on it to be sure that it would hold him. When he reached the top of the little building, he walked around for awhile as if to view the whole neighborhood. Then he came back down the ladder, this time unconcerned about the strength of the rungs.

Several mornings later, we looked out the back window and found that during the night the goat had not only relieved some of my mother's favorite shrubs of all of their foliage, but had actually stripped them of their bark. My mother could no longer be counted among the goat's friends.

Things came to a really bad end though when my father came out in the back yard to join in my frolic with the goat one Sunday afternoon.

The big animal which had always been docile became unpleasant. He lowered his head and with those big horns jutting out ahead of him started running full blast toward my father. Daddy ran into the goat house with the animal in hot pursuit. He escaped only by jumping through the window and running back into the kitchen.

At first I thought this was sort of funny, but the humor was lost on Daddy. The next day the goat was gone, and the explanation was that he was a dangerous animal and that my safety was more important than having a goat. I guess that was a valid explanation to an adult, but, to an eight-year-old boy, it seemed wrong. Things just were not the same without the goat.

# CHAPTER 10
# Marbles and Humility

Leaning forward from the desk behind me in Miss Kate Lasseter's fifth grade, Joe Adams whispered to me in a voice that was more audible than it ought to have been.

"Wanna shoot some marbles this e'nin' after school?"

"Suits me," I murmured back out of the side of my mouth, a little irritated that Joe interrupted my attraction to Miss Kate.

Of course I understood when he said "e'nin'," it was the local way of saying evening and meant afternoon, not night. That was a usage Southerners picked up from the old Scots. I also understood, in spite of my slight irritation, that I was about to have some fun without having to go to any trouble.

One of the good things about shooting marbles was that you could do it almost anywhere at almost anytime. Not many yards had much grass back then, particularly in the wintertime. Not many people enjoy cutting grass now, and I expect that nobody did in the days before power mowers. Instead they swept the bare ground clean and smooth with what we called brush brooms. You made the best brush brooms by tying dogwood branches together using the bigger end as the handle and the tip end as the sweeper.

Although effective, the brush broom did not add much to the beauty of the yard beyond a certain neatness. What they did was make some fine space for shooting marbles. But not all marble shooting went on in home yards. Most of the time we used the school grounds at Bank Stephens or the space around Mr. Winnie Rhodes's seed store across a side street from the school and across Johnston Street from the Depot. During one period, however, we made a real change and shot marbles inside.

That happened when our school decided to enter the statewide marble tournament put on by one of the big Atlanta newspapers. This was about 1937, and by that time I thought I had become a champion marble shooter. Some of the older boys who lived in the Trio mill village near our house let me shoot with them sometimes. Even their fathers took part in these games. The hard times had them on short time at the mill and this offered a little diversion for them. My mistaken confidence in my marble ability related from the kindness of those older fellows in letting "little Harold" win or at least compete reasonably. In addition, the boys in my grade just did not shoot marbles too well.

So when William King, one of the grammar school teachers, who later became president of Georgia Southwestern College, called us into the big hall at Bank Stephens for the fifth grade marble shootoff, I had little doubt of winning. Wearing my tweeduroy knickers, I was ready. But even the toughness of tweeduroy was not enough, and Mama always put leather patches on my knees because of the wear and tear on the pants from my marble games. She also grew a little tired of marbles wearing holes in my pockets, so she made me a marble bag out of some denim cloth with a draw cord at the top. Another piece of virtually required uniform was a sort of skull cap made from the crown of a man's felt hat. The bottom part of the crown was cut into a series of triangular peaks (I think women call that pinking) and turned upward. I was fully dressed for the occasion when I heard Mr. William's voice.

"You boys help me with the circles."

Miss Florie Childs, the school principal, looked on as we used a stout string and a piece of chalk to draw perfect circles, but that did not suit me. That meant we would play "big ring" marbles and not "pig eye." I liked pig eye better. This was a game in which you drew an enclosure shaped like a pig's eye on the ground and began shooting from a line about six feet away. The pig eye was only about eighteen inches long and six inches deep, but the distance from the line made the game hard enough. The object was to shoot from the line and knock the marbles out of the pig eye. If you knocked one out, you continued to shoot until you missed.

Big ring, on the other hand, meant shooting from the perimeter of the ring. Even though I did not like big ring, the day turned out okay because I turned away the other fifth grade challengers without too much trouble. That set the stage for the intergrade contest.

Mr. A. L. Willingham had just built an addition to his garage back of his Chevrolet place where they did repairs on all sorts of cars. He offered this site for the marble finals. As I walked from the school to the garage with my knickers making their distinctive sound, I almost felt sorry for the boys from the other grades, and a quick win over the fourth grade shooter did nothing to increase my insufficient amount of humility. But my next pairing was against the sixth grade champ, Bill Peters, and, without my knowing it, my humility was about to get a jump start upwards. I had never seen anybody shoot marbles like Bill. He put me to shame with his power and accuracy, and he taught me that bragging, even when it is just to yourself, can set you up for the lowest of lows.

Although they claimed to be pulling for our grade, I believe my classmates secretly enjoyed my comeuppance. They knew better than I that a little slice of humble pie would be good for me. I ate it, but I cannot say that I enjoyed it.

After all these years, Bill Peters and I have a different recollection of what happened after he beat me so badly. We agree that a Forsyth boy went on to Atlanta to win the state championship. We both recall the Atlanta newspaper said that boy could make a marble "do anything but talk." We both know that for years a big trophy sat among the many in the school trophy case as the most distinctive of all. On the pedestal rested a globe with the outline of the continents of the earth and on top of that knelt a boy wearing a crown with his hand poised to shoot his taw.

From there on our memories part. I am certain the boy on top of the world and in that news story was Bill Peters. Bill maintains that he lost to Lewis Treadwell, also from our school, and that Lewis won the state championship. Maybe Bill is just being more modest than I was way back then, or maybe I just cannot believe anyone who could beat me so badly could be other than the state champion!

The day we walked out of Willingham's garage Bill was on top of the world to me as a marble shooter. More than that, I was on the bottom of it right then. By the time Joe Adams and I shuffled down the Bank Stephens steps after his suggestion for the afternoon, marbles no longer meant showing off my imagined superiority. It was just another way for a young boy to have a little fun after school. But really it amounted to more than that because marbles has a set of lessons to teach. The game has its own code of etiquette, sort of like a poor boy's golf. Certain taboos impress themselves on the game:

1. *You do not hunch.* (That means moving your hand forward when you shoot to increase the speed and power.)

2. *Slippance is for little boys.* (That is, when someone makes a bad shot, he yells "slippance" and gets another shot.)

3. *You never, never use a steely.* (That is substituting a steel ball bearing for your taw and using it to break the other boy's marbles. If you broke his taw that way, a fight always followed.)

4. *Nice boys don't play keepance.* (Keepance is a form of gambling where you get to keep all the marbles you knock out of the ring.)

The game of marbles does not have much sophistication, but, like most everything else, you can learn something from it.

"Where we gonna shoot 'em?" I asked Joe as we reached the bottom of the school steps.

"How 'bout over at Buddy Rhodes's store," Joe said, pointing to the little red frame building near the depot.

He called it Buddy Rhodes's store because Buddy was running it while his father, Mr. Winnie Rhodes, was being treated at the state tuberculosis hospital at Alto, Georgia. Before Mr. Rhodes became sick, the store was nearer to the courthouse square in one of the regular brick store buildings.

That place particularly appealed to us young boys because Mr. Rhodes kept small wild animals in little cages on the sidewalk in front of the store. There would be squirrels, owls, and the like. I never knew where he found the animals or, for that matter, what he did with them. I just liked to look at them since it was the nearest thing to a zoo we had in Forsyth. In the store itself, Mr. Rhodes sold all sorts of seed, as well as school books and school and office supplies. When the state started giving school books away for free, about 1937, this knocked out a hunk of Mr. Rhodes's business.

Years later, Mr. Winnie also operated a real estate business, but he told me that he had a hard time keeping property listed because the ads he wrote made the place sound so good the owner would remove it from the list.

"After reading that ad," the owner is supposed to have said to Mr. Rhodes, "I came to realize this land is exactly what I wanted all my life. So I sure don't want to sell it."

When the store moved down past the school, they sold the same things but did away with the animals. Although I looked on this as a loss to the community, Buddy's willingness to let us shoot marbles beside the store building pretty much made up for it. We liked the place for several reasons. The ground was smooth with the right kind of dirt for marbles, but perhaps more important was that Buddy and his helper Jerry Mays were just good folks to be around. Buddy's brothers Sim and Jim spent some time there making it fun too.

Then on some days I might have a nickel and that meant I could buy a Three-Center and two penny packages of salted peanuts. Three-Centers were cola drinks which cost three cents and, when you bought one with peanuts, you did not just eat the nuts and drink the drink. You put the nuts in the drink and truly enjoyed the combination.

When Joe and I entered the store that afternoon, we did not have any money, but two or three others were there and ready to shoot marbles. By this time, the afternoon began to wane. Since Forsyth then observed Central Time, 3:30 left only about an hour and a half of winter daylight. But the lateness of the day lost itself in the fun of the game until the sun's warmth dropped to the other side of the Rhodes's store. The chill, more than the fading light, sent the message that home and supper called for my presence.

A winter sunset had begun. They are different. Summer sunsets linger lazily while the sun tries mightily to hold its grip on the heat of day. Children love summer twilights. They like the lengthened playtime, which delays bathtime.

On the other hand, winter twilights rush in almost unannounced and leave without taking time to say goodbye. In winter, the sun seems anxious to find a better place behind the horizon and quickly takes its warmth with it. While the transition from light to dark in the summer comes with a slow change in temperature, the winter transition triggers a blast of chilled air.

But there is something good about winter sunsets too. Before the sun makes it hasty afternoon exit, it paints a picture summer days seldom see. Summer sunsets are bland. Winter sunsets are brilliant. They spread across the sky a blend of colors which almost takes your breath.

Winter twilights give us at least one other beauty. That beauty is felt and not seen. That is the kind of sunset I faced as I walked up Johnston Street on my way home. When I turned on Kimball Street, a blast of cold slapped my face and wiggled its way through my jacket to my ribs, but it was not all bad. It brought something more than a shiver as it carried with it the homey smell of supper.

As I neared the first house on the street, I knew Mrs. Sikes was frying ham. At the next house, the unmistakable smell of fish in the skillet passed my nostril. Just then I began to feel my own hunger and remembered the lack of peanuts and a Three-Center. So I began to wonder what awaited in our kitchen.

Whatever it might be, I knew it was not dinner. You ate dinner at noon while the evening meal was supper. Although supper could not claim all the careful preparation of dinner, I liked it better. Often times supper took on the characteristics of a very large breakfast. We might have ham and eggs or perhaps battercakes (we never called them pancakes, hotcakes, or griddlecakes) or sometimes waffles. A pewter syrup pitcher always sat on the kitchen table.

That brings up another difference between dinner and supper. We ate dinner in the dining room while we ate supper in the kitchen. The formality of dinner was replaced by a warm coziness at supper that made everything more personal . . . a kind of family time.

Supper had its darker sides though. That is when you just had leftovers. Warmed-over turnip greens lacked the zip they had right after cooking.

We almost never ate sandwiches except at picnics, and I think I ate my first hamburger when I was in my early teens. I always wanted one because Wimpy in Popeye loved them so, but I guess Mama did not approve so we never had them. Mama had a thing about hot dogs, too.

"Weinies are made from the sweepings from the packing house floor," she would say while making a face revealing disgust.

Another of Mama's fetishes was eating before meals.

"Put that down," she would scold, "you will spoil your supper."

Now that bothered me right smart. It particularly hurt when I knew that fried peach pies were piled high on a plate in the kitchen safe. They made them with dried peaches folded into a heavy, half moon-shaped crust. Frying them in real lard emphasized the richness of the taste, and the use of almost no sugar allowed a tartness to balance the greasiness. If you wanted them sweeter, you just poured syrup over them.

Their calories and cholesterol content have long since removed fried peach pies from my diet. But sometimes I think maybe my waistline, heart, and arteries demand unreasonable sacrifices. Even so, the pies probably would not taste that good anymore because childhood tastes may be even more elusive than Thomas Wolfe's home. But I would swap all the broccoli, zucchini, artichokes, and avocados in the world for just one of those fat-drenched, health robbers.

# CHAPTER 11

# Other Kinds of Culture

The simplicity of life in Forsyth before World War II might lead to the impression that it was a cultural wasteland. Not so. The pursuit of culture held a higher spot on the community's priority list than in many cosmopolitan cities today.

Bessie Tift College, the second oldest women's college in America, offered a steady stream of concerts, plays, and recitals all well attended by the townspeople. The churches placed strong emphasis on the near professional choirs, and high school competition in literary meets drew as much interest as athletic events.

Memorizing classic verse and reading classic prose in school was expected by the teachers and parents and accepted as the norm by the students. But this should not be taken to mean that less serious events did not come along now and then.

During my fifth grade year, the teachers emphasized the natural sciences, and, to stir our interest in the subject, they brought several exhibits to Banks Stephens. To me the climax came with what we called the "snake show." They filled the whole stage with snakes—little ones, big ones, and one giant. The snake expert (we called him the Snake Doctor) described how and where these reptiles lived and pointed out their good and bad points.

The boa constrictor held my attention. Having a length of some twenty feet, the snake was as big around as a man's thigh and had a huge lump midway its length. The lump was its most recent meal, a small pig that it had swallowed a week earlier.

If that failed to grab you, the expert's next announcement did not.

"Now boys and girls, line up. I want you to come up to the stage and pet this big old sweet snake. He's my favorite."

Most of the girls screamed and withdrew. A fair number of the boys quietly retreated, but some of us felt compelled to show our manhood by going up and touching that big bad thing. Although terrified, I went. Afraid to touch it but ashamed not to, I placed my hand right on the spot where the boa constrictor's last meal was lodged in a semi-digested state.

To my amazement I learned that snakes do not feel slimy, they feel scaly. The big snake seemed to enjoy being petted. From that time on, I harbored a kinder feeling towards snakes realizing that all God's creatures deserve some respect.

After the snake show came an even bigger source of amazement. Late one afternoon a train disconnected one of its cars right near the depot and left it there. The next morning the people on the car covered the town with circulars advertising the exhibition of a whale, other sea creatures, and a special attraction to be announced inside the railroad car.

The nature of the show failed to interest the adults in Forsyth, but the formaldehyde odor from the car concerned them. The town echoed with demands that the whale be expelled. But for us young folks, it was something we wanted to see first.

Having saved up a little money, I resolved to see the show. On the way toward the depot, I encountered Marvin Waldrep. When we entered the railroad car, a woman with dirty fingernails sitting behind a card table looked up blandly.

"You wanna jes see the whale or the whole thing?"

"How much the whole thing cost?" asked Preacher (that is what we always called Marvin even though he never occupied a pulpit).

"Fifteen cents," the woman said disinterestedly.

Preacher and I both reached in our pockets hoping to find that much money, and surprisingly we did. On entering the car, we first saw a little seahorse floating in embalming fluid.

"Ain't that something?" Preacher said, in more of an exclamation than a question.

"Yeah," I responded, too amazed to elaborate.

Then along came the guide. He let us into the part of the car which housed the whale.

"Lord, it's big," I gasped.

Affected like I was earlier by the seahorse, Preacher said, "Yeah."

"Boys," began the guide, "your Mamas and Poppas have told y'all 'bout Jonah and the whale. I'm gonna show you that story cain't be true."

Right there I was afraid I had fallen into Satan's den and was about to be swallowed by the forces of evil. The leftovers from the teachings of my Presbyterian parents was saying to me, "Get out of here quick and pray for the cleansing of your soul." At the same time, the curiosity that goes with growing up told me, "You need to see this." Curiosity prevailed.

As the guide pointed out the small throat of the whale which could not possibly have swallowed Jonah, my faith faltered. But the teachings of my preacher Daddy and my devout Mama brought me back to the faith of my fathers.

"The Bible says a big fish, not a whale, swallowed Jonah," I said, looking the guide full in his grimy face.

He muttered something about knowing more than a boy from a hick town and led us on to the special attraction.

For decades, friends have laughed and even sneered when Preacher and I have told them about the special attraction. You do not have to believe it. I saw it, and I know that it is true. And Preacher, bless his heart, who died a few years ago, repeatedly attested to its truthfulness. So here it is.

We walked in the very back part of the railroad car finding a man standing beside a glass case about five feet long, three feet wide, and six inches deep. The case enclosed the most amazing show in the universe— a flea circus.

They had fleas running all over the place. Some of them were pulling little chariots with other fleas riding in them. They had a little bitty ferris wheel turned round and round by fleas on a treadmill next to it. Other fleas rode in the cars. I cannot even remember some of the other things the fleas did. The man called the fleas by name, and the fleas responded. About that time a woman with two little girls entered the compartment.

"How can you tell one flea from the other," she challenged.

"How do you," asked the man, "tell one of your girls from the other?"

Sneering, she said, "By the color of their eyes."

"That's what I do, too," said the man as he continued his comments.

For years, only Preacher and I remembered the flea circus and people always laughed when we told about it. I miss him for a lot of reasons, including this minor one. He always corroborated my flea circus story, and I always corroborated his. I know his spirit still supports me.

Lucky Teeter, the Evel Kneivel of that era, came to Forsyth once, but he did not impress me that much. The town was full of people who wrecked cars, so what was the big deal? I did get a kick out of Lucky walking blindfolded along the rim of a rooftop of Joseph's Department Store though.

Airplanes (we still called them aeroplanes) thrilled us most. If a plane flew over a grammar school class, every pupil ran to the window for a look. The teacher never complained because she probably wanted to see it as much as we did. So it is no wonder that when the occasional air show came to town, excitement fairly rolled on the streets.

In those days, emergency landing fields dotted the countryside, and one of the dots was on the Kimball Zellner farm just outside Forsyth. These fields had beacon lights which rhythmically waved across the night sky like a lightening bolt in slow motion. The barnstormers came to these fields to have their fun and sell their services.

The barnstormer king of our area was Doug Davis who, I think, flew the first airmail flight from the Atlanta airport. Even he came to Forsyth once, staying at the Boatwright Boarding House right across the street from us. The thrill of seeing these heroes of the sky was lessened by the flat "no" Mama and Daddy answered to my begging for a chance to "go up" in a plane. Still I liked to see the aviators and watch them fly.

My first chance to go up in an airplane came a little later and at most unlikely hands. John Boatwright was one of the four sons of our across-the-street neighbors. He was their most unusual son. In fact, he may have been the most unusual son anybody ever had.

His talent knew no bounds, and his sense of responsibility lacked bounds too. Sometimes John just disappeared without a word for months. After some of these absences, we awoke in the middle of the night startled by loud jazzy piano playing. Without a second thought, we knew this meant the return of John. He simply came in our house and started playing the piano which he did easily because no one locked doors then.

Sometimes John came home threadbare, unshaven, and hungry. Other times he came home driving a shiny new Packard and dressed fit to kill. We never understood this, and he never explained.

On one return, John walked over and found me alone.

"I got an airplane out at the Zellner's. You wanna go up?"

Naturally I jumped at the chance. My excitement allowed me to only say, "Uh huh."

I climbed into the little two seater and tried to settle down for life's greatest thrill. As the plane raced across the field which was really no more than a pasture, we bumped up and down roughly until the earth held us no more. The sensation of speed on the ground quickly turned into a motionless feeling as we lifted above the Zellner's farm and over the treetops. My dream came true.

After floating aimlessly over Forsyth for a few moments, John leaned over and yelled above the clacking of the motor.

"You want to see your house?"

Thinking he meant only to point it out to me, I answered eloquently, "Uh huh."

That unwise answer resulted in John diving the plane abruptly earthward until we almost brushed the top of our house. My little nephew, five years my junior, ran from the backyard into the house screaming to Mama.

"Ruby! Ruby! Harold is in that plane with John Boatwright."

"How do you know?"

"I saw him when they flew over the backyard," Billy explained.

Now that is what you call low flying.

John then laughed with his indescribable and sort of threatening laugh.

"Let's break up the court."

He tried to do this by swooping down by the courthouse. We flew so low that I had to look up to see the courthouse clock. From there we headed north toward Mr. Virgil Hooks's pond. A Georgia Power Company transmission line crosses the pond.

"How 'bout us flying between the wires and the water," John grinned.

By this time I had surrendered all hope of survival, so I just sat there pondering the hereafter. Mercifully, John did not carry through on this threat but rather returned to the landing field. My fear-caused numbness blotted all memory of my homecoming. I am certain my folks were not thrilled with the conduct of their little boy that morning.

Two other of John's airplane exploits bear telling.

About to take off from Zellner's one day, John found a problem with his plane's wings. Unable to straighten it out, he showed typical John Boatwright flair. Taking an axe, he chopped the wings off the plane then got in and taxied into Forsyth and all around the courthouse square.

But the worst came later. Mama answered the telephone and heard a voice.

"Miz Clarke, John Boatwright crashed his plane. It burned with John in it. Will you go tell Miz Boatwright what happened."

Shocked and saddened, Mama murmured, "Yes."

She decided at least two people ought to be there when she broke the sad news. She called another of Mrs. Boatwright's friends, Mabel Alexander. After they crossed Lee Street from our house and stood on the sidewalk in front of the Boatwright house thinking what to say, a car came by. A head stuck out of the car window with that patented laugh and a broad wave of the hand. John had jumped out of the plane before it exploded and was all right.

"I never saw two old ladies look so disappointed," he told me later, with the same fiendish laugh.

Occasionally John displayed a flair for ingenuity almost rivaling his capacity for audacity and outrageousness. This showed a few times in his business transactions, but more often in matters of less importance. One of those acts of ingenuity happened on a Sunday afternoon when the midsummer heat had stomped its oppressive heel on almost every human activity.

I had walked up to Castleberry's drugstore looking for most any small shady spots as I moved slowly across the two and a half blocks from my house to the store. Coming through the front door, I found Mr. Jep Castleberry and his son Edgar leaning against the soda fountain under a whirling ceiling fan. No matter how the fan labored, it offered little more than a movement of hot air, but not having developed a dependence on air conditioning, the old fan attracted me in as did the company of the Castleberrys.

Just as I settled in, John Boatright burst through the front door with a typical flourish.

"I'm not putting up with this damn heat any longer," he announced with his typical defiance.

"What you gonna do about it?" asked Mr. Jep, knowing he was about to hear something ridiculous.

John fixed his eye on the druggist and flung his right hand in the air holding in it a broiler. By broiler, I mean the oval, shaped, deep pan used mainly for cooking hens. This one had an enamel finish with a blue marbled pattern.

"Got any hot ice, Jep?"

"Yeah, I got some."

"I want all you can spare, and I want to borrow a curb service tray."

In those days they kept ice cream frozen while it was en route from the manufacturer to the drug store by packing it in "dry ice"—frozen carbon dioxide. Because it gave off a vapor that looked like smoke and burned you when you touched it, we called it hot ice.

With a smile of curiosity, Mr. Jep filled the broiler with hot ice and handed John the tray.

We followed John out the front door to his car. He let the right hand window up about halfway and attached the tray. Instead of putting the tray on the outside like you are supposed to, he fixed it to the inside. He then set the broiler, hot ice and all, on the tray. He closed the other car windows, but left the one with the tray open just enough so that the air coming into the moving car would have to pass right over it.

"Where you going?" asked Edgar, probably wanting to go with him.

"I don't know," answered John, with that eery laugh again.

"I'm just heading north. When I get to where it's not hot, that's where I'm going. Between now and then, this hot ice is gonna keep me cool."

Away he went, up U.S. 41 North.

I do not know whether he found a cool place, and I do not know whether the hot ice kept the car cool or for how long. I never thought to ask him about it later.

I do know that I saw my first automobile air conditioning that afternoon. Now they use freon, a condenser, and a mechanical fan. John used hot ice, an enamel broiler, and the wind blowing through the window. In principle, he was pretty close.

John survived many years, but advancing age, poor health, and hard living finally claimed the life which escaped so many daring and foolhardy experiences.

## CHAPTER 12
# Changing Sunday Afternoons

Sunday afternoons in the 1930s afforded a welcome opportunity for grown folks to rest. For young folks, though, they lasted forever. Boredom—not fear, pain, or stress—stands as the number one enemy of children. Sunday afternoons back then bored you.

Keep in mind there was no television. Although my parents allowed some playing, they set limits. The general proposition forbade boisterous playing and allowed those things which preserved the restfulness of the Sabbath. This resulted in a taboo list including baseball, football, rubber guns, swimming, other loud games, and, for some reason, fishing.

The okay list included kite flying and marbles, but on no days could you play "keepunts." Keepunts is a marble game where the shooter gets to keep the marbles that he knocks out of the ring. That, brothers and sisters, is gambling and ranks along with such sinful practices as pitching pennies at the crack.

As bad as the rules seemed to me, they were worse when my maternal grandmother visited us. Even though Daddy was a Presbyterian preacher and grandmother had left the Presbyterian church when she married my Methodist grandfather, she held onto blue stocking attitudes which went far beyond those of my father. Daddy and I had a regular Sunday afternoon custom of walking up town, buying ice cream cones, and then strolling around the courthouse square looking in the store windows. One Sunday while grandmother was there, I came in and asked if we could go for our walk and ice cream. You would have thought I had suggested going for a beer and a crap game. I sat through a long lecture failing to understand any of it. In due time, Daddy quietly took me out, and we had our walk and ice cream. None of this answered the childish questions in my mind about what desecrated the Sabbath and what did not.

Customs, ideas, and even values lack constancy. In some ways society suffers from this phenomenon, but in other ways it benefits. I do not think that anyone suffered much when they started letting me play loud games on the Sabbath. This did not happen overnight. Like most changes in the way people do things, our move came so gradually that I did not realize it was happening. It was almost as if one day I woke up and was playing baseball and "kick the can" and rubber guns on Sunday afternoon.

Nevertheless, some customs did not change at all. Mama still did little cooking on Sunday, and the modernization and moderation of our ways did not alter that. But down deep, we all knew Mama's desire for some free time was the main reason for that practice.

When we had enough people, we played baseball on what was then a vacant lot across North Lee Street from the city hall. When we were short of players, we played "rolling at the bat" on the edge of the street right in front of the city hall because the ball rolled more evenly on the street than on the vacant lot. In either case, we played without any adult supervision or coaching. We may not have learned as much baseball that way, but I am convinced that we picked up more lessons in initiative and self-sufficiency.

Rolling at the bat requires little planning. All you need is a baseball, a bat, and a few people. A glove or two helps but is not essential. The batter gets to continue hitting until somebody either catches a fly ball, catches the ball on first bounce, or grabs a hit ball and, rolling it at the bat which is lying on the ground, hits the bat with it. If any of those things happen, the person who does it gets to bat.

One day as we played rolling at the bat in the front of the city hall, Frank Wilder continued to bat for a long time. After hitting many balls far down the street, he pulled one squarely into the window at the city hall. We stayed frozen in our tracks until the city clerk ran out of the building. Sidney Burton looked more like a bulldog with a bad disposition than a city clerk. He could not have been as mean as he looked, and, fortunately, he was not.

"Frank," scowled Mr. Burton, "you broke that window. You got to pay for it."

Bad news. Like the rest of us, Frank did not have any money, and I think that Mr. Burton undoubtedly knew this too.

"If you can't pay for it, you'll have to fix it."

The kindness of this offer was lost on Frank because he did not know how to repair a broken window. Mr. Burton then showed both his wisdom and his compassion by producing the necessary materials and tools and working with Frank while the window was made like new. I wondered at Frank's new found ability, and Frank walked away beaming with pride. With adequate supervision, we would have avoided all this. With adequate supervision, Frank and the rest of us would have missed an important lesson. Frank later made his living as a building contractor. Maybe learning to fix windows at an early age had something to do with that.

If we played baseball without supervision, we played rubber guns without grown folks having any idea what it was all about. A rubber gun can inflict great pain. We made them ourselves or with a little help. You began with a plank one inch thick. Then you sawed out a barrel being one inch by about two inches and the length depending on your needs. At one end of the barrel you sawed out a handle kind of like that on an automatic pistol. To the backside of the handle, you nailed a clothespin and put a heavy rubberband around the top of the clothespin and handle to increase the tension.

The bullets for the gun are rubber bands made by cutting cross sections from an automobile innertube. You load the gun by fixing one end of the rubberband in the clothespin and stretching it to the point that you can loop the other end over the end of the barrel. To fire the gun, you simply squeeze the handle which opens the clothespin and releases the rubberband causing it to propel forward. Obviously, the longer the barrel, the greater the tension and therefore the greater the force of the shot. But the longer the barrel, the harder it is to load the gun. So little boys had guns with short barrels, and big boys had guns with long barrels—some more than two feet.

One Saturday, I heard the big boys planning a rubber gun war against another bunch of big boys for the next afternoon. The idea really excited me. I had missed World War I, and World War II had not happened yet. So this loomed as my chance to see what I viewed as a major war first-hand.

It seemed Sunday school, church, and Sunday dinner would go on forever. When they finally finished, I took off for the edge of the Boatwright yard where Fred Boatwright's troops were already marshalling. Hugh Chapman and Joe Tribble came first. Then Walter Bramblett and some others.

Walter looked to me like the world's champion rubber gun soldier. He had a couple of long pistols under one arm, a short one stuck in his belt, and, under the other arm, he carried a rifle and a machine gun.

The machine gun was shaped like a rifle and had notches on the top. A string attached to the end of the barrel was stretched across the top of the gun so that when you loaded rubber bands in the notches, the string lay under them. To fire, you simply pulled the string. Walter understood the importance of fire power, both as to volume and force. His guns were real blister raisers.

All this convinced me that if the Confederacy had this crowd, it would have been Grant not Lee who surrendered his sword at Appomattox. I almost pitied the boys who would face this mighty force.

Battle plans called for a mutual attack to occur a block or so down the street at Mr. Virgil Hooks's lumberyard. Mama flatly denied me any right to go into that place. All sorts of dangers lurked down there. There was machinery like fast-moving belts and saws and particularly the lumber stacks.

Mr. Hooks stacked his lumber in a triangular shape leaving a big triangular space in the middle. In the mind of a little boy, this made an ideal space for a fort or a hideout. And to one who lived close by as I did, it had vast drawing power. Despite the lumberyard's appeal, I had resisted the temptation pretty well, but this day differed from all others because war clouds gathered over the lumberyard. I just could not miss history. So trying to remain unnoticed, I followed the big boys from a distance expecting to see them massacre their foe.

It did not turn out like I had thought. All the power and force I had seen in my heroes paled in the face of the breathtaking might and sheer ferocity of the other gang. When the forces met in pitched battle, rubber bands filled the air and yells of pain and cheers of victory breached the peace of the neighborhood. The trouble was my crowd did the howling, and the other crowd did the cheering.

At the beginning, I watched unseen lying in some tall Johnson grass near the edge of a lumber stack. But when things really turned bad, I decided a better hiding place was necessary. I sought refuge by risking the dangers of climbing some eight or ten feet up a lumber stack and then down into the triangular hole thus trapping myself.

Settling down in my hideout, I could not see, but I still heard frightening sounds of warfare. Then one of my heroes hollered.

"Let's get out of here. These people are gonna hurt us."

So there I was. The unbeatable rubberband army had retreated in fear of a superior force.

"Lord," I thought, "I'm glad they don't know I'm here."

Then I heard a terrifying statement.

"Let's look in these stacks. One of 'em may still be here hidin'."

As I lay in the hole of the stack, I prayed for my mother's faith and tried to tell myself I was too big to cry. I curled up in the corner of the hole as the voices of the tormentors got closer and closer.

"Nobody in this un," yelled somebody from the stack next to the one where I lay.

I silently asked both the Lord and Mama for forgiveness for going to the lumberyard as I heard an executioner climbing my lumber stack. Peeping up I first saw the barrel of a rubber gun coming over the top of the stack. It continued coming and coming. The size of that gun made Walter Bramblett's gun look like a pea shooter. But that was not the worst of it. Once the whole gun crossed the top, I saw its holder. Not only was he big and mean-looking, he gave the impression he just liked to hurt people.

"There's one of 'em in this stack," he yelled.

Just as I thought I had faced the end of everything, the big mean-looking boy glared at me and then sneered, "Ah, never mind, he's just a little un. Let's leave him be."

They left. I just lay there for awhile. Then I remembered what Mama said so often.

"All things work together for good to them that love the Lord."

I thought to myself, "I got to start loving the Lord more."

CHAPTER 13

# "Playlike" Adventure

The subject of the latest adventure picture show had a lot to do with what young boys played along North Lee Street.

Once they showed a picture about the Crusades, and we all rushed home to find the makings for a sword and shield. All of us used a piece of wood about two inches by one inch and some thirty inches long. We nailed a six-inch cross piece up close to where we held the stick. We made our simulated swords; the shield came more readily by just borrowing the garbage can top.

With these implements we fought many a battle against the infidels until another picture show came along with another subject. When the show told the story of the Alamo, the latticed fence around our backyard became the walls of that little mission in San Antonio.

When the show concerned what we called the World War (because there had not been but one), we used the ditch down the street as the trench from which we charged "over the top" to attack the Kaiser's army. Marion Dorner, who lived a few doors down Lee Street from me, often played as the German leader because his father came from Austria.

But with all this variety, we always came back to one everlasting theme—cowboys. Our heroes came from the picture shows. I picked Tim McCoy as my favorite. Others listed Tom Mix, Hoot Gibson, Buck Jones, and Ken Maynard. They were real cowboys. It seems a little strange that I picked Tim McCoy as my cowboy because I had at least some reason to have selected either Buck Jones or Tom Mix. I saw Buck Jones riding on his horse Silver in the Ringling Brothers parade in Macon once and saw him later that day in the circus itself. Buck Jones had a horse named Silver before the Lone Ranger was ever thought of. I also had a Tom Mix pistol which I received from sending off Hot Ralston Cereal boxtops.

It changed when Gene Autry and Roy Rogers came along. Not only did they sing, they had automobiles in their shows. To me this finished off the cowboy show era. But until they came along, we enjoyed our games. All of this required that we divide into two gangs to do our "play-like" cowboy wars. I was not too smart about this, ending up on a gang of little boys including Norris Sykes, Billy Hill, and various others who might come along. The older boys made up the other gang led by Tubby Boatwright and Cecil Brown. Even though he was about our age, Edgar Castleberry threw in with Tubby's and Cecil's bunch and by doing this showed good sense. He always won or at least almost always.

The gangs counted as their treasure pieces of paper about the size of a dollar bill which represented the cowboy money. As part of the game, each gang hid its money, and the other tried to find and take it. Much of this money came from the scrap paper drum at Daddy's print shop.

One hot summer afternoon, Bubba Williams and I sneaked over to Edgar's yard hoping to find the other crowd's treasure. Instead they found us and sentenced us to prison.

The Castleberry chicken coop had only recently been emptied of its feathered occupants, so they selected it as our place of incarceration. A worse afternoon I do not remember. The coop stood about three feet high and measured some six feet by six feet on the ground. The top was open except for wire, so the searing summer sun looked down directly and unkindly, baking us as we crawled around. But even worse, the drippings of the lately de-parted chickens covered the ground to a depth of several inches. Just as Bubba and I thought life had gone bad, we made a wonderful discovery. A backyard shed formed one side of the coop and Bubba crawled over there trying to escape the sun. For no good reason, he reached through a crack in the wall, just to be reaching I guess.

"Great day," Bubba bellowed. "I found it."

"Found what?"

"Found it all," Bubba said, looking like it was Christmas.

"I found all their money."

Little by little, we pulled the enemy's treasure through the crack and stuffed it in our shirts, feeling rich and flushed with success. Bubba and I had never bested that gang before and now all we had to do was wait to be turned loose. They finally let us out and although we felt on top of the world, our troubles had only begun.

They say if you shoot at the king you had better kill him. Well if you capture the big boys' money, you better get beyond their reach. Our trouble was we could not get far enough away to escape the revenge of Tubby and Cecil. After all, we lived in the same neighborhood, and they could outrun us whenever they wanted to. They did an even meaner thing. They kept telling us the terrible things they were going to do to us. For weeks we lived in horror of the bad, bad things that were waiting at every turn for us. I think they knew the threats were worse than actions. But nevertheless all this time I wished that I, like Edgar, had joined up with the other gang.

Not long after I quit worrying about what they would do to me, Karl Hill came over to my house one afternoon wanting to do a war with the other gang.

"Just the two of us can't get in a war with that bunch," I told him. "They'll wear us out."

"Then why don't we find one of them by himself and capture him?"

"That ain't so easy either," I explained. "Most of them are so big they can whip both of us."

"Edgar is not so big," Karl reasoned. "Together we could handle him."

"Uh-huh," I smiled, as we took off looking for Edgar.

But he had gone fishing or hunting or something. We could not find him.

"Maybe we could capture Tubby," I thought aloud. "He's been sick." We did not find him either.

About to give up and find something else to do, Karl and I headed back across Lee Street toward my house when we saw Cecil Brown coming our way. Now Cecil was the biggest and fiercest of the members of the other gang. Just seeing him scared me because I still wondered if he might hold a bad grudge over what happened to his gang's money.

"Let's get him."

In saying that, Karl had made the most ridiculous statement that I had ever heard, but I felt a rush of foolhardiness overcome me.

"Let's do it."

So we took off at full foot speed toward Cecil who just stood there looking surprised. As Karl grabbed one arm and I grabbed the other, my better judgment returned in the company of total terror.

"G-u-r-a-ate day," I thought to myself. "He'll kill both of us with one swing."

To my utter shock, the mighty Cecil crumpled in the face of our attack.

"Okay, I'm your prisoner," he said, between pants, "whadda you want me to do?"

Lord, we had not given any thought to that. Then Karl, flush with the confidence of a conqueror, spoke up.

"We're gonna put you in the prison over Harold's garage."

Cecil nodded, and we led him to the garage and up the ladder to the loft. I always kept a length of plow line up there which looked just right for tying up Cecil.

As I took the rope and started wrapping it around Cecil's wrist, he threw his arms wide apart, undoing the rope, and tilting me over backwards in the process.

Then with no words, he leapt out of the loft window and onto the ground some ten feet below. Absolutely astounded, we stuck our heads out the window to better understand this unbelievable feat. A smile and a wave greeted our four young eyes as Cecil walked easily toward home.

With very little effort, Cecil could have beaten up both of us, but he chose a better course. He humiliated us.

After things calmed down some, we all went to the picture show one Saturday and the news reel showed a soap box derby. That set us on fire.

"I got to have me one of those," murmured Cecil with a determined voice.

We all felt the same way, having visions of the sleek vehicles in the news reel.

We built them all right, but nowhere near the fancy ones we had seen at the picture show. Tubby and Cecil finished theirs first followed by Edgar while I still struggled with mine.

A big board served as the chassis and they mounted axles on two-by-fours secured by nails bent over the axles. The back axle was simply attached by nailing the two-by-four crosswise the big board, but the front axle took more doing.

They attached a heavy bolt to the front axle two-by-four and bored a hole through the big board so the axle could turn. Belts were fixed on either side of the two-by-four and wrapped around the steering wheel post (usually a mop stick). Model T Ford steering wheels were thought to be ideal if you could get one. For a hood, they nailed a large nail keg at the front end of the big board. Their wheels came from anything—children's wagons or even wheelbarrows.

The one thing they used that I wanted for mine was a Model T steering wheel. But I wanted two other things better than theirs. First, I intended to build a hood looking like a Packard instead of a nail keg. Then I really wanted wheels with ball bearings for speed.

At long last I put it together and all on my own. Glory be! Because of the ball bearing wheels, mine ran the fastest of all.

We raced regularly, and, for the only time, I more than competed with the other gang. Through all the gang battles Edgar and I remained good friends, but we frayed the edges of that friendship sometime. One of those times related to the racer.

"Lemme ride it down the hill," Edgar asked as we stood in front of my house.

"Go ahead."

About half way down the hill, the racer went off the sidewalk and into a deep ditch, banging it up pretty bad. For the rest of his life Edgar said it was an accident. Even now I say it was on purpose. We always argued good naturedly.

Not everything was competitive along North Lee Street though. Some of our adventures took cooperation. Like the time we got the idea that we could sell owls if we could catch any.

"I know where there's an owl's nest," Marion Dorner said, nodding over toward the woods near Blue Hole.

Away we went, envisioning great riches from owl sales.

"There it is," Marion pointed at a tree.

"You go up and get some of them," Tubby said to Marion.

Getting a little ways up the tree, Marion reached into the nest and began yelling.

"Ow! Ow! Ow! Ow!" he yelled. "Something's got me."

None of us expected to find the mama owl in the nest, nor did we know how violently a mama owl reacts to an invasion. After looking at

Marion's bloody hand, we knew. So we never had a chance to test the owl market, if one ever existed.

Along about this same period of time, we all received our Melvin Purvis Junior G-Men badges from having sent off Post Toastie boxtops. The Junior G-Man badge vested us with a considerable feeling of authority and duty. The trouble came when we tried to exercise this authority.

Wearing our new badges, Bubba Williams and I stopped at the water fountain on the wall of the back side of the city hall where two massive pumps pulled water from two deep wells. Upon slaking our thirst, made acute by the heat of a summer afternoon, we happened to look over toward the rear of the business buildings across the street.

"Looka yonder," Bubba whispered.

Sure enough, a businessman had retrieved a bottle of whiskey from a stack of cardboard boxes behind his business and, of all things, drank directly from the bottle.

Knowing Forsyth as a legally dry town, Bubba and I recognized our duty as Junior G-Men to do something about what we considered a heinous crime.

"Let's sneak the bottle out and turn it over to the police," I suggested.

Bubba nodded his head in agreement.

After the imbiber returned his bottle to the box and walked back in to his business, we eased over to the scene of the crime. Looking into a box about two feet square and a foot high, we found the contraband, a quart bottle of Four Roses nearly one-half full.

"We can't tote that up the street with everybody looking at us," I protested.

Bubba had the perfect solution.

"Let's just take the whole box," which we did.

Fast as we could run, we took off for the city hall, carrying the box containing the bottle and looking for the police chief, Lyle Hollis. When we found the chief, we were panting heavily from our running with our awkward load and more particularly from our excitement.

"We found this behind James's place," I boasted, between heavy breaths, "and we saw James drink some of it."

Now Lyle was not a very vigorous enforcer of that sort of law, and he liked most everybody, including James and Bubba and me. Undecided on what he should do, he first bragged on us some, then with a look of relief on his face, he came up with his solution.

"Boys, I don't have jurisdiction over things like that. Why don't you carry it over to the sheriff."

That sounded reasonable. So across town we went, jointly carrying the box and the Four Roses. When we got to Bittick Motor Company, which Sheriff Cary Bittick owned and operated, we retold the story.

"Lyle told us to bring it to you," I explained.

"You did good, boys," the Sheriff said, with kind wisdom. "You just leave this with me, and I'll take care of it from here on out."

We left, thinking how proud Melvin Purvis would be of us. Later we discovered not everybody felt that sort of pride.

The word of our exploits as Junior G-Men made it back to Mama and Daddy, and they let me know in the firmest of terms that I had better leave law enforcement to those who had real authority. From then on, my Junior G-Man's badge was for play only. For me that turned it into the cheap piece of metal it really was. The thrill and excitement of wearing it just kind of faded away.

Marion Dorner led us into another safer activity.

"The National Guard drills tonight," Marion said while we played an army war game on a Tuesday afternoon. "Why don't we go up to the courthouse square and watch it."

We not only watched, we lined up in the rear and marched with them. The Guardsmen, one being my brother, did not like it much, but they did not do anything about it at first. When we came back the next Tuesday, we joined in again.

The local guard unit had a proud history going back to 1826 which included service in two wars and on the Mexican border in 1914. The very idea of a little gang of ragtag boys strutting along behind them made them feel insulted. So they turned the insult around and chased us off.

Our banishment from the drills suited Mama just fine. During the peaceful years between the two big wars, lots of National Guard members used their gatherings for more than just learning military science and tactics. Besides their weekly drills, the tank company as they were called spent two weeks each summer at Fort McClellan, Alabama.

These summer camps offered a chance for a fair amount of poker and dice and more chance than that for drinking whiskey. Some of the stories brought back from Alabama amazed us little boys.

One of the best concerned Otto Couch, known to everybody as Tobe. During the rest of the year, Tobe worked as a competent bookkeeper, but even then his interest in the cup sometimes interrupted his toil with the numbers. According to other guardsmen, camp for Tobe turned into a solid two week interruption.

When it came to drinking, he did his with ingenuity. Legend says that upon arrival at Fort McClellan, Tobe quickly staked out a lower bunk. He proceeded to hang a jug of shine liquor from the springs of the upper bunk. In the jug he put a syphon tube long enough to reach his mouth as he lay below. To control his consumption at a level he could manage, Tobe fixed a clothespin on the tube.

So while the others marched and did whatever else they did at National Guard camp, Tobe lay there relaxed with a tube in his mouth, squeezing the clothespin when the urge for a slug hit him.

Some of his friends found him useful. While talking to a friend and straightening up the place in the late afternoon, a barber discovered somebody had left a fruit jar of liquor in the restroom. Being the appropriate time of the afternoon, he decided a libation might be in order.

"I'm just not sure about this stuff," the barber said, shaking the jar looking for beads. (Beads are the tiny bubbles which mean shine liquor probably will not make you go blind or die.)

"Here comes Tobe up the street," reasoned the friend, "Let him try it first. He'll drink anything."

"Tobe," called the barber, "You want a drink?"

"Oh y-e-s-s-s-s," came the expected reply.

Taking the glass with at least a triple shot in it, Tobe threw it down and followed it by twisting his face into a grotesque shape and uttering the inevitable guttural sound they always made after swallowing moonshine straight.

"Ah-h-h." Then he walked out.

Reassured, the barber relaxed in his own barber chair and enjoyed a down home old fashioned happy hour. But that did not end it.

The friend who observed it all told the story at the pool hall, and they decided to do some funning.

Mr. Edge walked into the barbershop.

"Sure bad about Tobe, ain't it?"

"What?" asked the barber, with obvious concern.

"Well, he was just walking up by Castleberry's Drugstore and just dropped over dead."

Panic struck. It got so bad the barber's friends had to fetch Tobe and parade him up and down in the barbershop to prove his presence in the land of the living.

All levity about the National Guard ended in January 1941. While America still clung to peace, the government called the tank company to active duty. The churches of the town conducted a union service bidding guard members farewell. One preacher refused to take part because he believed in "peace at any price." The song "Goodbye Dear, I'll Be Back in a Year" made the Hit Parade. Little did any of us know.

We missed the Guard, but a lot of time had passed since we marched behind them. That was little boys stuff, and we felt the effects of growing up. Sports had supplanted child's play in our lives.

Some of us moved toward team sports, but Edgar heard the call of the wild. Hunting and fishing appealed to him. He and George Bailey went squirrel hunting before day one morning and unwisely they decided to go separate ways when they got into the woods.

Not having seen anything to shoot at all morning, George heard a rustle in the brush. Quickly he pulled the trigger of his shotgun, and a howl of pain answered the gun blast. George had shot Edgar in the back of the neck. Luckily the bird shot did not injure Edgar too much, but, when I saw him later that day, he looked like a mummy with all the wrappings they had put on him.

Later Edgar had the unique experience as a combat medical corpsman in the Navy of participating in two of the real big ones of the war. He was at D-Day at Normandy and landed on Iwo Jima in the Pacific only seven months later. Through all this he suffered not a scratch. George Bailey did to Edgar something even Hitler and Tojo could not do. I could have told Hitler and Tojo in the first place because Edgar always figured out a way to come out okay. A most admirable trait.

He died recently. I miss him.

CHAPTER 14

# At the Old Swimming Hole

In every life a few special moments emerge when you feel totally free as though you were released from gravity and relieved from all of the world's cares. The childhood day in May or June when school lets out is one of those times.

On those days, I experienced the kind of euphoric relief which a captured eagle must feel when he is released and allowed to soar into his natural environment. Unnatural bonds were cut. Natural freedom was experienced.

As you walk out of the schoolhouse, you pull off your tennis shoes (tennises we called them), then you massage the warm dirt with your toes. You look up at the topless sky where the only things separating you from the endless blue are one or two fluffy clouds and three or four buzzards coasting on far away wind drafts. For a time you do not want to do anything. Then your mind leaps from quiet satisfaction to thoughts of excitement and some danger . . . swimming.

Swimming in today's context is a fairly commonplace activity. Forsyth in the 1930s had no swimming pool, so my parents set limits on swimming to those unusual times when Mama took me to Indian Springs or some like place to enjoy a pool.

Now that school had turned out, my job was to reach beyond those limits and find places and times to swim on my own. In this effort I was not alone. Forsyth swirled with boys sharing that intent. The network reached into every household where a boy lived. I received the signals.

The possibilities ran from several farm ponds to places called Slippery Rock and Blue Hole—all forbidden. Pippin's pond, Vaughn's pond, and Willingham's pond all lay beyond easy access on foot or by bicycle, so that left Slippery Rock and Blue Hole.

Slippery Rock possessed many assets, but it was not well suited for swimming. There creek water flows rapidly across smooth rocks into a pool with a sand bottom. This makes the spot ideal for sliding down the rock with the water flow into the pool. But the pool itself was never deeper than two or three feet; it was all right for playing and splashing but hardly prepared anybody for the Olympic freestyle.

Though falling short as an aquatic arena, Slippery Rock could then and even now lay claim to being a considerable attraction. It is pretty. Located behind Mary Persons High School, Slippery Rock nestles below a cluster of huge boulders.

Many warm afternoons I lay on my back on top of the biggest rock watching the sky. The summer clouds offered an unmatched art exhibit as they formed shapes which, through the use of a little imagination, became living things speaking their silent thoughts and revealing their hidden emotions. The quick and jerky motions of sparrows and swallows also grabbed my attention as they flashed and darted by.

But the buzzards always stripped my mind away from these other things and held it still. Buzzards boast no beauty close up. Their neck feathers stick out in unkempt disarray, and their heads resemble that of a feathered Uriah Heap. Their unpleasant odor coincides with their disgusting eating habits. What good then recommends the buzzard to a young watcher of nature?

His flying. Lying face up at Slippery Rock, I followed the soft glide of the buzzard. His easy circular path of flight at altitudes reached by no others, the grace that he exhibited, and the great distance that he covered erased all thought of the personal repulsiveness of the ugly scavenger.

My friends abused me because of my buzzard affection. With only Barrett Sutton expressing any agreement, I settled into silence on the issue, thinking of myself as something of a freak. Years later my friend Tom Watson Brown gave me a pamphlet written by his great grandfather, Thomas E. Watson. I found there an essay entitled "The Vulture," in which Senator Watson extolled the virtues of the buzzard, writing: "He has no enemies: envy, jealousy, unreasoning prejudice, aim no poison shafts at him: no other bird wants his job, and he himself is contented with it." He finishes his essay with these lines:

> Poor old weatherbeaten mariner of the skies!
> Tireless swimmer of the invisible waves! Lone sentry of the trackless beat!
> You're not pretty, and you probably smell bad, and you eat in a way that we despise—although we daily devour dead things ourselves —you've never had a "write-up" by one who appreciates your advantages and sympathized with your limitations.
> Well, you've got one, at last, such as it is.

Now he has another, such as it is.

Ralph Gregory, who lived four or five houses down North Lee Street from me, using an ordinary worker's chisel and hammer, fashioned two life-like faces on the big rocks at Slippery Rock. Without any training at all, he chipped away at the rocks until the likeness of an Indian Chief appeared on one rock. On another rock, he hammered out in detail the distinctive face of Eleanor Roosevelt. No one knows what he might have done with training. I lost track of Ralph; I do not know whether he ever acquired any training.

Many years later my son Hal came home one afternoon telling me, "Daddy, I found the neatest place. This pretty creek runs down a big rock into a pool but the main thing is on an even bigger rock, the Indians carved out the face of their chief."

I had to tell him that my neighbor and not the Indians did the carving. That makes me wonder if some other supposed historic monuments may have been created by some other Ralph Gregorys in other places and other times.

Slippery Rock remains nearly like it always was except for one thing. Some thoughtless person has chiseled over Ralph's masterpieces.

Blue Hole was the best spot for clandestine swimming and its advantages abounded. First, the trip from my house to Blue Hole took about ten minutes by foot. Second, it too was pretty with a clear stream running gently through the woods until it reached a little cliff dropping off about two feet into Blue Hole.

The cascade of clear water made a continuous bubbling sound in the hole. The three banks surrounding Blue Hole enclosed a pool of blue water with a clean sandy bottom. I do not know the depth of Blue Hole, but I do know it was over my head. This is one of the reasons I learned to swim there. The choices boiled down to swim or drown, and I opted for swimming.

The swimming holes did pose dangers. My neighbor Curtis Waites found that out when he decided to go to Blue Hole by himself one day. The problem was multiplied by the fact that Curtis could not swim. He might have drowned except that Johnny Ward happened along and pulled him out.

Sometimes I went to Blue Hole by myself, but usually in hopes of finding someone else there to swim with. On one such day, I found no one, and I contented myself to wander around looking at the wonders of nature. I happened upon one of the finest patches of maypops you ever saw. Maypops grow on a vine. They do not get ripe until late August usually, but, during the early summer, they have a beautiful purple flower which resists being picked by wilting almost immediately, regardless of whether you put it in water.

Maypops have only two uses that I know of. First, they serve as ideal ammunition for little boys' battles. That is, we used them to throw at one another. They do not hurt when they hit you, but they make a loud popping sound when they burst. So the victor knows when he has made a hit on his victim.

The maypop's other use has to do with the making of little animals. Being a green, oblong, vegetable-like thing, more round than a cucumber, and hollow inside, it is simple enough to take four kitchen matches and stick on the underside for legs. We then took another kitchen match and stuck toward the front top and topped it off with a smaller maypop for a neck and head. On the back of the top we took the sixth kitchen match and made a tail. Most little boys referred to these animals as pigs. I liked to think of them as either a hippopotamus or rhinoceros. When I made a rhinoceros, I generally took another kitchen match and stuck right on the snout of the head for the tusk. This kind of activity did not cost anything, and it provided a way for a little boy to pass some time.

That is exactly what I did on my way to Blue Hole that day. Then I heard somebody coming along. Looking up, I saw John Bland Jr., who lived not far from Blue Hole.

"What you doin'?" asked John.

"Just playin' with some maypops and waiting for somebody to come go swimmin'," I answered. Then I had a question to ask. "Why do they call 'em maypops when they grow in August?"

"Because when you hit somebody with one of them, they may pop," laughed John.

"I guess that's right, but there's some other things I don't understand, too. Why do June bugs come out in July and July flies come out in August?"

"Aw, come on, let's go swimmin'," said John, shaking his head with a little bit of disgust at my silly questions.

So away we went with me gaining one little bit of knowledge but making no progress on two other unanswered questions. I do not know the answers to those questions yet.

I never looked at Blue Hole as a danger because its beauty and peacefulness belied its hazardous threat. Many days I gathered with friends and set out from home with a sack of peanut butter crackers for a sort of snack picnic. Most times, swimming was not involved at all. Just getting there and being there was enough.

We started from my house, turned left just across the railroad, and then right into the woods after the street passed a wet weather stream. The trip then passed through gorgeous hillside woods behind Mr. Will Hill's house until Blue Hole appeared below. Often though the trip there was for swimming.

Understandably, this purpose lacked parental approval. Eight- and ten-year-old boys really ought not to be swimming unsupervised. I knew the consequences of breaking that rule. Mama developed a surefire detection device. When I came home on a hot day, she simply felt my head, and, if she found it wet, appropriate punishment was administered. This called for defensive action on my part, and I took it. Before going home after swimming at Blue Hole, we stopped on the railroad track where no shade deflected the direct sun rays. There we stayed until our hair dried, and we could go home safely. Ingenuity prevailed.

Throughout all this, the overwhelming wish of Forsyth young people was for a community swimming pool. Adults told us there could not be one because Forsyth's little water system could not support a pool. Mama worried about infantile paralysis. That is what we called polio.

Back then our water came from wells. Some of them were behind Bessie Tift College, and a couple of them were in the back part of the old city hall. These wells had big cast iron pumps with long plungers which made a "swush, swush, swush" sound each time they reached to the depth of the well. A new water system drawing from Tobesofkee Creek solved the problem.

By the time Forsyth had enough water, the federal government offered the WPA to build the pool. It took a long time to complete it, far more than a year I think. We would ride our bicycles out the dirt road to watch the workers as they dug the hole with picks and shovels and hauled the dirt out with wheel barrows. Some people said WPA stood for "we piddle around" instead of Work Projects Administration. The old New Deal organization may have moved slowly, but it got the job done and made jobs for those who needed them.

As the bright new green of the spring of 1940 deepened into the duller old green of midsummer, the pool completion neared and the excitement rose. The city hired Ouida Rhodes to manage the pool, and Walter Bramblett and Robert Bailey to work as life guards.

Then a controversy arose. A group of citizens protested that boys and men must not be allowed to swim unless their bathing suits had tops. Although the fuss delayed the pool opening, they finally resolved it in favor of toplessness . . . men and boys only of course.

Then came opening day. Each of us wanted to be the very first to hit the water, so every boy tried to position himself close to the pool during the opening ceremony. None of us foresaw the length of the ceremony. Almost everybody made a speech, and we did not want to hear any of them. Judge Ogden Persons made the final talk, and mercifully he held it short. When he finished, we all made the plunge; no one knows who entered first.

That day began a long relationship between me and that pool. Much of our summer social life centered there and I later became the life guard and after that managed the youth recreation program at the park where the pool is. Blue Hole became a nearly forgotten remnant of the past. It was old fashioned and countrified, and now we were up-to-date and city-like.

The city still operates that same pool. But I do not see much of it anymore. I think more about Blue Hole now, but nobody will ever see it again. When they graded out a shopping center parking lot, they covered up Blue Hole. Ain't progress wonderful.

CHAPTER 15

# Country Newspapering

"Where Uncle Remus Came of Age"—those words appear on a historical marker at the courthouse square in Forsyth. They refer to the fact that Joel Chandler Harris had his first newspaper experience working for the *Monroe Advertiser* there from 1868 to 1871. He later achieved fame with the *Atlanta Constitution* with his stories about Bre'r Rabbit and Bre'r Fox and their friends.

Not many people remember Harris worked in Forsyth. In fact, fewer and fewer folks even remember the *Advertiser* itself. Not so with me because I, like Uncle Remus, came of age there. For about thirty years, the little newspaper deeply affected my life. The paper started in 1854. My father bought it in 1917. He made it into one of the most widely quoted weekly newspapers in Georgia. Hardly a week passed without some of his writings appearing in the Atlanta papers.

Shortly after taking over the *Advertiser*, he wrote of his first newspaper experience during his sophomore year at Presbyterian College in South Carolina:

> The editor of the Clinton paper was addicted to drowning his sorrows in drink. It was before the advent of prohibition and his sorrows were multitudinous. One week the editor's spree coincided with the time during which the paper had to be issued. My roommate and I took up the task of the alcoholic publisher and issued in our opinion a notable

edition of the paper. No author of a book of many editions has ever been prouder than we were.

Thus began his career in newspapering.

The *Advertiser* could justly boast of considerable literary achievement. But it totally lacked physical opulence. Located in an austere brick building at the corner of West Johnston Street and Phelps Street, the *Advertiser* was heated by coal stoves and cooled by whatever air Mother Nature moved through the windows and doors. The news and business section of the building occupied only a minimum area; my father's desk with his Underwood typewriter and a couple of bulky wooden cabinets filled it. Besides Daddy, the news staff was composed of my mother, Mrs. Fred Stokes, and a varying number of contributing correspondents.

The print shop took up most of the building with bare floors, cracked plaster walls, and tongue-and-groove beaded ceiling which portrayed a kind of dingy substantialness. The people working in the back made up an interesting collection of characters.

Frank Thompson held the dominant role. He seemed old and was nearly deaf. But as a linotype operator and printer, he approached every job with an eye demanding perfection. When I began learning about printing, I first learned to dislike Mr. Thompson because I could never satisfy him. I now know that more teachers of his sort would create a better society. Next in line was Homer Dungan who set his sights upon being the world's next Frank Thompson. Although he fired at that target often, the bull's-eye was elusive because Mr. Thompson was one of a kind. Then there were the Blackman brothers, Gene and Robert. They fed job presses, cast cuts, and performed whatever tasks needed to be carried out.

I brought up the rear being too young, too inexperienced, and too clumsy to help very much in a print shop. This was the personnel structure—although it periodically included my older brother and sometimes my sister Rachel who did not know anything about printing but who wrote well.

This crowd made up a curious combination, but one person in the organization stood out from the others. That was Daddy. He appeared as an island of neat orderliness in a sea of disorder. He was the only person that I ever knew who worked around a print shop with clean fingernails and an unsoiled white shirt.

His concession to county newspaper fashion came in the wearing of a green celluloid eyeshade. He fit the country editor mold in another way by seeming to move so slowly while covering a lot of ground. I never thought he worked hard, but he always got a lot done. Maybe some of that resulted from his work schedule. His schedule dictated his absence from our breakfast table because he ate Post Toasties before daylight and went to work while the streets still lay quiet. The solitary early time of day undoubtedly provided better opportunity for writing and bookkeeping while freeing other hours for other things including his passion, fishing.

Advertising and subscription revenues in those days failed to meet the needs or wants of an editor and his family. This made job printing necessary. In our shop, this meant printing letterheads, envelopes, circulares, forms, and paperback books and pamphlets.

Some of the regular booklets contained the minutes of organizations bearing interesting names. For instance, the U. B. & S. of L. (United Brothers and Sisters of Light), the H. C. & U. B. (Home Circle and Union Brotherhood), the Grand Order of the Seven Wonders of the World, the New Towaliga Missionary Baptist B. Y. P. U. and Sunday School Convention, and Old Folks and Orphans Home.

Some not-so-regular publications had forgettable names but unforgettable contents. I remember one in the late 1930s written by a man from Griffin predicting the end of the world on an early and certain day. He said that he and other believers would be taken up to heaven and non-believers would be left here to suffer. To prove his confidence in his prediction and his compassion for unbelievers, he said that he mailed all of his clothes to Mussolini. The idea was that the author would not need them in heaven and Mussolini would still be here, thus needing them. The day of his prediction came and passed, and I do not know what the author did without clothes. For that matter, I do not know what Mussolini did with the clothes either.

The operation of a small town newspaper requires all sorts of skills: literary, mechanical, and business. Beyond that, it requires at least some understanding of people. Daddy wrote about that:

> The editing of a county newspaper gives a man a rather accurate cross section of the elements which enter into human life. It falls his lot to

weep with those who weep, to laugh with those who laugh, and to lie with those who lie, if one is to judge by some of the death notices and wedding write ups which are published.

Occasionally, country editing calls for a demonstration of bravery. On that subject, Daddy recorded:

> The career of the editor has a place not only for mental courage and the championship of the right, but there's also a call at times for a degree of physical fearlessness in order to cope with the results of writing. I recall that soon after I took charge of the *Advertiser* I wrote an article concerning a man who was fined for bootlegging and whose fine had been paid by a Baptist deacon. Soon after the paper had been placed in the mail, there came into my office a gentlemen over six feet tall with the sinews and war-like appearance of a Roman general. My mind reverted to the writings of those who recorded the events of the times when giants were said to be in the land. The abnormal specimen of hostility demanded my authority for writing him up as a Baptist deacon. I immediately passed the buck to the county sheriff who, with too much regard for the dramatic and too little for the truth, had given me the information for the story.

But being in my early teens, none of that meant much. My great concern was feeding a job press right. If I fed the paper crooked, missed feeding one paper so as to cause the next to offset, or failed to regulate the ink, I incurred the wrath of Mr. Thompson.

Even though I was his boss's son, Mr. Thompson failed to take any edge off his instructive tirades. The Blackman brothers who held positions only slightly more important than mine in the shop became my soul mates as we three attempted to bear up under Mr. Thompson's fearsomeness. Gene and Robert were older than I and were black, but neither of those circumstances altered our kinship born of a mutual fear of Frank Thompson.

I learned other reasons for liking Gene and Robert. Robert taught me to ride a bicycle. Gene tried to give me some instructions in boxing, and, when the three of us went fishing with Daddy, we would find our own spot where fishing was not taken so seriously.

Robert, the younger of the brothers, demonstrated more ambition than Gene. He undertook a moonlighting project of repairing and cleaning typewriters for people throughout the community. At my early age, it seemed that he was earning a great fortune at this enterprise. Gene, on the other hand, pursued his fortune by engaging in a weekend moonshine whiskey business which I think involved nothing more than transporting the contraband from the still to the dealer. In any event, it resulted in his landing in the chain gang.

The judge imposed a brief sentence on Gene, and the warden favored him by making him a trusty. He worked around our school helping with the building of the lunchroom, and I would talk to him during the recess period.

The striped suit did not seem to bother him much, and I do not think the work was any harder than that in the print shop. But lack of freedom makes a difference. In fact, it made so much difference to Gene that when he walked away, he never returned. That was more than fifty years ago. I heard reports that Gene has lived the life of a useful citizen. I hope that is true.

Robert did not get into the liquor hauling business with Gene, but sometimes he drank too much of it and caused disorder on a public street. The authorities charged him with public drunkenness and when court came along, Daddy went over to appear with Robert and pay the fine.

After the fine was imposed by a judge visiting from another circuit, the judge granted Daddy's request to make a statement. The statement went something like this: "I don't understand the liquor business. It's legal to make it, it's legal to sell it, it's legal to drink it, but illegal to show the effects of having drunk it."

The judge did not put Robert in jail, but I think that he came fairly close to locking up Daddy.

I learned of another one of Robert's talents when Daddy sent him and me to our house to do some furniture moving for one of Mama's spring cleaning episodes. As we waited for Mama to show up and tell us what to do, Robert looked over and said, "You ever hear me play the piano?"

"Aw, you can't play the piano," was my reply.

He then undertook to prove his point and proved it well. Moving easily onto the piano stool, he began playing in fine jazz style "What's the Reason I'm Not Pleasing You."

Our relationship had another interesting twist which came to light because of our fascination with boxing. Joe Louis reigned supreme, but the smaller and white Billy Conn mounted a serious challenge just before World War II. Robert made no bones about the fact that he favored Louis because of his blackness just as I made no bones about my favoritism for Billy Conn because of his whiteness. That conflict in our interest never shamed either of us or resulted in any change in our feelings for one another.

The day of the fight, we went fishing with Daddy and got home just as the fight was beginning. We sat in the car and listened with intent and emotion as Conn maintained the upper hand going into the thirteenth round. But thirteen turned out to be his unlucky number. The ever-stalking Brown Bomber found his target and ended the fight. Robert's yelling and jumping showed so much happiness I could not find it in my heart to be sad at Conn's loss. In fact, seeing how much the fight meant to Robert had a lot to do with me becoming a permanent Joe Louis fan.

A few months after the fight, America began its first peacetime military draft. Even though we had not yet entered the war, lots of young men were drafted, and others joined up. So one night not long after that, Robert came by the house.

"I'm leaving tomorrow," he said, "going to the Army. I'm gonna whip Hitler like Joe Louis whipped Billy Conn. I'll see you after the thirteenth round."

I never did see Robert again although I talked to him once on the telephone from New York. I understand that he has been reasonably successful, and that does not surprise me.

One of the curiosities about small town newspapers during the 1930s was a phenomenon called the tramp printer. These men went around the country from town to town stopping at print shops. Custom obligated the owner of the print shop to offer a day's work to the tramp printer and allow him to sleep in the shop on the following night. I particularly remember one.

After he worked all day long, Daddy said, "I guess you want to sleep in the shop tonight." The printer turned around and replied, "No. When the weather's nice like this, I like to sleep in the cemetery."

Now that gained my attention.

"Why," said I, "would you want to do anything like that?"

"I like to sleep on the ground and the ground in the cemetery is level with soft grass and besides that, they ain't nobody what's gonna bother you out there."

Truth is what you ought to get at a newspaper, and, to my childish notion, the last part of what the tramp printer said was the absolute truth.

CHAPTER 16

# The Politics
# of the Times . . . All Times

"Editor through necessity, minister by the grace of God, and Mayor by accident." My father wrote those words by way of self-description while he was serving as mayor of Forsyth in the late '20s. Although he appeared non-political in almost every way, he was a serious student of politics and never failed to assert himself when he saw a need.

My mother, on the other hand, was openly political having developed this interest as a child from her father who served in the Georgia legislature and on the bench. For her, the announcement of a political rally was like a fire bell to a firehorse. She could not resist it.

Mama and Daddy exhibited other differences in their political interests and responses. Perhaps a review of their heroes helps to understand this. In my father's view, Woodrow Wilson stood out as what a president really ought to be. In fact, he even had a secret admiration for Calvin Coolidge. Being a native Virginian who spent most of his life in Georgia, the Republican party was of course unthinkable to him. I believe, however, he might have been a card-carrying Federalist if that organization had been available during his lifetime.

My mother's attitude differed sharply. It probably grew from her father, Hugh Lumpkin, who had been something of a populist reformer in his public life. He favored many of the policies of Thomas E. Watson.

His claim to fame in the legislature was a vigorous effort to enact child labor laws. Many opposed this about the turn of the century.

Mama had two heroes, William Jennings Bryan and Franklin D. Roosevelt. She had a personal brush with each of them.

As a small child, her parents carried her to a chatauqua in Chattanooga where the principal speaker was the silver-tongued orator of the Platte, Bryan. She used to recount to me the story of the summer heat that night in the tent in the Tennessee River Valley and, how during the course of the program, Bryan came down into the crowd and sat in an empty seat next to my mother and fanned her with his palmetto fan. She may not have known much about the wisdom of the silver standard, but she was dead certain that Bryan ought to have been president.

Although the Roosevelt appeal was universal, my mother felt a personal need to be his champion. Among her well-remembered experiences was her attendance at a luncheon in Atlanta for a committee of Georgia Women for Al Smith for President. No less a personage than Franklin D. Roosevelt ate with and spoke to the group. Later in that year of 1928, he appeared as the principal speaker at a huge Smith rally in Atlanta. But the first one was more intimate and never forgotten by my mother. She could never have been anything but a Democrat.

So my mother and father had some different philosophies about politics because of their differing experiences. But, on the broadest issues, they seldom if ever disagreed. Both of them abhorred demagoguery and racism. Buffoonery also offended them. I mention this to show something about my own political background and to explain the political climate for some of the political events of my childhood years in Forsyth.

The Democrat-Republican question never meant much in Forsyth, Monroe County, or Georgia for that matter. You do not build much excitement in a contest participated in by only one side; we had Democrats but no Republicans. That is not exactly true. We did have Mr. Jim McCowan.

This solitary, unusual gentleman made up the entire list of white Republicans in Monroe County. He had an impact on me. The poor man suffered from arthritis or some like ailment and, as a result, walked with his back bent far forward and with an inability to turn his neck in either direction. I had never seen a person with this sort of disability other than Mr. McCowan. I had never seen a Republican other than Mr. McCowan. So I naturally assumed a relationship existed and concluded: if you become a Republican, you will end up with a stiff neck and a bad back like Mr. Jim.

If there were not other reasons for my thinking of myself as a Democrat when I was little, this reason was enough. The absence of a two-party system did not mean the absence of partisan politics. Quite to the contrary, conflicts in the political arena were part of the lifestyle of the time and developed so uniquely they became almost an art form.

In the time before my recollection, I understand the real split in city politics in Forsyth and perhaps county politics followed the line separating the Ku Klux Klan group and the anti-Klan group. As I understand it, the Klan of that era, while less than admirable, differed substantially in character from what we have known in the last generation or so. To begin with, a number of substantial citizens apparently participated, and it became a vehicle for political advancement. In his book *J. J. Brown and Thomas E. Watson, Georgia Politics 1912-1928*, Walter J. Brown explained his recollection of the status of the Klan in Georgia of that era:

> In the early 1920s, Klan membership was a fact of life for most successful politicians in the South, as well as in many other states, particularly in the middle West. No social stigma was attached to Klan membership. Revived in 1915 by Methodist minister Colonel William J. Simmons, the organization spread rapidly after World War I. Somewhat of a reform movement, it supported the enforcement of Prohibition laws, the protection of society against the corrosive influences of increasingly lax moral codes, law and order and the cleaning up of government.

Mr. Brown also wrote, "the Ku Klux Klan was a dominating political influence in the South, as well as the mid-West, in the early '20s and most successful politicians gravitated into that order." Thus many people joined the Klan not because of anything it stood for, but rather because it might lead to political gain. I think the Klan pretty much acquired control of the city government of Forsyth during most of the 1920s.

The Klan had a meeting hall in town and periodically conducted marches. My older brother used to tell me about watching when he was a little boy. As I recall the story, the local postman was a man named Jackson, and he had a little black and white spotted dog which followed him on his rounds delivering the mail everyday. Mr. Jackson belonged to the Klan, and, when he entered into the parade, he donned his robe and mask but the little dog at his heels always tipped off his identity.

The little boys in the town would follow along yelling, "There's Mr. Jackson and his dog, Spot. "

Mr. Jackson would kick at the little dog.

"Git, git, git. "

Spot would not "git," and everybody knew who Mr. Jackson was.

After some period of Klan dominance over the city government, a number of local leaders decided time had come for a change.

A hardware store stood at the corner of Lee and Johnston Streets in a building built for that very purpose in 1873. The Bramblett family built the building, and Walter Bramblett Sr. operated it for a long time along wit his partners, Charlie Hollis and Lewis Zellner. It became a gathering place for persons interested in politics, and Mr. Bramblett achieved a position of political leadership without ever holding public office. In fact, one member of the opposition group always referred to Bramblett Hardware and Furniture Company as Forsyth's Tammany Hall.

The store was the focal point for the anti-Ku Klux group. One day Mr. Bramblett and some of his other friends gathered with the intent of finding someone to run against Maynard Zellner, the Klan's candidate for mayor. Nobody seemed interested in undertaking the job. Finally, somebody looked over at Daddy and said, "Jack, you're it."

Daddy appeared an unlikely choice. Forsyth put great stock in being an old family, and my folks had just moved to Forsyth in 1917. Being a Baptist or Methodist and having deep Georgia roots counted for a whole lot. Daddy did not qualify on either score. Being a Presbyterian minister from Virginia who held graduate degrees from Union Theological Seminary in Richmond and Johns Hopkins University in Baltimore where one of his children was born, he did not fit the mold. But fit or not, he entered the race.

The attacks came almost immediately. The Klan people began by saying that he was a Yankee and a Catholic. It did not matter to them that he was a Presbyterian and a native of the home state of Robert E. Lee. After all, a Virginia accent did sound a little strange, and so did Presbyterians. He was clearly different. It may be that my mother's involvement in the Al Smith campaign added some fuel to the fire.

Additionally, Daddy had openly supported ill-fated political campaigns and endorsed unpopular positions. In 1920, he backed Governor

Hugh Dorsey in his campaign for the United States Senate despite the popularity of his opponent, Thomas E. Watson. Dorsey lost, but Daddy continued his support.

About the time of the election, Governor Dorsey wrote a pamphlet entitled "The Negro in Georgia." In it he recounted reports of mistreatment and injustices accorded black persons in some counties in the state. The pamphlet met with loud protests from a highly vocal portion of the population which may or may not have constituted a majority. The critics contended Governor Dorsey had slandered the state by making those reports public.

Quickly Daddy defended the Governor and his pamphlet. In a long editorial he wrote:

> There is thus no ground for the charge of slander. Viewing the matter from a broader standpoint, it is a well-known fact that Georgia has a regrettable record in the matter of lynchings. Court records would also confirm the charge that peonage exists as well as other forms of injustice in connection with the Negro. In view of the facts a charge of slander is plainly out of place and has its basis in the application, by some, of that brand of soap which is known as soft. There are too many men who cannot write without keeping one eye on the typewriter and the other in the direction of the polls.

The editorial further set out that the cases of lynchings cited by Governor Dorsey had been reported more completely in a majority of the newspapers of the United States, and that for Georgians to refuse to face the issue would be like sticking their heads in the sand. The editorial ended:

> A certain organization in demanding the impeachment of the governor compares him to Sampson, who in dying, destroyed the temple also. The organization does not press the comparison to the point of recalling that Sampson destroyed a heathen temple and along with it the enemies of law and righteousness. Such temple destroyers are much needed today.

Even so, during the course of the mayoral campaign, Daddy restrained his editorial treatment of the Klan. An example can be found in an editorial saying:

We are against the usurpation of rule by any clique or organization. As we see it, fraternal orders and patriotic organizations, regardless of the merit of the principles for which they stand, were never intended as a tool to elevate their members to office or keep them there.

As the campaign went on, my father wished many times he had never entered it. Particularly when they told him he would need to go from door to door soliciting votes. This came hard for him. One day he rapped on a door, and a little old lady answered. Daddy reached in his pocket, pulled out a campaign card, and handed it to the lady.

"I'm Jack Clarke. I hope you'll vote for me for mayor."

The little lady looked at him with a quizzical eye.

"You don't know who I am, do you? I'm Maynard Zellner's mother."

"Well, if you and Maynard have a falling out between now and election day, I hope you'll vote for me."

"I don't reckon that'll happen," she said, closing the door.

The campaign was a hard one with charges and some statements that could have even been considered veiled threats.

Election day arrived. Late in the afternoon, the Klan members assembled behind their meeting hall donning their robes and masks and pointed hats and organizing their torch light victory parade through the streets of Forsyth. Then came the shocker. The parade had to be canceled because Daddy won. After the election day, Daddy remained suspect in the eyes of the more ardent racists. A dentist from Atlanta wrote a letter to one of Daddy's friends complaining thusly:

Sept. 17, 1929

Dear Mr. Goodwyne:

There is a rumor started here in Atlanta and I am writing you to find out if it is true. It was said here that the mayor of Forsyth had entertained Ben Davis and his wife [the Republican National Committeeman who was in power until recently] and it was further stated that the mayor entertained the president of the school at Tuskeegee and his wife who were about to be received and entertained by Bessie Tift College but were stopped for some reason.

Please answer telling me if these are facts that exist or not.

Thanking you for a prompt reply, I am

Yours truly,

B. H. Mobley

Both the Republican chairman in Georgia back then and the Tuskeegee president were black.

I find no evidence of a response. I did find a photograph taken on the courthouse steps about that time showing three black men, two Asians, and three white men. The black men were the President of Tuskeegee, Professor William M. Hubbard of the Forsyth school, and Dr. W. F. Boddie, a Forsyth physician. The white men were Daddy, Superior Court Judge Ogden Persons, and Dr. Aquilla Chamblee, president of Bessie Tift College. I never uncovered the identities of the Asians.

Even though the campaign was bitter, my father and Maynard Zellner had been friends before the campaign, during the campaign, and remained warm friends for the rest of their long lives. That just proves that political candidates can often possess better qualities than some of their supporters.

In 1930, Daddy again opposed the Klan by supporting former Governor John M. Slaton for the United States Senate. Slaton became a Klan target by commuting the death sentence of Leo Frank in 1915. A Jewish pencil factory manager, Frank was convicted of the murder of a young female employee and sentenced to death. After the Governor commuted the sentence to life in prison, a group of night riders hanged Frank. Governor Slaton escaped mob violence but never escaped the political enmity of those who felt strongly about the Frank case.

When he ran against incumbent Senator William J. Harris, Slaton still bore the political scars he incurred in 1915 and lost badly carrying only Evans County. Nevertheless, Daddy used glowing terms in introducing him during the campaign. He referred to the former governor as "one from whom the people could expect statesmanship in times of national need, and you would no longer be forced to be satisfied with clerical skill and the placing upon the pronoun 'I' of a burden which it is not able to bear."

He went on to say this about Slaton, "I am introducing to you a man of courage and conviction, one who in the past has walked in ways of truth and justice even when those paths were dark; a man who does not become the champion of a national issue when it appears to be popular and then plays the traitor to that issue in later years."

After the Klan disappeared as a political influence, the need again arose for the structuring of the politics in the community to provide two sides so that everybody could be on one or the other. About this time,

Eugene Talmadge emerged as a political force in Georgia. This created two factions ready-made for Georgia politics: Talmadge and anti-Talmadge. The division fit Forsyth and Monroe County because the Talmadge family was among its earliest settlers. Gene Talmadge was born there, and his father, Thomas R. Talmadge, was a prominent and well-to-do businessman and farmer. The Talmadge personal, political, and business contacts ran deep in the community.

At the same time, some did not agree with the Talmadges and their sentiments ran equally deep. The dissidents however were a minority in Monroe County. There never was a doubt as to which faction my folks would fit into. The Talmadge approach did not fit their taste. Even so, that fact never had a chance to come into play because of an earlier occurrence.

Sometime during the twenties, a feud arose among the members of the County Board of Education. As I heard it, my father was a member of the board as was Mr. Tom Talmadge. The dispute had to do with the sale of the school books and the possible audit of the board's books and resulted in a public meeting being held one night in the courtroom in Forsyth. I relate the story as it was told to me by my father and remembered by me. I have no doubt of his truthfulness and accuracy. I do have some doubt of the accuracy of my recollection of details. But here it goes anyway.

Daddy, along with some other younger members of the Board of Education, favored a more economic sale of the school books and an audit of the board's books. Mr. Talmadge and the older members of the board opposed. At this time it appeared that the public agreed with the younger group so when Daddy got up to speak at the mass meeting, his words were met first with applause and as they became more moving, with cheers.

"I guess I got carried away with the public reaction," he told me.

With his enthusiasm buoyed by the crowd's enthusiasm, Daddy said he looked at Mr. Tom Talmadge and continued his oration.

"They're either a bunch of fools or a gang of crooks."

At this point, Mr. Talmadge, who often carried a cane, jumped out of his seat and started rushing toward my father. Dr. J. O. Elrod, who was Mr. Talmadge's brother-in-law and one of Daddy's closest friends, jumped between them, and looked at Daddy. "Don't hit him, Jack. He's an old man. "

Things quieted down, but it pretty well finished up the meeting. I have no idea what was ever done about the sale of the school books or auditing of the board's books. It was one of those events in which the issue was lost in the controversy surrounding it.

A humorous twist was that the next day Mr. Frank Thompson, the Linotype operator at Daddy's newspaper, sat with a crowbar by his side to fight off the Talmadge invasion of the newspaper office should it occur. Of course, it never did.

The fallout from this event was that the line was drawn between Daddy and the Talmadge family. As far as I know, he always opposed every Talmadge in every race they ever ran and actively supported the opposition. That was not an unusual position to take, though, because most people in our area at that time were either Talmadge men or anti-Talmadge men (women had opinions too but they did not express them as openly). The twains met only rarely.

My first personal participation in a political campaign came when I was nine in 1936. Gene Talmadge ran against Dick Russell for the United States Senate. His protege, Charlie Redwine, ran against Ed Rivers, the anti-Talmadge candidate for governor. Rivers and my father had developed a friendly relationship, and I went to a number of his rallies. In my view, Rivers made a better political speech than anybody in that era. He sure excited a young fellow like me who had already developed a deep interest in politics.

I do not know who thought the idea up or who organized it, but a bunch of youngsters in Forsyth formed what became known as a bicyclecade. We collected political posters and cards from the campaign forces of Senator Russell and Ed Rivers and decorated our bicycles with them. Then, as the election day approached, we rode up and down the streets of Forsyth showing our interest in our two candidates.

It had no effect on the election and certainly not on the diehard Talmadge people, but when Russell and Rivers won statewide, we were convinced that we had a part in the victory. Thus was born a personal political interest which never died.

If 1936 was fun, 1938 became fascinating. This time, Gene Talmadge decided to run against Senator Walter F. George. Since George lived in Vienna, Georgia, as did my oldest sister, our family dived in actively beginning with the campaign's opening in Vienna and continuing through the summer. One of the big events was a rally at the city auditorium in Macon. Daddy was asked to give the invocation.

"Bring your boy on up here on the platform, too," the senator said, as the rally was about to begin.

This cemented my support for Senator George.

The big occasion, however, took place in Barnesville, Georgia, late in the summer of 1938. Under the financing of the Rural Electrification Administration, electric co-ops strung electrical wires throughout the countryside. At long last, kerosene lamps could be discarded and electric lights provided illumination for country homes.

To celebrate the turning on of the electricity, they invited President Roosevelt to throw the switch and make a speech in Barnesville. My mother and her best friend, Katherine Sutton, agreed to carry me and my best friend, Barrett Sutton, to Barnesville to witness this historic event.

We arrived there early and even then the heat was terrible. Red Cross tents had been set up around the edge of the Gordon Military College football field to accommodate those of the crowd overcome by the heat. Before the day was over, the tents were overtaxed.

The football field lies in the lowest spot of a valley with banks on the north and south sides accommodating the stands for spectators. The Barnesville people built a temporary platform in the east end zone, and the crowd filled not only the stands but the entire field.

Before most of the people showed, Barrett and I made our way to the very front row, fairly close to the football goal line. A rope was stretched across at that point to keep the crowd back, and soldiers stood in full dress winter uniforms on the other side of the rope. As the day progressed, the soldiers began to fall from heat exhaustion. But as it turned out, the biggest fall of the day would not be from the climatic heat but from the political heat.

As I have already said, both Walter George and Eugene Talmadge were candidates for the United States Senate, George being the incumbent. Roosevelt favored neither. Talmadge had been a thorn in his flesh from the earliest of times, and George fell into the President's disfavor because of his opposition to some New Deal measures. Another candidate, Lawrence Camp, endorsed every Roosevelt program and, consequently, became recognized as the New Deal candidate for the United States Senate from Georgia. This set the stage for the speaking at Barnesville.

After spending a good deal of time extolling the virtues and describing the wonders of rural electrification, FDR finally got down to what he came for.

"Mr. George and I do not speak the same language," he said.

He went on to endorse Lawrence Camp for the United States Senate. In doing this, he made no mention of Talmadge and a curious chain of events was set in motion. A crowd which had a short time earlier exhibited wild enthusiasm for Roosevelt began to turn surly.

Senator George spontaneously took the microphone at the end of the Roosevelt speech.

"Mr. President, I accept the challenge."

Then the crowd which undoubtedly had been pro-Talmadge in the senatorial race burst into cheers for Senator George.

Roosevelt's purge attempt failed in Georgia as it did in South Carolina, and the effect in Georgia was almost amusing. The effort saved George from probable defeat at the hands of Talmadge who was an even stronger enemy of FDR and the New Deal programs.

Some observers even said that this was the President's real intent anyway and that he played a monumental joke on the Georgia voters to keep old Gene out of the Senate chamber. I do not know about that, but I do know that Lawrence Camp never had any possibility of winning, and stranger things have happened.

As a footnote, it is interesting that FDR never got around to his avowed purpose for being in Barnesville—throwing the switch to provide electricity for country folk. Apparently the Secret Service demurred to this.

W. Y. Andrews threw the switch. W. Y. was an employee of the rural electric co-op and was the son-in-law of my father's crowbar-wielding linotype operator, Frank Thompson. Mr. Thompson never did in Tom Talmadge with the crowbar, but his son-in-law became a part of an event which had the result of doing in Gene Talmadge in his race against Senator George.

# The Imperfect Anglers

Fishing occupied an important place in Daddy's life. He fished two or three times a week for almost the last fifty years of his life.

Daddy's devotion to angling contrasted starkly with the passionate, competitive pursuit of fish by some of those activist-type fishermen who buy expensive equipment, continuously wade and cast, and become frustrated at the failure to catch fish.

He used cheap fishing gear. He not only did not wade or cast, he never used artificial lures. Worms mainly served as bait for him, but he often baked a dough-like bread of three-fourths flour and one-fourth meal for catfish and carp.

Occasionally he seined for minnows to attract bass and crappie. At that time no one ever called those fish by those names. We knew bass as trout and crappie as white perch.

Not only did Daddy not wade and cast, he did not even hold a pole. He threw his lines from two or three poles in the water, stuck the poles in the bank, sat down and lit a Chesterfield, and waited for the cork to move.

Daddy never carried fish home because he did not like to eat them, and Mama sure had no interest in fooling with them. Logic says sitting in beautiful surroundings outside in nice weather pulled Daddy to the banks of a stream. That conclusion has logic but misses the factual mark. Daddy sometimes fished in ugly places like the mill race behind the big grist mill at Juliette. He often sat in rain, manning his poles and lines even when not a single fish had nibbled at his bait all day. More than once I watched from the car as he patiently waited in the sleet for the fish which had not bit.

Consider the possibility of a stimulating and intellectual association as Daddy's reason for fishing. There was Daddy's eclectic group of fishing companions. They ran the gamut from a cotton merchant and warehouseman who lost his business, a city clerk, an overly talkative printer, the Blackman brothers, a railroad foreman, a fireman, a black undertaker, the town liar, and sometimes me. Of course, this does not complete the list of fifty years of fishing cronies, but it illustrates their types.

The cotton merchant moved to the house across the street from us when the Depression caused him to go broke. Without work for himself, he brought his wife and five children to our neighborhood where she ran a boarding house, and he just sat on the front porch in the mornings and fished with Daddy in the afternoons. Mr. Boatwright was a good man ravaged by the brutal economy of the thirties.

The city clerk was a dear man from a dear family. His grandfather helped in the founding of our church, and he superintended the Sunday school.

The fireman was a good-natured fellow who enjoyed the blessings of spiritous liquors. When I brought a watermelon fishing with us, I offered him some. He looked at me astounded.

"Good Lord, no, I don't eat those things. You never know when somebody might come along and offer you a drink."

According to the wisdom of those times, the drinking of whiskey and eating of watermelon on the same day inflicted the foolish partaker with some dread and painful physical ailment. The fireman lived long enough, though, to learn the fallacy of this old wives' tale and enjoyed many a day on the creek bank eating watermelon while sipping bourbon.

The expert prevaricator, Bill, made the days different and sometimes trying. He did not tell mean lies or even ones from which he reaped any special benefits. I think he just found fiction more satisfying than fact and liked to live in what he thought of as a satisfying world.

Flat Shoals on the Towaliga River above High Falls was a favorite fishing haunt for Daddy and friends. Making our way downstream from where the car was parked, Daddy and I stopped at his favorite fishing spot. The yarn-spinner moved on downstream to a bend where the water pooled at a greater depth. We happened to see him pull up a fish basket (a illegal trap made of chicken wire) which somebody left to catch catfish. We watched as he put the biggest fish from the basket on his hook and eased it into the water.

A few minutes later, he made a big to-do out of pulling the poor old fish all around.

"I got a big 'un, preacher," he yelled, excitedly.

"Yes," Daddy answered calmly, "we saw him the first time."

A month or so later, Bill called Daddy suggesting fishing that afternoon. Daddy begged off, citing the work he needed to do. But, as noon approached, the urge to fish increased, and Robert Blackman and I took off with Daddy for Buck Creek. As usual, we caught little or nothing, but I will never forget Robert bragging about how he could hit a bird on the wing with a rock.

"Naw, you cain't," said I.

Robert hurled a rock and knocked the bird into the water. No matter how much I taunted him, he would not try it again. If you have already succeeded, why tempt fate with the possibility of a failure?

Caught up in the excitement and fun of Robert's bird-knocking feat, Daddy and I forgot all about Bill's call that morning. The next morning Bill called again. Having no excuse this time, Daddy agreed to go fishing that afternoon with Bill. On the way to Buck Creek, Bill told us about driving the most powerful truck ever built from Valdosta to Macon the day before.

When we reached Buck Creek, Daddy commented, "The water is up since yesterday."

"I thought you couldn't go fishing yesterday because of work," fired back Bill.

"Oh it wouldn't have made any difference to you," Daddy said, as he opened his tackle box, "You drove the big truck from Valdosta yesterday."

Bill gathered up his things and quietly walked to his usual fishing place. Daddy had done him in again. It was almost like a game they played.

If you looked for an intellectual among this bunch of fisherman, the black undertaker would come closest to qualifying. John Ham, known for some reason as Johnny Boy by both black and white, who talked, moved, and acted with great dignity. I always heard he went to a college up north somewhere. Maybe he acquired his way of speaking with those beautiful pear-shaped tones there.

I enjoyed going fishing with him and Daddy. They talked about things that sounded important and made me think. Maybe I missed the laughs and down-home fun on those days, but they intrigued me.

I wish I knew how Daddy selected his fishing companions. They lacked political influence, social status, great intellect for the most part, and particularly money.

Right here it might be well to point out that wealth did not matter much as a status symbol then. An often repeated phrase in that era was "genteel poverty." Even though poverty can be degrading, most folks back then truly appreciated those who could deal with their lack of worldly possessions in a genteel way.

So perhaps gentility in its own fashion was one of the standards Daddy employed in selecting these companions. But more than that, I think he looked for genuineness. Even the friend who played loose with the truth had an oddly twisted genuineness about him.

The selection standard possibly flowed from a youthful impression. After Daddy died, I came across something he wrote about his boyhood in Virginia which may provide an answer.

> I remember it as a land of oak and chestnut forests and broad fields of tobacco. Social life there was dominated by an aristocracy, so called, which had degenerated into a form of ancestor worship. This brought some of life's darkest moments to those who were more democratic and considered that some of life's dearest friends could be found in circles which were proscribed.

I also found this from one of his sermons:

> If you need further proof of the selfishness of human friendship you have only to turn to those instances in which the world bows down to men of wealth and fame. Many a worthy man has been ignored by the world simply because wealth and reputation were not among his possessions.

Mama dwelled a little more on the question of personal status. To her there were two particular categories of people: those who were "nice" and those who were "common." I have difficulty coming up with a clear definition of who fell in each category to Mama's way of thinking, but it seems to me it went something like this: a nice person was "brought up right." That meant a nice person had good manners. Some amount of higher formal education might help, but Mama never viewed that as essential. Culture she valued, but felt it could be acquired by the individual. A sense of values held a high place in the determination of whether you could be counted as nice. Wealth had nothing whatsoever to do with it. "You can be rich as Cresis," Mama said, "and still be common as gully dirt." I think her main ingredient for niceness was a kind of social responsibility and concern. In her view, its antithesis was crassness.

The afternoon fishing outings accounted for some fun but did not match the trips to Midville, Georgia. Midville is a small farming town on the Ogeechee River in east Georgia lying several hours from Forsyth by train.

We generally went by train for a couple of reasons. First, the Central of Georgia Railroad paid for its newspaper ads with what they called mileage. That was a booklet which allowed members of the newspaper family to ride a certain number of miles each year. When you told the conductor where you wanted to go, he would tear coupons from your yellow mileage book. The railroad assigned books to each family member and cautioned us of their nontransferability.

Another reason for train travel was that Daddy did not drive. I do not know why, he just did not. On ordinary trips, Mama drove but not for fishing. Unless somebody else went along with us, we had to go by train since I was too young to drive.

I talked to my friend Marvin Waldrep about going with us on one of the train trips to Midville. I told him he could use my brother's mileage and avoid the payment of a fare. Both of us knew the mileage was not transferrable. Preacher, as we called Marvin, liked the idea.

Getting on to the train, Preacher and I found seats near the front of the car while Daddy sought out a spot in the back. About fifteen miles out of Forsyth, in the middle of a remote area during the middle of the night, the conductor came in the back of the car, moving along taking up tickets and mileage.

He stopped and talked to Daddy for a few minutes. I wondered why Daddy would waste time with a conductor. They always seemed grouchy to me. When he got to us, he took my mileage matter-of-factly.

Then he took Preacher's mileage which was really Bubba's. He looked at it, then at Preacher, then back at the mileage book where Bubba had signed.

"What's your name, boy," growled the conductor even more unpleasantly than usual.

Preacher's ordinarily ruddy complexion turned ghostly white. He made a sort of gurgling sound and then sputtered.

"Jack Clarke Jr."

"Sign your name right here," barked the conductor, pointing to the back of the mileage coupon.

Looking at Bubba's signature, Preacher signed. A better job of forgery you never saw. The conductor stalked off saying nothing else.

I learned later that I witnessed Preacher's first train ride. All I knew at the time was that both of us thought the ride faced a quick midnight end for Preacher, and he was some sort of scared. I now wonder if the conversation between Daddy and the conductor might have been a planning session for a trick on Preacher. If so, it worked.

We always went to Midville on Thursday night after Daddy put the paper out. We walked the quarter mile or so from our house to the depot carrying only one change of clothes and Daddy's tackle box. Fishing poles lay waiting for us in Midville from the last trip.

The train left Forsyth close to midnight and reached Midville just ahead of the early sunrises that come in the summertime. Making our way through the dimly lit streets of the little town, we walked a short distance north of the depot to the home of a Mr. Drew. He operated a cafe in town and accommodated Daddy by renting us a bedroom on our fishing trips and allowing us to leave our fishing poles under his house between trips. After quietly getting the poles from under the house, we headed in the opposite direction for the river.

A sort of path, which at some point had been a wagon trail for logging purposes, led through some scrubby oak trees trying to survive in a ground that was more sand than soil. Just before reaching the river, the sound of constant water flowing and splashing could be heard.

Someone long before had driven a pipe about two inches in diameter into the ground, and out of this pipe there flowed an endless supply of cool clear water from an artesian well. It splashed on a rock and the portion which was not either drunk or soaked up by the sandy ground made its way into the Ogeechee River.

A few steps from there, we also made our way to that gorgeous stream. Nature endowed the Ogeechee with a peaceful beauty in spite of its almost ominous-appearing black waters caused by the dye seeping from the knees of giant cypress trees.

As we reached the banks of the Ogeechee, I always looked quickly downstream where you could see the faint glow of the sunrise through the Spanish moss and hear the awakening sounds of birds. Even the early rays of sun made visible one of the spectacular sites of the Ogeechee, the dawn frolic of the mullet.

It all began with the smallest of this species, about two or three inches long, jumping a foot or so out of the water and making a "spit" sound as they reentered. When their number grew, the bigger ones came out—at first just a few and then by the hundreds, propelling their flat silver selves in a graceful arc maybe three feet above the water. Polite society looks with disfavor on the mullet, but anyone who has seen the "Ogeechee mullet ballet" knows they are fishes of art and culture. I have even learned that truly fresh mullet is a delectable dish.

Before long the sun would tell us whether the river was low or high, a matter of importance. Low water meant good fishing, high water meant bad, according to the natives. I have seen it both ways and I never could tell much difference either way.

For that matter, the natives always told me, "You should have been here last week, they were really biting."

If the water was too high or even slightly stained, we gave up the ghost on the Ogeechee and hired someone to drive us to McKinney's pond. The pond water was always clear, and the mill race even clearer. Handsome bass swam lazily in full view in the race, but if anyone ever caught one I do not know about it. They would swim right around your bait. McKinney's pond looked pretty, but we caught more eels than fish there.

On the Ogeechee, our quest was the redbreast bream although we caught an occasional bass. We never caught a mullet because their mouths are too tender to hold a hook. We fished the simple direct way with cane poles and worms and looked for those elusive spots where the hungry fish waited to feast on red wigglers.

While some of the natives followed the same pattern we did, others practiced a more complicated method they called jigging. They used a long limber cane pole with a line only about eighteen inches long holding a big hook. Using yellow jacket larva (they called them baby jackets) as bait, the overall-clad locals wiggled the hook on the top of the water to the delight and eventual horror of unsuspecting bass. Because of the short line they could not "play" the bass so they just jerked them out of the water before the fish knew what was happening.

All that fascinated me, but we never tried it because we had no baby jackets and neither Daddy nor I were willing to reach into a yellow jacket nest in search of them. Besides we did not have the instinctive skill to jerk the bass out. So we stayed after the bream. Daddy had the only copy of Izaak Walton's book, *The Compleat Angler*, that I ever saw. As a little fellow I read Walton's description of a bream as a "large and stately" fish. This hardly fit the bream we knew.

"Either bream in old England differ from ours or Walton has more of the nature of a fisherman than a scientist," Daddy explained, chuckling.

Without saying so, I decided that the large and stately bream lurked somewhere in the dark Ogeechee water, and that one day I would catch him. I never did.

Our days up and down that stream were good ones, even with what appeared to be the world's highest population of huge mosquitoes and swarming gnats. I was told you could tell whether a person was from North Georgia, Middle Georgia, or South Georgia by the way he handled the gnats. If he fanned them with his hand, he was from North Georgia. If he tried to blow them away with his mouth, he was from Middle Georgia. If he just did not pay any attention to them, he was from South Georgia.

Sometimes we caught a good deal of fish. Sometimes we did not. Nevertheless, we stayed with it constantly, all day Friday and all day Saturday, broken only by a walk up to Mr. Drew's cafe for a little food.

The train carried us home just as it brought us there. It left at about ten o'clock Saturday night. This meant we had some time to waste after supper at Drew's cafe. This we generally did by joining the firemen sitting on their cane-bottom chairs across the street from the depot.

I learned some lessons of economics from them as well as a whole lot of trivia. The economics lesson came in response to my question about why Midville had several blocks of empty buildings. They explained that the dethroning of cotton did it to them. They pointed out the empty warehouses, the gins that operated no more, and the stores that had closed for lack of customers who could pay.

It was always good to get back to Forsyth even though Sunday school came awfully early the next morning.

I do not fish anymore. Memories of those fishing days are good ones. At least most of them are. One October day was different.

October days usually treat us well. In an apparent effort to hold back the brutality and dreariness of winter, nature sends an October sun unrivaled in brilliance. It reaches the earth at angles highlighting the beauty of even the most ordinary objects. October heat never burns and October cold never chills. Little boys understand that only a few of these days remain before winter heaps its restrictive weight on their freedom-loving spirits.

Such a day was Saturday, October 3, 1936.

Daddy came home a little early for dinner and asked, "You want to go fishing with me, Boatwright, and Mr. Anderson this afternoon, Big Boy." He mostly called me Big Boy until I became a teenager.

"Yes sir," I answered, really a little bit undecided.

We ate dinner (which at noon on Saturday was more of a lunch than other days), and for some reason I had second thoughts. I told Daddy that I believed I would not go. He shrugged it off as he gathered his things together.

The afternoon went smoothly enough until just after dark when Mama, Baby, and I were sitting in the library waiting for Daddy to get home for supper. Bubba burst in looking horrified.

"We're the luckiest people in the world," he blurted out, gasping for breath. "The train just hit Mr. Boatwright's car. Mr. Boatwright and Mr. Anderson are dead but Daddy's all right."

Even today, I can recall the stunned feeling of the moment. Sadness and joy mixed together. Grief and thanksgiving came from all of our lips, and about that time Daddy came in. His face was ashen, his eyes were glazed, and his steps were halting. Words just did not come.

Mr. Boatwright furnished the car for fishing that day. It was an old two-door Chevrolet with Mr. Boatwright and Daddy in the front seat and

Mr. Anderson in the back. When it stalled on the railroad tracks, Daddy looked out the right-hand window and saw the train coming around the bend.

The fishing poles tied on his side of the car made opening the door difficult but the age and frailty of the cord fastening them allowed Daddy to jump. Mr. Anderson tried to follow but not in time. Both his legs were severed. Mr. Boatwright apparently remained in the car trying to start it. With his head in Daddy's lap, Mr. Anderson lost consciousness and died shortly afterward.

In all of the horror and sadness, we rejoiced in Daddy's safety and wondered at my decision not to go fishing. Had I not changed my mind, I would have been in the backseat. Daddy then would have undoubtedly spent his time trying to get me out—which would have meant that none of us would have survived.

I remember Daddy sitting in his bedroom that night as visitors came by to comfort him and he seemed not to know they were there. His eyes sort of looked through us as though they saw into a region beyond. Maybe he was reliving that terrible time, or maybe he saw his friends Boatwright and Anderson in another world.

I have a vivid memory of Mr. Bob Persons sitting beside Daddy that night. He was a slight man with enormous animation, but this night he sat quietly on a chair that went with a little child's rolltop desk which I received for Christmas years before. Under other circumstances the sight of this little energetic banker sitting on a small child's chair beside Daddy in his big rocker might have looked funny. But this night it was a sad site of a man trying to comfort a friend who could not see or hear him.

For some time, Daddy could not find it in his heart to go fishing. But finally, just as the call of the spirit always drew him back to the pulpit, some other call drew him back to the river banks and creekside. Thinking back, I know now that fishing had a spiritual connotation for Daddy. Late in his life he wrote these lines:

> To some of us heaven, if we get there, will not be perfect if there is no opportunity to sit with our old cronies upon the banks of an eternal river and if there are no everlasting lakes there in which we may tempt the fish with our celestial lures.

CHAPTER 18

# Lazy Days of Summer

More cosmopolitan people call it the Summer Doldrums or some other fancy name. To us, though, the heavy, hot, humid days of late July and August are Dog Days.

Some scientist said this relates to the location of the dog star, but every Southerner knows that is hooey. We call the period Dog Days because you see more mad dogs then. And the dogs that do not go mad spend most of their time lying in the grease spot under the car or in the cool dust under the back porch.

Little boys of the 1930s did not face options that simple. We did not go mad, lying under a porch did not hold much of an attraction, and our Mamas would not have liked us wallowing around on a grease spot. It was too hot for baseball. No wind blew for kites. Marbles is a winter game, and Forsyth had no swimming pool. All that left a lot of time for slow walking and cloud watching which became boring pretty soon. As a result, little events became major attractions for us.

The city water tank towered over the dead end of Morse Street near our backyard. On rare summer days when the water filled the tank to its capacity, the water ran over and spilled on the sun-withered grass below. The sound of this artificial rain reached the sensitive ears of bored little boys living nearby and happy yells notified the rest of the neighborhood.

Within minutes a whole gaggle of boys romped in the sprinkle from the tank like geese who had been deprived of water for a long time. Only the Dog Days of long ago could make so simple a happening into a major event.

Other sounds sometimes broke the quiet of a Dog Day and issued their call to hot and restless children. The bell on the ice truck signaled that Howard Wynn was about to make a delivery of ice. Most folks did not have electric refrigerators then. For the few who did, the tradename Frigidaire took on a generic meaning because that is what they called all refrigerators.

For the rest of us, an ice box served the purpose. They put a block of ice from the nearby ice plant in a container at the top of the box, and the section below held the food needing cooling. As the ice melted very slowly, the cold water dripped down through little tubes inside the walls of the cooling compartment and then into a pan at the bottom. It did the job tolerably well.

About once a month, Mama bought a book of ice coupons. Each green coupon paid for a certain number of pounds of ice. Mama would leave one or more coupons on top of the ice box on the back porch; the ice man took the coupons and put the appropriate amount of ice in the box. As he approached he always rang the bell in case anyone forgot to put out the coupons. The bell meant Howard would chip a long sliver of ice about the size and shape of an ice cream cone and give it to me to lick until I ate it or it melted.

A less appealing part of our ice experience came on those days when Mama failed to put out the coupon, or we just needed some extra ice. Then she sent me down Kimball Street after it. I liked going to the ice plant; it was the coming back that I did not like.

Hanging around the ice house intrigued me as I watched the huge slabs of ice come sailing down the chute on their edge. Ice came out about a foot wide, three feet high, and four feet long. As soon as it hit the old tire-padded timber at the bottom of the chute, one of the workers grabbed it with tongs and attacked it with an ice pick. Quickly he broke it into virtually exact sizes and shapes before slinging it into the frozen storage room. I always wondered at the sight. How could anybody do that with an ice pick? I still wonder.

"Mama sent me for ten pounds," I told the man with the tongs and the pick, handing him the coupons.

In a flash he flipped a big block of ice on a little shelf and chipped out what I always assumed was exactly ten pounds. But nobody weighed it. We just trusted their skill and integrity. They tied a piece of what we called grass cord around the ice and slid it out toward me.

Unless you have walked a couple of blocks with grass cord cutting into your seven-year-old fingers from the weight of ten pounds of ice, you cannot really appreciate why young boys did not like going after ice.

A couple of blocks in the other direction from our house, another business offered equally interesting action, without the drawback of ice toting. Mr. Willie Webb and his sons ran the Seminole Bottling Company in a building shared with the National Guard on Jackson Street.

The continuous line of bottles moving along on a track first were thoroughly washed and were then filled with soda pop and capped. All this made a wonderful sound as the rattle of the track provided the rhythm for the harmony of the swishing washer, the scooting filler, and the popping capper. This audio turned into a video with the bottles doing a dance of wiggles and jumps on their way to becoming colorful holders of Double Orange or Double Grape.

Sometimes a different shaped bottle was filled with Jumbo Cola. This drink gained particular popularity because some of its caps had a number under the cork padding inside. The number might be five, ten, or twenty-five. If you got found of those, they gave you that much money for it—a great windfall. Of course the windfall was in cents, not dollars. That ended when Double Cola replaced Jumbo Cola as the trademark.

Billy Hill and I made frequent visits to the bottling plant, partly because we liked the sight and sound, but an even better reason drew us there on hot days. The operator sometimes gave us a cold drink. No liquid ever tasted quite so good.

The too-full water tank went splat, the ice truck bell went ding-a-ling, and the bottling machine went swish, scoot, pop, making some of the sounds of my childhood.

But another more common sound told the story of what was perhaps the towns focal activity . . . the railroad and its trains.

The powerful chug of the steam engine combined with the clickety-clack of the tracks and the mournful wail of its whistle to lend a little town importance and hope. Towns with railroads survived. Towns without railroads dried up. The tracks acted as the town's arteries and the trains as its lifeblood. They moved people; they moved goods; they brought news, ideas, culture, wealth and progress. They also brought dreams.

I spent a lot of time watching trains go by. They did not go to far away lands across the sea, but for me the Flamingo speeding through Forsyth on its way from Chicago to Miami triggered just about as much imagination. I particularly liked to see the people sitting in the dining car eating what I thought must have been the finest food on earth.

I also saw visions of the towns they came from and the towns they headed for. The thought of Chicago and Melvin Purvis shooting down John Dillinger as he came out of the Chicago picture show with the lady in red always excited me. That is why I prized so dearly my Melvin Purvis Junior G-Man badge which I got in return for Post Toastie box-tops.

Miami, on the other hand, painted a different mental picture for me. In fact, the picture was not just mental. It hung above the fireplace covering most of the wall in the brick Victorian passenger depot in Forsyth. In vivid color, the painting revealed what seemed like a whole lot of a well-shaped bathing beauty lounging on the sands of Miami Beach in a late twenties or early thirties swimsuit.

Funny, the picture was really just a poster advertising a train, but for me it held all the fascination of a work of one of the great masters. Not only did it show the glamour of Miami's white beach, blue ocean, and palm trees that seemed to sway in an unfelt sea breeze, it aroused my interest in feminine comeliness from its latent state in tender years.

The Flamingo shared with the Dixie Flyer and Dixie Limited the special place of being the "fast trains" through Forsyth. These trains stopped in Forsyth only when the station agent, Miss Laura Frye, wired ahead with her telegraph key telling that somebody waited with a ticket, or when somebody wanted to get off.

A whole bunch of other passenger trains came through, and we called them locals. They stopped just about everywhere and had no dining car or Pullman berths, but they meant a lot to us.

The four o'clock train brought the *Atlanta Georgian* and the six-thirty train brought the *Atlanta Journal*. The *Constitution* came on an early morning train, but we did not see much of it because small town folks mainly liked afternoon papers. I think this was because they rushed off to work in the morning but had plenty time after supper to read the paper because there was no TV.

Buddy Rhodes, who was the chief of the paper deliveries, told me that they delivered only fifty-two copies of the *Constitution* everyday.

Interestingly, fifty of those went to black subscribers and one of the white subscribers was Oscar McCommon. Buddy does not remember who the other one was.

Mr. McCommon ran the combination wagon, buggy, and blacksmith shop across from the city hall on North Lee Street. He had interesting curiosities spotted in front of his place. One I remember most vividly was an oversized musket hanging on the outside wall under the shed extending over the sidewalk.

A sign over the big gun said "Just like Hitler, all bluff."

Mr. McCommon might have been right in 1936, and, if we had called Hitler's bluff then, much of the agonies of World War II might have been avoided.

Watching the train people throw the papers off and Buddy Rhodes and Leon Brooks grab them up for delivery added something to a dull afternoon. I liked to watch the mail pickup and dropoff too. I do not know whether Emerson Woodward worked for the railroad or the post office, but I do know he carried the mail in a pushcart from the depot to the post office and vice versa.

A jolly fellow, Mr. Woodward held the favor of all of us young folk partly because of his cheery way of saying "Hello." He yelled, "Yeehoo." He also told stories of the past. He used to tell me about his father or grandfather helping load and unload trains.

As a slave, the elder Woodward loaded food and other provisions for the Confederate troops in North Georgia before the fall of Atlanta. He then unloaded wounded soldiers still wearing their gray uniforms in the heat of July 1864, after the Battle of Atlanta.

This all happened at a stone depot on Adams Street. They built that building when Forsyth sat at the northern end of the railroad being the terminus. Right after that, the rail lines moved beyond Forsyth to another community, first called Terminus. The name of that settlement became Marthasville, and finally Atlanta.

The old stone depot in Forsyth predates all buildings in downtown Atlanta and still stands. In 1896 the brick depot replaced the old structure as the passenger depot, but the freight activity stayed on until recent years.

In my young days Mr. J. E. Bogle was the freight agent while Miss Laura Frye took care of the passengers in the new building. The Forsyth stations held important positions on the railroad.

We had plenty of freight trains. I watched them for a different reason. They evoked no dreams of glamorous people and places. They revealed to me the hard realities of hard times. Every freight train carried numbers of hoboes riding on top of the cars, between the cars, and even on the rods underneath the cars. They came from nowhere and seemed to be headed nowhere. They only looked for something better wherever that might be. During this time people learned to be "string savers." They wasted nothing and even the young ones like me still cling to some of the frugality which flowed from the Depression.

Despite having lived during the most prosperous era in history, I still have some of the funny habits of the deprived. I find it hard to throw anything away. I find myself eating food when I am full and know it will make me fat—just so it will not be wasted. Wastefulness still offends me mightily. Watching hoboes can do that to you.

These experiences drew a great dividing line. On one side stand those who not only remember but lived in the hard times. On the other side sit those who know only the comfort of the years after the Depression. I worry about America when all the "string savers" are gone.

There is another thing about trains. They can nearly about scare you to death and with good reason because they are big enough and fast enough to do bad things to you.

"Don't get too close to the track," Mama used to say. "That train will suck you under its wheels."

I believed her. Most anybody else who has been fairly close to a speeding steam locomotive would believe it too. I also knew what a train could do to people because of the tragic experience of Daddy and his friends on their way home from fishing. But somehow we tend to forget dangers and tempt them with our own foolishness.

As Buddy Howard and I walked toward the courthouse square on an August afternoon, we heard the whistle of a train travelling south toward the crossing on North Lee Street. We wheeled around and ran at top speed toward the track.

Earlier we had decided to place some pennies on the track for the train to flatten in interesting shapes. But we grew tired of waiting for the train, so we decided to walk up town. Now the sound of the whistle signalled the opportunity, and we naturally responded to the signal. However, our response was not well thought-out. Thinking the train might reach the North Lee crossing before we could get there, we ran toward a street further south which deadended at a deep and steep bank at the edge of the track.

Upon getting to the bank, I hesitated not at all. Down I went. Only then did I realize my momentum down the almost 90° embankment some twenty feet deep was thrusting me onto the track where the train and I were about to tie in our contest to reach the same spot on the track. I right then realized the train might be about to turn me into a spot on the track. But fear allowed me to violate the law of gravity and principle of inertia. Frantically grabbing at the honeysuckle and Johnson grass on the bank while I scrambled upward turned me around one hundred and eighty degrees. An object hurdling downward had abruptly turned its movement upwards.

When I reached the top of the bank I saw Buddy sitting on the ground laughing uncontrollably. While he laughed, I panted heavily not so much from exhaustion as from fright. I had just learned something physicists probably do not believe . . . fear can cause you to overcome natural laws.

# A Photo Album:
## The Clarke Family & City of Forsyth

The Monroe County Courthouse, Forsyth, 1940. As was the case with many small towns of the era, the courthouse was the center of activity in Forsyth and a symbol of its past and future.

PLATE 1

*Top left.* Rosa Gravely Clarke, maternal grandmother of Harold Clarke. *Top right.* Jack H. Clarke, his mother, and his sister Sally. *Bottom.* Jack H. Clarke, Harold's father, posing with his fraternity as a student at Presbyterian College, 1903. He is second from the right, second row.

PLATE 2

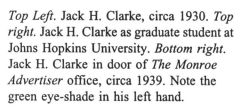

*Top Left.* Jack H. Clarke, circa 1930. *Top right.* Jack H. Clarke as graduate student at Johns Hopkins University. *Bottom right.* Jack H. Clarke in door of *The Monroe Advertiser* office, circa 1939. Note the green eye-shade in his left hand.

PLATE 3

*Top.* The tri-racial gathering, 1929. Back row: Dr. Acquilla Chamblee, Dr. L. B. Boddie, Professor William M. Hubbard, Jack H. Clarke. Front row: Unknown Asian, the president of Tuskegee Institute, unknown Asian, and Judge Ogden Persons. This picture was taken shortly after Mr. Clarke defeated the Klan candidate for mayor of Forsyth, Georgia. *Bottom.* Mr. Clarke fishing on the bank of the Ogeechee River. His objective was relaxation.

PLATE 4

*Top.* Judge and Mrs. Hugh P. Lumpkin, paternal grandparents of Harold Clarke.
*Bottom.* The home where Ruby Lumpkin, Harold's mother, grew up in Lafayette, GA.

PLATE 5

*Left.* Ruby Lumpkin, Harold's mother, as a young girl, circa 1895. *Top right.* Ruby (Lumpkin) Clarke as a young wife and mother about the time the Clarke family moved to the town of Forsyth. *Bottom right.* Ruby (Lumpkin) Clarke with three of her children, Jack (Bubba), Rachael, and Rosa Emiline.

PLATE 6

Jack, Jr., Rachael, and Rosa Emiline Clarke posing for a photograph.

PLATE 7

*Top left.* Harold's sisters, Rosa Emiline and Essie Black, circa 1927. *Top right.* Rachel (Baby), Essie Black, and Rosa Emiline. *Bottom left.* Jack Clarke, Jr. (Bubba), Harold's older brother, circa 1929. *Bottom right.* Rosa Emiline Clarke, circa 1932.

PLATE 8

*Top left.* Harold Clarke (*right*) and cousins at the 1939 World's Fair in New York. *Top right.* Billy Crowder, school picture 1938-1939. *Bottom left.* With cousins: Virginia Coffee, Harold, Emmalee Wyly, and Lumpkin Coffee, 1939. *Bottom right.* Ruby Clarke and Harold, 1935.

PLATE 9

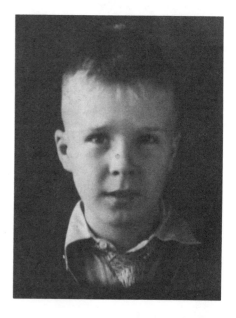

*Top left.* Harold Clarke as young boy. *Top right.* Harold's school picture, 1937. *Bottom left.* Harold in window of the "goat house." Mr. Clarke jumped through this window to escape the attack of Harold's "pet" goat. In this picture, Harold is wearing a pair of tweediroy knickers, which he detested. The pants, however, were popular with mothers because the material could withstand the wear and tear of shooting marbles and other games their mischievous children devised.

PLATE 10

*Top left.* Harold in his homemade soapbox racer, 1937. *Top right.* Harold's Ninth Birthday Party. Standing: Banks Worsham, Harold. Seated: Sonny Ensign, Barrett Sutton, and Billy Hill. *Bottom left.* Harold and Banks "making up first grade," the summer of 1934.

PLATE 11

*Top left.* Major Boulware, the grandfather of Barrett Sutton. *Top right.* Sheriff Ty Holland and two of his daughters, circa 1914. *Bottom left.* Harold and his mother sitting on the steps of the Georgia monument at the Chickamauga Battlefield.

PLATE 12

*Top left.* Forsyth high school students observing Confederate Memorial Day, 1939. *Middle.* Postcard of Bank Stephens Grammar School. *Bottom left.* Confederate Memorial Day, 1939.

PLATE 13

The Rhodes Seed Co., Forsyth, mid 1920s. Note the books on the extreme right. Mr. Rhodes (*left*) sold school books before they became free. The young boy is Sim Rhodes.

PLATE 14

The Bramblett Hardware Co., Forsyth, 1920s. *Lf to rt*: C. D. Hollis, Lewis E. Zellner, and Bob McCowen. The store, the site of political debates, was called the Tammany Hall of Forsyth.

PLATE 15

The Clarke family purchased this home on Lee Street in 1920. The house was built in 1820, and the T. J. Hardin family (photographed here in 1913) remodeled and enlarged it in the 1890s.

PLATE 16

## CHAPTER 19
# Trains out of Wonderland

We did our share of riding on the trains too and not just for long trips. We used them to go to Macon and particularly to go to Atlanta. One of the reasons was convenience but the mileage books given to the newspaper office probably formed a stronger reason.

The train made a trip to Atlanta an easy one. Rich's sat near the terminal station and offered just about any sort of sight a young boy could want to see, from the toy department on. There was always the danger of wandering off and getting lost so Mama always gave me a bit of good advice.

"If you get lost, go to the man in the store who's not wearing a hat. He's the floorwalker and will find me for you," she always explained.

That statement carries with it a commentary on the times. The first thing is that all big department stores had people called "floorwalkers" on each floor stationed there just to be helpful. Another commentary is that all men wore hats in stores and on the streets. Those without a hat one were bound to be store employees. If we revived that custom, we would reduce the incidents of skin cancer.

The train got you to Macon quicker but it was a heap more confusing. In those days the line between Eastern and Central time zones ran pretty much down the middle of Georgia. This put Atlanta and Forsyth on Central time, and although Macon is only twenty-five miles from us, it went by Eastern time.

The train trip from Forsyth to Macon took about forty minutes, but the clock said otherwise. If you left Forsyth on the eleven o'clock train, you got to Macon at twelve-forty. It sounded a lot like an hour and forty minutes to me. Coming home puzzled me even more. If we left Macon at five o'clock, we got to Forsyth at fifteen minutes to five. Now that is fast.

The train to Macon crossed a long trestle with no sides or guard rails and I always thought it might fall off. That was one of those deeply felt childish fears that you are ashamed to admit to.

For a time, my aunt lived in Thomaston, and we made trips there to visit her and my two cousins, Lumpkin and Virginia Coffee. It is less than thirty miles from Forsyth to Thomaston, but at that time part of those miles were on some of the muddiest roads anybody every saw. So we often went by train. This meant a two-leg journey, taking the better part of a morning or afternoon.

We began by riding a regular train from Forsyth to Barnesville and then having what seemed like an awfully long wait for a one-car train which went from Barnesville to Thomaston. They called this vehicle the "dummy," and although it rode on the railroad track with railroad wheels, I think it was moved by a gasoline engine. Certainly it had no steam locomotive attached to it.

On one trip to Thomaston, I visited for several days enjoying the life of what seemed to me to be a big town compared to Forsyth. My aunt carried us to a ten-cent store and bought three little boats we called putt-putt boats. They were made of tin and were about two inches long. A more ingenious toy no one ever devised. A little indenture on top of the cabin would hold a few drops of water. Inside the cabin you placed a birthday cake candle which heated the water and created steam which went through small pipes causing the boat to go forward with a "putt-putt-putt" sound. We spent happy hours playing with those little boats in the bathtub.

On one afternoon, Virginia and Lumpkin and I went over to a playground. They had heavy swings hanging on long heavy chains, and I had visions of swinging high enough to loop the bar far over our heads. I was never able to do that but I did swing high enough to fall out of the swing.

Hitting the ground did not hurt so much but then the swing came back down and hit me in the head, opening a right ugly gash. As I lay there trying to be brave, Virginia looked down to see the blood running from my head and began to cry.

"Your head's bleeding," she sobbed. "When your head bleeds, you die."

My manly braveness caused me to resist crying from the pain, but it was not big enough to cover things like dying. So I joined Virginia in the crying business. The cut turned out not to be as bad as we thought. It healed up and I did not die.

Another funny train that took a long time was the small and slow train leading through Cedartown and going to Mama's old hometown Lafayette near Chattanooga. Either the Thomaston or Lafayette train, I cannot remember which, had a conductor who was one-legged. His train did not have a lot of passengers, so he liked to spend time and conversation with the few that it had. After we had ridden with him off and on for a couple of years, Mama saw a newspaper account of his death. The writer had lots of good things to say about the one-legged conductor on the train with few passengers and how he spread some sunshine along the rails. We felt saddened by his passing and commented that the train would not be the same.

The next trip we took on that train there stood the same one-legged man just as alive as he ever was. We did not want to ask him about his obituary and memorial article so we never knew why all that appeared in the paper.

CHAPTER 20

# A Southern Christmas Carol

"Merry Christmas. I'll see you in January." With those words, Mr. Frank signaled the beginning of Christmas holidays in 1938, and all of us in his sixth grade class rushed for the door. We left behind a teacher with one of the biggest supplies of raisins anybody ever saw.

Almost every day at recess our teacher, Frank Williams, ate raisins, explaining they contained lots of iron. So naturally I thought of a big box of raisins as the perfect Christmas present for him. The whole class thought the same, resulting in his oversupply.

Mr. Frank's raisins concerned me little as we rushed down the Bank Stephens school steps. Chilled by a stiff wind from the winter's first cold spell, I half ran and half walked home where I knew the "getting ready" for Christmas process would be in full blast. Mama turned "getting ready" for Christmas into something almost as big as the holiday itself. She began it the day after Thanksgiving by making three fruitcakes— two dark and one light. Most often she summoned me to the duty of cutting up the dried and candied fruits. The big scissors usually caused a blister or two on my fingers.

Sometimes I helped stir the fruit into the batter. Once, in a flash of insight, I broke the monotony by stirring clockwise for awhile and then switching to counterclockwise—that is until Mama noticed.

"Don't change your stirring direction," she said softly, patting my shoulder. "It will make the cake unstired." I could not figure that out then, and I still cannot. But if Mama said it, it is so.

Mama's cakes contrasted sharply with the store-bought fruitcakes of today. Hers had none of the gumminess of commercial fruitcake, and instead of tasteless sweetness, they stimulated the sense of smell and taste with lots of spices and a slight tinge of bitterness.

When Mama took the cakes out of the oven, she put them in big silver-colored tin containers we called lard cans. Standing about two feet high, they had about an eighteen-inch diameter. We could stack as many as three cakes in one can. As each cake was put in the can, Mama poured grape juice over it. Since we were a preacher's family, we did not use wine or bourbon like other folks, and this may have been an advantage because the juice did not overpower the spicy flavor of the cake. Before sealing the cakes for some three weeks of seasoning, we put fresh apples and oranges around them. This added moisture and flavor.

When I walked into the kitchen on that first day of Christmas vacation, I faced surroundings different from those of my first or second year in school. A white enamel natural gas range stood before the fireplace where the old green kerosene stove used to be. A wooden icebox no longer sat on the back porch. Instead, a Frigidaire hummed in the kitchen. The ancient kitchen safe with its screen doors had given way to a kitchen cabinet that Mama had traded newspaper ads for. Daddy had hired A. B. Dannelly to brick up the little open grate coal fireplaces in each room of the house, and natural gas radiant heaters occupied all the hearths now. All this displayed the coming of the modern era. It also tipped off the fact that some of the pains of the Depression had subsided.

The prosperity that everybody yearned for was not upon us, but the sharp edge of the economic blade no longer cut ugly gashes in people's lives. Bruises and abrasions persisted, but deep lacerations had become rare.

Our two or three years without a car ended when Daddy bought a 1935 Chevrolet. I no longer overheard the whispered concerns Mama and Daddy expressed to each other about trying to hold onto the house and the newspaper. I did hear them talk with relief about how the Home Owners Loan Corporation had saved things for us. But even at the darkest of times, Mama always maintained her eternal optimism and over and over again said, "Don't worry about *things*. There are more important concerns in this world."

Our family had seen other changes too. My sister Baby married that year and seemed happy. I had no way of knowing that neither the marriage nor the happiness would last. My brother Bubba was drinking so much he could not keep a regular job. Again, Mama's emphasis on the positive surfaced. "He will pull through this. It's just a stage in his life," she reassured me and herself. Time proved Mama wrong. Bubba never pulled through it, and Baby never experienced sustained happiness. Two talented and loving people just never got life in sync. But none of these misfortunes weighed on Mama or any of the rest of us on this day. This was the Christmas season, and Mama was truly a Christmas person.

"Harold," Mama called in a lilting voice. "Baby's home and Bubba will be here in a few minutes. You all need to go to get a Christmas tree."

I knew this meant a fuss because it always did. We did not buy our trees, we went to the woods to find and cut one. (In fact, I never bought a Christmas tree until I was sixty-three years old.) Back then, Bubba, Baby, and I did the job. Cutting the tree and carrying it home was not the hard part. The trouble came in the business of picking out the tree. Baby always thought the one that Bubba picked out was too little, and I always figured both of them wrong.

"Here's one that's just right," Bubba said about the first cedar tree that we came across.

"Don't be silly," Baby sneered. "That little thing is dinky."

"Here's the one I want," I yelled from down a hill.

They both just laughed at me without answering. I answered their laughter by pouting.

As always, we compromised and brought home a tree nobody particularly liked. Without a trace of a smile among the three of us, we carried the tree into the house where the consummate peacemaker met us.

"O-o-o-oh," Mama exclaimed. "It's gorgeous! I do believe it's the prettiest tree we've ever had."

As years went by, I began to realize that she said that every year. Although repetitive, it did the peacemaking trick and restored our Christmas spirit.

The decorating of the tree created less controversy because each of us had separate roles. Bubba put on the lights. Baby hung the ornaments, and I handled the tinsel. The lights interested me most because they were fairly new to us. Until I was about six years old, we only had ornaments and tinsel on the tree, with lights being nearly unknown in Forsyth as Christmas tree decorations. I saw lots of magazine and newspaper ads where people had candles on the tree so I begged Mama to let us do that. She refused, explaining the dangers of fire and that they just light those in the ads for a long enough time to take the pictures.

The first Christmas with lights on the tree was doubly exciting for me. Homer Dungen, who worked in the print shop, claimed to be an electrician as well as a Linotype operator and printer. He made a big production out of testing, arranging, and plugging in our first lights, all of which seemed like magic to me. Those old Christmas light cords were troublesome because each light served as a connector along the cord to the succeeding light. If one light burned out, the entire string went dark. Of course we did not know which light had burned out, so we were constantly testing every light on the cord to replace a solitary bad one.

While the three of us did the tree, Mama busied herself putting red and green crepe paper around the light fixtures in every room so the house would have what she called a "Christmas glow." Daddy never took part in any of this activity. In fact, he usually made it his business to be out somewhere fishing when all this went on. I puzzled over what caused Daddy to be what I thought was a non-Christmas person. About his only participation in the yuletide season was the reading of the biblical Christmas story to all of the family on Christmas Eve night and following that with a prayer. His one other Christmas involvement had to do with fireworks.

In my boyhood, we did not shoot fireworks on the Fourth of July, but we sure did at Christmas. In fact, fireworks formed a big part of Christmas for young boys. Several teenagers put up three or four little fireworks stands along the streets of Forsyth where they sold everything from the smallest "lady crackers" to the biggest "Dago bombs." Naturally, boys my age loved to hang around the stands, so I headed for the one on Johnston Street near my school the first chance I had.

By the time I arrived there, a crowd had already assembled. They stood around a fire that the Allen brothers had built because the afternoon was getting colder and colder. The few boys who scratched up a nickel bought a package of Chinese firecrackers. I was one of the lucky ones. Opening my pack of twenty firecrackers, I separated each one unwinding the funny little tangle that held the fuses together. Every time a boy join-ed the crowd, he would hold his hands close to the fire to warm fingers nearly frozen from the wind that rushes by the handlebars of a fast-moving bicycle.

When they were close enough, I would throw a firecracker in the fire and watch the boy jump. This was fine and innocent fun. The fun grew less innocent when Wilson Grant sidled up to the stand boasting the possession of a dime.

"I'm not fooling with the little old firecrackers. Give me one of those Roman candles."

Just then Ogden Allen set upon Wilson with a series of good-natured insults. At first Wilson tried to respond in kind, but Ogden's quick wit was tough to overcome. So Wilson's temper took over. He stuck the end of his Roman candle in the fire, lighting the fuse. Then he turned the thing into a weapon by aiming it at Ogden.

Small but quick, Ogden took off like a scalded dog. He ran with Wilson following him in hot pursuit. Wilson yelled in anger. Ogden yelled in fear. The rest of us followed, yelling in delight. Wilson could not move as fast as Ogden, but the fireballs could. A couple of them hit Ogden, but they did not wound him much.

All of us thought this fun, but when the word of it reached the adult community, the fireworks stands faced an early extinction.

After that, Mama limited my fireworks use to Christmas night. That is when Daddy brought out a whole box of big ones—Roman candles, sky rockets, and Dago bombs. Despite the size of the display, the strict supervision took away from the excitement, and fireworks faded as a Christmas attraction for me.

By 1938, the attraction of Santa Claus changed as well. By that time, I knew all about Santa, and certainly Mama and Daddy knew that I knew. Yet we acted as though I did not. I had no intention of bursting the bubble and risking a void around the tree on Christmas morning. But most of all, Christmas was beginning to mean a whole lot more because an eleven year old begins to have feelings that a five or six year old never thought of. Even then, I knew I wanted to preserve and expand upon those feelings.

I felt a sense of pity for Daddy who never seemed much into Christmas. What I did not know about Daddy was that his mother and two sisters had died during three different Christmas seasons. Something else I did not know was that he did indeed have strong sentiments about Christmas. He expressed those sentiments that very year in a column he wrote for the newspaper. This is what he had to say.

There are few of us, perhaps, who do not lead a double life. A part of the time we live among the things that are real, the things that we can see and touch. At other times we find ourselves living in a kind of fairyland of the imagination. In every stage of life we are to a large extent dream-children, and whether we will or not, find ourselves following in the footsteps of fancy.

In this land of fancy the mind of childhood delights to roam and revel. It was in this land in the early days that I found Santa Claus. I knew not at that time that he was only a dream, only a creature of the imagination, only a tradition handed down by parents to children. It is true I never saw him, never heard his voice, never felt the touch of his hand, but I believed in his existence with all the clinging trust of a little child. Many a Christmas night did I wait for his coming, trying to push away the heavy hand of slumber. Many a time did I fancy that I could hear the ringing of sleigh bells and the patter of reindeer feet upon the roof. No picture was more clearly engraved upon my mind and heart than the cheery face of Santa peeping above his well-filled arms.

No questions appealed more seriously than whether the chimney was large enough to admit Santa and his team, or whether my stockings were hung just where they would attract his keen eyes. Among all the letters of my childhood, I am sure that none came so straight from my heart as those I wrote to dear old Santa. To him I could unfold all my hopes and the desires of my childish heart. I believed that his love was with me and he would understand.

My mother and father were great and powerful people to me but their power was small when compared to that of Santa, generous patron of the Christmas season, who was able to bring whatever he desired to the children who had pleased him.

In such ways as these, Santa played a happy part in my dreams and prayers. Three cheers for him and long may he wave! Long may he live in the hearts of childhood. Long may we continue to weave our romances around him and make him a real person to the little ones who welcome his coming.

Many years have passed and the days of childhood are only a memory to me now. I learned long ago that Santa Claus was at best only a mythical saint. There are people around me who will regard as folly the romance of an ancient custom. They ask, "Shall we lead the little child to feed his faith upon a delusion?" But all the wisdom of the years cannot steal from me the tender feeling for the Santa Claus who was real. Wherever the paths of life lead, he will have stored honey in the hive of my memory.

Somewhere just after a child's age reaches double digits, Christmas Eve becomes more important while Christmas Day begins to be viewed as almost anticlimactic. This must be true because I remember the Christmas Eves of that time better than I remember the Christmas days. I remember Daddy reading the scripture and praying, and I remember Mama playing the piano while we all sang Christmas carols. I remember looking forward to hearing Bing Crosby give his annual Christmas Eve performance of "Silent Night." ("White Christmas" had not been written yet.)

And I remember the most important Christmas Eve event of all. When Mama finished her tiring day, she took me by the hand and led me into the backyard where we talked about the Christ child and about love. Then we looked for the star in the east. She always picked one and said, "That's it." Then she hugged me lightly and said a little prayer.

Even now I go into the yard on Christmas Eve night. I look for the star, say a little prayer, and think about the Christ child and love. Then I murmur to myself,

"Merry Christmas, Mama. Merry Christmas, Daddy."

# CHAPTER 21
# Mama: The Guiding Force

Her ankles made little popping sounds when she walked. You heard that as she moved from room to room straightening pictures which always hung crooked because the house shook some when the train went by the crossing two doors down the street.

The scene repeated daily, demonstrating Mama's near obsession with straight pictures.

She had another obsession—making something out of me. Considering my first grade fiasco and reading disability, the second obsession appeared to call for at least as much persistence as the first and a good deal more ingenuity.

The ingenuity that Mama employed in straightening me out tested her patience and self-control. She apparently recognized my suffering self-confidence and attempted to deal with it in two ways. First, she boosted me by looking for even the slightest opportunities to heap praise on me. Second, she continuously thrust me into one activity after another, seeking one which might grab my interest and at which I might possibly excel.

Among Mama's interests, three stood out—music, politics, and just plain "going." So she tried all these on me.

When it came to music, she claimed no unusual talent, although she taught piano for awhile and played a little at church. Her performing ability was marginal at best, but the piano served her as an emotional prop.

When she worried she made a bee-line for the piano to play a hymn or, more likely, a popular song like "The Isle of Capri" or "When I Grow to Old to Dream."

When I was in the second or third grade, she decreed that I must take piano lessons from her good friend Louise Heard. In doing this, she overlooked that a little boy who cannot read words cannot read music. That fact coupled with dear Miss Louise's volatility brought my piano career to an early end. When Miss Louise started lightly slapping at my errant fingers, I called it quits. Later, I made another stab at the music world when Miss Louise's sons, John and Charles, and I made weekly trips to Gordon Military College in Barnesville where John and I took trumpet lessons and Charles studied the clarinet. This I enjoyed because I liked the afternoons with John and Charles. But even though this went on for a couple of years, neither John nor I ever gained much ground as trumpeters. We were older than Charles, but he possessed the quality age could not bestow on us—talent.

So my musical education finally retreated to courses in music appreciation, and Mama decided the world of melodic sound would never shore up my sagging self-esteem.

During this whole span of time she made strong efforts to interest me in her other favorite activities—politics and "going." She involved me in these at every turn, and they often merged with one another, like when "going" meant riding somewhere to a political rally.

But to take a real step toward the real politics, you need speaking ability. Accepting this, Mama signed me up to take expression from Antoinette Bramblett. She emphasized what you might call "cultured Southern speech." This meant pear-shaped tones by avoiding lazy lips and always sounding the final *g*'s. She admonished us that we should never sound *r*'s harshly. For instance, you never said the word "door" as "doorrr" in the manner of the mountain folks, Texans, and most Yankees. You most certainly did not pronounce it "doe" with no "r" at all.

Antoinette taught us to say "doah" in something similar to the English manner of speech.

As a matter of fact, this "proper" Southern pronunciation received some wider attention when Miss Susan Myrick of the *Macon Telegraph* was sent to Hollywood as a technical advisor for the film production of *Gone With The Wind.* Her job was to make things as authentically

Southern as possible, which involved helping the actors sound Southern without overdoing it as was usually the case.

When she came home, she said that her toughest task centered around softening Clark Gable's Western speech pattern. Being English, Vivian Leigh presented no particular problem, but Gable was something else.

So Miss Susan came up with a one sentence drill for Gable to practice on.

"I can't afford a four-door Ford."

She said it took some doing to round off the edges of all those *r*'s.

My lessons from Antoinette developed into the first progress toward self-confidence for me. It began when I recited Frank L. Stanton's "Keep A'going" at grammar school chapel. The crowd gave no ovation and I deserved none, but I made it through without getting the gong or dying of stage fright.

Next I did "Ferdinand the Bull" before an audience of both children and some grown folks, receiving a right favorable response. But the best lay in the immediate future.

Antoinette happened upon a comedy piece which was a sort of burlesque parody on a sermon using the Old Mother Hubbard rhyme as the text. I practiced and practiced. Sometimes before Mama and Daddy, sometimes before Antoinette, and sometimes just by myself walking around the backyard.

When she thought me ready, Antoinette scheduled me to "preach" this sermon before an impressive group of grown folks at the high school auditorium. Dressed in a dark preacher-like suit, at the age of nine, I walked on the stage and launched into my mock sermon.

Instantly, waves of laughter filled the hall. As I preached on, the crowd showed its approval over and over with more laughter and finally with a really big ovation. I walked off the stage with the kind of internal smile you have when you are proud of yourself.

"You're good," I whispered to myself, taking my seat while grown people patted my back.

This first brush with personal success expanded as I received several invitations to preach the sermon at adult gatherings. They all went well. It was several years before I realized that the public acclaim came not so much because I did the piece well. The crowd liked it because a preacher's son did it. But whatever the reason, it helped me.

Mama also believed that to understand politics, you must first appreciate history. Without any particular scholarship in the area, she began dangling the political events of the day before me with one hand and the parallel historic events with the other.

This led to long talks about the influences of Jefferson and Hamilton upon our government. I found myself a Jeffersonian one day and a Hamiltonian the next. But after a long period of vacillation, I resolved that we are fortunate that neither of them dominated. Jefferson without the counterbalance of Hamilton's influence could have led the country toward a government so lacking in power that it could not survive a serious crisis. Hamilton without the checks of Jefferson could have fashioned a government so strong that it could not survive the dissatisfaction of the people. I concluded that the coinciding presence of these two brilliant minds preserved the infant republic. They left the middle for the less dynamic but greatly important Madison. Providence must have played a hand.

The trips to political rallies reinforced my enjoyment of politics and taught me to love barbecue. They also ignited an ambition.

Somewhere along the line, I set aim on the office of secretary of state of the United States. This ridiculously high goal was as unexplainable as it was unattainable. I think that I have found some explanations even though the unobtainability of course has remained. The first question needing an explanation is this: If I shot that high, why not shoot for the big one and aspire for the presidency? There are answers.

For starters, in the mind of an adolescent, the secretary of state dealt with the truly interesting and important things while the president had to put up with a whole lot of junk.

Then I greatly admired Cordell Hull, Franklin Roosevelt's secretary of state. Maybe a subconscious thought came through in this connection because Secretary Hull came from Tennessee and even as a Southerner he became secretary of state. Yet Northern bias had excluded Southerners from the presidency since the Civil War regardless of ability or appeal. Simply stated, a Southern boy could be secretary of state, but, in those days, Northern prejudice barred him from the presidency.

Mama's penchant for "going" stayed with her for her whole life. She kept a hat, gloves, and pocketbook close by so she could respond quickly to any invitation to go.

Her positive feelings about "going" canceled out any inclination to do some of the things which require much staying at home. For example, she never owned a washing machine.

"I wouldn't have one of those things in my house," she often exclaimed.

In my young days, we sent "washing" out to a wash woman. Later, it became known as laundry and went to a commercial enterprise for appropriate handling.

For many years Molly Hamm did our washing and ironing at her house. Her neighbor, Alf Hanson, picked up the washing on Monday mornings and brought it back on Thursdays, always in a very large basket. It came back sparkling clean and with a wonderful smell coming from the strong soap and use of an old fashioned flat iron.

Alf Hanson was an older black man whom we all called Uncle Alf. For the pickup and delivery, he used a wagon pulled by a bay horse rather than the traditional mule. Uncle Alf provided two other important services. Using the horse, he plowed the vegetable garden behind our house every spring, where I always attempted but pretty much failed to grow big watermelons. In the fall, we always visited his house to walk through his garden to pick our pumpkin for Halloween use.

After I reached adulthood, my sister Baby came in one day to tell me of seeing the then old-aged Uncle Alf sitting on the roadside. His teary eyes were fixed upon his equally aged bay horse.

The horse had died in harness still hitched to the old wagon. Not long after, Uncle Alf died too.

Mama did make a concession to household activities though when it came to making blackberry jelly in the summertime. With the help of Gladys Powell, she spent hot hours in the kitchen, boiling the blackberries and then straining the juice through the fabric of sugar sacks before mixing it up with sugar and some sort of gelatin to create the jelly. While doing this one horribly hot afternoon, Mama looked up to see her friend Katherine Sutton walk in the back door.

"Ruby," asked Miss Katherine incredulously, "Why on earth are you wasting your time doing that?"

"Because we like the jelly," came Mama's reply.

"Well, if you want to suffer through all that," Miss Katherine said sort of looking up at the ceiling in disbelief, "it's all right with me, but I don't think it can compete with Libby or Cross & Blackwell."

The "going" mainly involved non-exotic outings. Sometimes we just rode around to cool off at night and sometimes we drove to Indian Springs for a cup or two of the sulphur water that some people did not like.

Visiting kinfolks in the summer and Mama's "must" visit to the mountains annually amounted to a little more. But I liked best the occasional trips to the beach and the trip to the 1939 World's Fair where I saw and spoke to Dorothy Lamour. She spoke back, making me a permanent fan.

The New York trip afforded me several personal firsts. We rode on a limited-access highway for the first time, a hair-raising experience. I rode an escalator for the first time, and I watched Mama argue with a Yankee for the first time.

Mama and Baby took turns driving because I was just twelve and could not drive yet. So I helped with the maps and looked at the sights.

Following a pre-arranged plan, Baby pulled the car into a garage in New Jersey and a young man drove us to our hotel near Times Square. On several days, he came back to drive us on sightseeing tours.

Right off I knew he was different because he talked funny. He called the Holland Tunnel the "toob." It took us awhile to figure out he was trying to say "tube."

About two hours into our first tour day, he asked a question.

"Wanna stop for a bottle of pop?"

We had no idea what he meant. In the first place, he pronounced bottle in a sort of guttural way which was foreign to us and besides that pop sounded a little ominous. Finally it came across that he was talking about a soft drink. All this seemed strange to us, and really it seemed strange to him when Mama made her reply.

"Thank you, I think it's about time for a dope."

The young Yankee no doubt thought he had happened upon an addict from Dixie, not understanding "dope" meant Coca-Cola to us in those days. When he did understand, he began making fun of Coca-Cola and bragging on Pepsi. This inflamed Mama, because to her the comparison between the two drinks was like the comparison between Lee and Grant.

From then on, the relationship between Mama and the driver grew worse.

"This your first trip to New York?" the driver asked Mama.

"Yes."

The driver laughed.

"When have you been to Atlanta?" Mama asked.

"I never was there."

Mama laughed.

I kind of enjoyed it all.

At the beach, I sat with my sisters by the radio one night listening to Young Stribling fight Max Schmeling in Chicago. Stribling lost and my sisters cried. In the early '30s, every Middle Georgia girl loved the handsome, swashbuckling Stribling.

Some years later, in 1940, we went to Jacksonville Beach. The trip was especially fun because some of my friends from Forsyth went at the same time. Banks Worsham, Katheryn Zellner, and Gloria Chapman joined me at the beach during the day, and at night we went to the boardwalk. But best of all was the pier. On the pier you could dance for a nickel a dance while an all-girl orchestra played.

But the real excitement came from an event across the sea. Nazi Germany had just overrun Denmark, so a Danish sailing ship in use as a training vessel hurried up the St. Johns River and into the docks at Jacksonville. The presence of German U-boats dictated its action.

Because the United States was still neutral, the harbor people faced a dilemma. International law placed a time limit on the docking of ships from warring nations in a neutral port. In fact, the German pocket battle-ship *Graf Spee* had that problem in South America a few months later. As a result, the crew scuttled the ship just off the coast to prevent its capture.

The Danes met a better fate. The townspeople displayed their admiration for the young Norsemen by sneaking food and other goodies to them. I do not know what finally happened to the sailors on the ship. I suspect we took care of the sailors by interning them comfortably until our entry into the war. I know that the ship came out all right. It gained fame as one of the world's most beautiful tall ships at big ceremonies like the Bicentennial Celebration in New York harbor in 1976. It is called the *Danmark*.

Daddy did not go with us on these excursions. He did not want to. He had his fill of travelling at a younger age, living in various places and even taking a boat trip to New York. Following the same pattern, he mostly sat in his and Mama's room in the evenings reading while the rest of us gathered in the library across the hall. Mama was the more social of the two and loved parties.

The summer before I reached twelve in September, Mama came to me with a novel idea.

"I think you ought to have a prom party," she announced.

A prom party meant I had taken another important step toward growing up. Before that, there had been the children's parties, and, little by little, our social life became more adultified. We had tacky parties where the boys and girls dressed up in outrageous looking old clothes discarded by their parents or older siblings.

Then when I reached twelve, a lady named Ann Fleming came to town and organized what she called a dancing club which met every Thursday night for a couple of hours. This really amounted to a set of dancing lessons where we learned to do the Big Apple (including trucking, Sissy Britches, and the Suzy-Q), the Polka, and mainly the Fox Trot. The Fox Trot is what young folks this day and time call the slow dance. As the highlight, Miss Fleming staged a big Christmas dance.

We even were invited to the President's Ball that year. The ball took place on January 30 each year, that being President Roosevelt's birthday. Almost every community put on one of these dances to benefit the March of Dimes. Of course, the President had a deep interest in the March of Dimes because of his bout with polio.

All these things framed part of our early party life, but prom parties seemed bigger.

The boys wore coats and ties, and the girls wore long dresses, usually with ruffles. The festivities centered around the front porch where everyone gathered before the promming began. Each one had a card with a line for each of the twelve proms of ten minutes apiece. The boys asked the girls for proms, and the names were filled in.

We came sternly admonished that no girl should be left with a blank space on her card. As far as I know, the boys always answered the call to duty and the girls were spared the horrible embarrassment of sitting unescorted.

When the promming started, you could walk up and down the street till the bell rang or you could stay on the porch and eat little sandwiches, cookies, cheese biscuits, and salted pecans and drink punch. We were blessed in my view that we had not even heard of chocolate chip cookies.

My party succeeded except that a little girl standing by the punch bowl on the round part of the porch under the cupola was bumped. Red punch spilled on her pretty, new white dress, and she ran into the house weeping. We did not know what to do.

Mama's love for parties lasted on and on. Many years later, I took her to the hospital for an operation. She was nearly eighty but had driven to another town for a party the day before.

I am sure that she straightened the pictures just before we left the house for the hospital. She never returned to that house she loved so much for more than fifty years.

I still own the house which is now an office. When I go in it, I smile at the crooked pictures and think of Mama.

When my daughter Julie walks, I hear the cute ankle-popping that she inherited from her grandmother, and I remember the undeserved praise Mama gave me. I also remember her patience in the way she gently nudged me toward some degree of success.

I hope she knows I recognize all this and how much I appreciate it.

CHAPTER 22

# Traveling around Wonderland

Getting around town in the Depression days did not present much of a problem. Folks walked just about everywhere they went. While it took a little longer to get there, it did not matter when you had plenty of time anyway.

Walking to school comes natural when everybody does it. Daddy always walked to the newspaper office just like most other businessmen walked to their places. Some farmers came to town in a car or truck, but just as many or more came in wagons or buggies sometimes pulled by horses but mostly by mules. Hitching yards filled the backside of the blocks facing the courthouse. People saved their cars, if they had one, for longer trips or really bad weather except when they used them for "riding around."

Of course, the trains and buses provided long distance travel, but no one felt any particular need in town for public transportation. Nevertheless, we had several taxicabs. Although you almost never saw the taxis carrying a passenger, you could see passengerless cabs traversing residential streets regularly.

Not until my teen years did I learn that the true purpose for most of the taxis had nothing to do with transporting passengers. It had to do with delivering illegal whiskey. The twentieth century had put the bootlegger on motorized wheels.

An enterprising and entertaining black man began a legitimate taxi business in my early teens. I do not know his real first name, but his initials were S. T. Someone must have thought that S. T. Stroud ought to have a real name, so years ago they decided a person who went by the initials S. T. just had to be called Saint.

Saint Stroud. Now that sounds truly ecclesiastical. Unfortunately though, the passage of time and laziness of speech and pronunciation corrupted that impressive moniker into something a whole lot less clever or important. Most people began calling him Sink instead of Saint.

Saint or Sink, never claimed any high degree of saintliness, but he was a good friend and made his contribution to the community life. A big part of that contribution came from his sense of humor.

When Saint started his taxi service, he knew that he needed to advertise on the taxi itself. So he neatly painted the word TAXI on the right hand side of the windshield. That sounds like a good idea except for one thing. He did his painting while sitting inside the car. So it came out looking-glass backwards to the people outside the car.

The uniqueness of the letters making up the word taxi compounded the humor of the mistake. In capitals, they look the same frontwards or backwards. So to anyone seeing Saint's cab from the outside, it was not a TAXI, it was an IXAT.

People laughed at what they perceived as Saint's dumb mistake. But I have long since believed that Saint's sign was neither a mistake nor dumb. To the contrary, it made the cab locally famous. People joked about it so much that in Forsyth we had a new synonym for taxicab—IXAT. You do not ordinarily get that kind of exposure or attention so cheap. Think what Saint could have done if Madison Avenue had discovered him.

Goods, merchandise, and farm products moved in, out, and around Forsyth by varying means. Trains and trucks did their part. Cotton and produce came to town mainly on wagons pulled by mules, but one transportation means stood out from the rest. That is the way Mrs. Boatwright transported the groceries to the boarding house across the street from us.

She and Matilda Moore did the cooking at the boarding house. I ate there more than a few times, and the food tasted extra good. I liked the desserts, usually homemade ice cream, and they brought it on what looked to me like an antique tea cart. Then there was the player piano sitting in the room in front of the dining room. The whole place was all right to me.

Mrs. Boatwright and Matilda loved to talk and laugh. They had almost identical laughs, high-pitched and with even higher volume. While the boarders ate dinner at noontime, the two of them would sit on the front porch waiting for time to serve the dessert. As far away as our house, you could hear their laughter as they sat in the swing and talked. I always wished I could hear what they were saying because it had to have been powerfully funny.

Matilda did the grocery shopping for the boarding house. About every other day you would see her heading up the sidewalk toward town pushing an oversized iron-wheeled wheelbarrow. About an hour or so later, she came back down the street, having visited about every grocery store in town comparing prices. This time the wheelbarrow wheels made a scraping sound on the pavement from the weight of a great load of food stuffs.

In all my years, I have never again seen anybody else use a wheelbarrow for grocery shopping. This might have been the forerunner of the present supermarket carts or buggies.

# CHAPTER 23

# Aunt Rachel:
# A Study of Contrasts

$F$ate and irony sometimes conspire to create strange results. That happens when people who have the least driving abilities end up with jobs requiring constant driving. That is about what happened with my Aunt Rachel.

To say that Rachel Wyly had a distinctive personality is like saying a winter fireside is cozy or tornadoes are turbulent. Some things are just too obvious to need stating. Rachel (I called her Aunt Rachel until my teen years, then just dropped the Aunt) combined countless qualities and characteristics of stark contrast.

She was at the same time among the most generous and frugal people I have ever known. She could be sharply decisive on major questions and could be the master of indecision on minor points.

When it came to keeping up with car keys, Rachel looked like a miserable failure in the art of organization and management, but, in running a household as a widowed mother of a small daughter, she was a master.

She cooked wonderfully, particularly cakes and pies, yet she ate about nothing, making her the skinny sister among plump siblings.

She loved art, music, and poetry. In fact, she wrote vast numbers of poems, and she published many at her own expense. This demonstrated her values and showed where she was willing to spend money which she ordinarily tightly held.

Among the volumes she published, I found a small collection of little rhymes about her daughter Emmalee and her nieces and nephews. She just did these for fun, and they lacked the literary quality of some of her poems. But their words conveyed a message of love. Here is one she did about me.

Harold's Pet

I think I've had all kinds of pets,
But, since I've grown so big,
I have no time for rabbits and goats
And a spotted guinea pig.

For now I like my story books—
I can write as well as read—
So my terrier, Skip, and my greyhound, Prinz,
Are the only pets I need.

In a more serious vein, she did another little poem involving my mother, me, and ultimately my own son Hal, who is really a "junior." I must say she exaggerated my high school career, but here is the poem anyway:

Birthday Cakes

She mixed the batter of his birthday cake:
Two cups of sugar, eggs all beaten light;
And with each whirl the wooden spoon would make
Went thoughts of other days—a small boy's bright
And eager face, his lips pursed tense to blow
The gleaming birthday candles that had stood
To deck his frosted cake long years ago.
Years passed. The candles grew to six, and then ten.
And she recalled the joy that had been hers
His sixteenth year. A football hero then,
He had a host of high school worshipers.
With the spoon's last beat, she turned and smiled to see
His dear little "junior" standing by her knee.

Considering her contrasting traits, it is not surprising that her work would demand her to perform an act which she did about as poorly as anything in the world—drive. I do not think it every occurred to Rachel that she could not drive so good, but it sure occurred to everybody else who knew her.

One day while leaving a filling station, she backed into a gas pump knocking it cattywhompus. While none of her mishaps ever hurt anybody or did any serious damage, they amounted to a veritable mountain of near misses.

After her husband, Uncle Robert, had become an invalid, he decided one day to ride to town with Rachel. She had three of her famous near misses within fifteen minutes or so and never even realized it. Uncle Robert was a better observer.

"As near cripple as I am, I'm getting out of this car," he announced, signaling his last venture as one of Rachel's passengers.

"I'm walking home before you kill me." There was something of a chuckle in his voice but not unmixed with seriousness.

In spite of all this, Rachel gave up her career as a classroom teacher to become a caseworker for the relief. That is what they called the welfare program in the early Roosevelt days. The job put her on the road constantly visiting the homes of the poor to process relief benefits for them.

One summer when I was about eight, I rode with Rachel for several days while she visited the people who needed help. She taught me about driving as it ought not to be done. But I also learned about life as it ought not have to be lived.

As she zoomed her Chevrolet across the dirt road without apparent concern for the numerous hazards, I often ducked in fear. She approached hilltops or sharp curves in a one lane road without any concern for what might be coming in the other direction. It was bad enough to bump haphazardly over the deeply rutted dry roads with the car bouncing from one ditch to the other, but it was worse after a rain when we would skid and fishtail from one ditch to the other.

Rickety wooden bridges carried the little country roads across the numerous streams (we called them branches). Curiously Rachel had some concern about these bridges, but her means of testing them was even more curious. She would pull the car to a stop, get out, and walk over the bridge. With all of her 100 pounds, she would jump two or three times on the bridge to see if it could hold a 2500-pound car. Even at an early age, I had little confidence in this test. It satisfied Rachel though.

On one hot dusty afternoon, we bumped along a little road between Forsyth and Russellville when Rachel's car came to a stop. Her absent-mindedness had struck again. We were out of gas. After sitting there for a time, thinking that we might never see civilization again, we heard the sound of an old truck coming up behind us. Going out to the middle of the road waving both arms Rachel hailed the driver of the truck. He turned out to be known to both of us.

He made his living as a jack-of-all-trades who specialized in plumbing. His ingeniousness in the business of making do with whatever might be available kept him in demand. "You and the boy got some sort of trouble, Miz Wyly?" he asked as he pulled himself out of the truck with his nearly shaved grey hair shining in the sun.

"My heavens, I'm so glad to see you," exclaimed Rachel, "If anybody in the world will know what to do with a car that's given out of gas way out here, it would be you."

"Aw, this won't be no trouble. I got a syphon tube somewhere here in the back of the truck."

As he fumbled around with the various tools and pieces of materials, I did not know that I was about to get a lesson in physics which would astound me. Even to this day, I am amazed at what makes a syphon work. He turned his truck around and backed it up to the backside of Rachel's car. He then removed each gas cap and placed one end of the syphon tube in the gas tank of his truck. What he next did I really could not believe. He began sucking on the end of the tube. In a moment or two, he spat the tube out, closing his eyes and screwing his face into a contortion that looked like a twisted prune. Then came a series of coughs, wheezes, and grunts.

Having done this, he quickly stuck the other end of the tube into Rachel's gas tank, and gas flowed easily from the truck to the car. The only trouble was that he had just sucked a little too hard.

"Oh," Rachel said with obvious concern, "I know that was just awful."

"No'm, Miz Wyly, I've drunk whiskey that tasted a whole heap worse than that."

Rachel had trouble keeping a straight face.

"Well, I certainly appreciate everything you've done," Rachel responded, as she reached into her pocketbook, "Here, I want to pay you for your gas and your trouble."

"No'm, it ain't right to get paid for helping somebody in trouble."

The good Samaritan actions of that afternoon stood him in good stead for future plumbing business because Rachel told the story over and over around the community. Maybe he understood this possibility, but I really think he did what he did out of a willingness to be helpful.

Between the wild rides, we stopped at poverty-ridden homes where eyes betrayed the hopelessness of the times. Children ran to meet Rachel's car because they still held to hope and thought she brought something better. The mammas and daddies hardly moved at all; they expected nothing. Thinking back, the most surprising thing was the absence of anger in the eyes of the people. They did not seem to blame anyone. Their look just painted a picture of despair which they accepted as a product of fate rather than a result of exploitation. I guess it was some of both, but mostly fate.

No one could do much about the boll weevil or about the drought that even caused the wells to go dry so that water had to be hauled from the creek. Maybe somebody could have done something about the Depression if they had planned right and acted in time. I still do not know.

I do know all this moved Rachel deeply, and she helped these people in ways beyond her official duties. Her kindness and concern caused many of these folks to admire and even love her for many years to come.

Her decisiveness in dealing with these weighty problems simply did not square with her constant trouble with everyday minor things. Deciding what to wear on special occasions really stumped her. So she did the natural thing, she sought the advice of her older sister Ruby, my mother.

The vision remains.

"What in the world should I wear to Ruth's tea?" she would say as she walked into Mama's bedroom carrying an unopened Coca-Cola in one hand and the car keys she was about to misplace in the other.

"Should I wear my blue silk or my beige wool?"

"Well, let's look at them," was Mama's usual reply.

The same little exchange happened countless times on countless small issues, but the most frequent question remained: what to wear? On the other hand, there was one question neither of them hesitated on for a moment. That was whether to make a trip to LaFayette, their home town.

They never ceased hearing the call of the mountains or of the valley between Lookout, Pigeon, and Signal Mountains where LaFayette sits. At least once a year the sisters went back to the place of their beginning.

"I just have to breathe mountain air every now and then," Mama explained. "It renews my spirit."

More than a few times I went with them on the trip that seemed awfully long to a little boy. Even driving to Atlanta took almost two hours, and that was just the beginning. Today's super highways existed only in the dreams of some unknown engineer. We went right through downtown Atlanta, out Marietta Street to the old steel-sided bridge over the Chattahoochee River. A fruit stand stood just before the bridge and provided out first stop for a break.

Mama generally bought me some bananas, parched peanuts, and a Coca-Cola. This fortified me until we began seeing and crossing the mountains. That is the part I liked. First, though, we went right through the middle of Marietta, which seemed about the size of Forsyth with old men playing checkers on the courthouse square. I never would have anticipated the giant it has become.

After Marietta, things took on a different look. Some wag once said it was easy to give directions from Marietta to Chattanooga.

"You just head north from the courthouse and stay between the bedspreads."

That was pretty near true, because the people of the foothills made and sold chenille bedspreads by the thousands. They hung on something like clotheslines all along the highway displaying about every design and color. Some might have an enormous peacock, others something equally colorful, and all were for sale.

Amazingly, within a few years, this cottage industry became one of America's major industrial enterprises. Some bright person saw something in the tufting process unseen by others. Early Appalachian settlers from Scotland brought the tufting process with the simple up and down motion which created chenille. Somebody finally discovered that carpets could be made in the same way. Because of this North Georgia became the carpet capital of the world. It remains such.

But this was a long ways away when Mama, Rachel, and I rode through North Georgia between the bedspreads. Cotton mills were the only major industry then, and Rome formed the center of this activity. Sometimes labor relations turned bitter and even violent.

On one of our trips, the ever cautious Rachel issued a warning.

"There's a strike in Rome, and they called out the National Guard. So we must be careful going through there."

We faced no danger in Rome and saw no violence. But what we saw excited me. The National Guard troops had piled up sandbags and set machine guns on them. Sitting behind the sandbags and guarding their flanks, the guardsmen wore steel helmets, canvas leggings, and webbed pistol belts. I thought it wonderful.

I gave no thought to the hardships, bitterness, and deprivation underlying this incident of social disorder. Little boys don't worry much about things like that. Sad to say, most older people don't either.

From this scene of conflict, we moved easily into the lovely scene of peacefulness as the hills grew higher and became ridges giving warning of the real mountains ahead.

The ridge that means the most to me is Taylor's Ridge just south of Summerville. The road winds in a snakelike fashion to the crest of the ridge. Then you see it, the gorgeous valley with mountains lying on either side and beyond. Not long ago, I drove the same road, and, reaching the top, I had the same sensation as I did so long ago . . . except for one thing.

When I was little, I liked the sight, but I liked watching Mama see it even better. You could see the pleasure in her smile and then the sentimentality in her eyes as a tear or two trickled down her cheek. Then a look of general satisfaction as she took a deep breath of what she called "mountain air."

"Glorious," she would sigh.

The middle-aged woman was a little girl again.

I know Rachel must have had the same feeling that Mama did about all this, but I naturally did not watch her as closely. Since then, I have read what she wrote about the valley in those hills.

Mystery of the Mountains

I.

And I would lift my eyes unto the hills—
The blending place of earth and rocks and sky,
Where ridges smile and nod as clouds go by,
And mistiness of daybreak quietly chills
The beads of dew the frostiness distills.

My gaze is winged to plains where meadows lie,
And soon my thoughts are following the eye
To peaks beyond the valley daffodils.

In hushed serenity, I stand alone
Beholding mountain roofs and skies they touch
To learn the secret charm they have for me—
Their strangeness and their stirring undertone.
And from the stillness comes a gleam I clutch
As it reveals their haunting mystery.

### II.

In mountain strengths, I see the Master's face,
In fold on fold, I feel His restful arms.
Their crystal falls and timbered Alpine charms
Show me His tranquil loveliness and grace.
Then comes assurance out of viewless space
That nobleness brings quietude, and calms
The searching one who felt unreal alarms;
And peacefulness is found in its embrace.
And so the mountain's lure for me is found.
Then with the Psalmist King of long ago,
I seek my help from hills as they intone
This anthem which the fields and plains resound,
"As mountains watch the villages below,
So God's embracing arms protect His own."

These trips always meant a visit with the Hall family. Miss Annie Moore Hall had been Mama's best friend, and her husband Ed was Mama's first boyfriend. Mr. Ed owned and operated the local newspaper, *The Walker County Messenger*. All this linked us together neatly.

We sometimes visited the Chicamauga Battlefield Park where my grandfather Lumpkin fought the Yankees, and a few times we went to visit a Mrs. Rogers at Menlo. Mrs. Rogers was the aunt of Aunt Rachel's husband and claimed some kinship with Will Rogers. She liked to recount her experience as a child when the Yankees came to their house on the pretense of searching for Confederate soldiers, but apparently really looking for silver.

She said that her mother had thrown all the silver in a well so the Yankees could not find it. She showed me the bottom of the locked secret drawer in her buffet which the Union soldiers had roughly sawn out in their unsuccessful quest for the silver.

But her best story had to do with the very short and slightly built Yankee captain who began going through all of her mother's dresser drawers.

"What in heaven's name do you expect to find in there?" inquired the indignant mother.

"I'm looking for Rebel soldiers," came the brusk reply.

"Well," said the lady of the house, looking down at the diminutive captain, "I can see you grow dresser drawer-size soldiers up North, but in Georgia we grow them man-sized."

While we were in Lafayette, one thing stayed the same. Rachel still could not decide little things. Who should we visit first? Where should we eat? Where should we stay? In all this, she looked to Mama. This continued into their old age.

Rachel was right at seventy-nine when Mama died. On the morning of the funeral she was about to get dressed and began talking to my cousin Virginia Tribble about the ever present problem of what to wear. Then with a bright smile, she announced her solution.

"I know. I'll call Ruby."

Her smile suddenly turned to a look of horror. Then exploding in tears, she covered her face with her hands and ran into her room.

Now even a trip to Lafayette could not make her a little girl again.

# CHAPTER 24

# Winter Wonderland

Wintertime and childhood do not go together. Cold wind and rain go with winter, while little boys need the outside, baseball, kite flying, and swimming.

Growing up before TV, winter days could be long. Norris Sikes and I spent many afternoons thumbing through the Sears, Roebuck catalog, picking out the equipment and clothes necessary for our imagined African safari. (Additionally, there was an occasional peep at the lingerie section of the catalog).

Only one thing could relieve the boredom of winter—snow. The Sunday funny papers always showed people like Skippy, Freckles, and Henry frolicking in the snow having a wonderful time ice-skating, throwing snowballs, and making snowmen. We had rain, mud, and the Sears, Roebuck catalog. Yankees had it pretty good.

On those rare occasions when snow came, we rejoiced exceedingly. As the first flake fell, boys and girls bolted out the door imagining themselves as Jack London or a character from an Oliver Kirwood book. Most times the snow did not amount to much. Either it did not stick, or it stopped snowing pretty soon. Like an old gold prospector, we kept waiting for the big one to hit. Once we got a couple of inches—not bad, but not good enough—then came January of 1940.

The snowfall began in the morning. At noon, it was still coming down, and, for the rest of the day, it fell. Over six inches! It grew colder and colder. The temperature dropped to about 0° each morning for a week; this caused the heavy snow to crust over and the pipes to freeze. Even ponds froze fast and thick. After the week in deep freeze, the thaw set in turning the dirt roads into thick bogs. They let out school the first week because of the snow and cold and the second week because of the mud on the school bus routes. Snow and no school. At the same time? Providence had smiled on us mightily.

When the snow started that first morning, I immediately thought of my friend Karl Hill who lived on Indian Springs Drive. That was one of the fine old residential streets in Forsyth but had not always had such an imposing name. For generations it was known as Railroad Avenue because it paralleled the Central of Georgia Railroad, and it was not until Karl's mother, Miss Cora Hill, started a campaign that the name was changed to Indian Springs Drive.

When Karl was a little fellow, it still had the old name, and, being an energetic, intellectual, and enterprising youngster, he began publishing a neighborhood newspaper called *Railroad Avenue Journal*. He printed the journal through the use of a jelly-like substance known as "ditto." The journal contained interesting and sometimes almost spicy tidbits about the goings on up and down Railroad Avenue.

Later Karl became a scholar with degrees from the University of Chicago (Phi Beta Kappa) and Harvard Law School. He excelled as an editor with a book publishing company, international consultant, Washington official, banker, and businessman. I admire and respect Karl for all of this and for his many other fine qualities. But, something else will always stand out in my memory.

Because of some sort of medical advice, Karl's parents decided that he should go barefoot all winter. This began getting interesting to me about the middle of October. By Halloween I was amazed, by Thanksgiving I was astounded, and by Christmas I was shocked. At my house, my parents imposed regulations based on the calendar, not the thermometer. Therefore, I could go barefoot beginning the first of May and go swimming beginning the first of June.

So I envied Karl's license to trod the outdoors unshod in the wintertime. Now, though, the snow and terrible cold would put Karl to the ultimate test. Not even he could stand this. So wearing my overshoes, gloves, and about all the clothes I owned, I headed for Karl's house, satisfied that he would have surrendered to the elements. I felt delighted that Karl would be either wrapped up like me or sitting inside by the fire.

That is when I learned never to underestimate Karl Hill. I found him in his front yard busily rolling snow for a snowman. Those feet—kind of big for a boy his age—stood there in the deep snow exquisitely bare. Just as bare as Mother Hubbard's cupboard. That was a sight I will never forget.

As years have passed, my friendship with Karl has grown beyond anything I might have imagined back then. My appreciation of him as an intellect, a businessman, and a human being have expanded substantially. But even now as I watch him across a conference table pondering an important business decision or sit across a dinner table enjoying interesting, stimulating and just plain fun conversation, an old vision materializes. I still see the eleven-year-old boy with a fourteen-year-old's feet, standing happily in snow piled above his ankles.

After the coldest of the mornings, Barrett Sutton and I went beyond his house on Johnston Street to Persons' Pond with the thought of seeing the pond and even playing on it if it were truly frozen over. We saw something more.

Nat Hardin had recently graduated from Harvard Business School where he picked up some Yankee skills but not many Yankee attitudes. That was the first time I ever saw someone ice skate except in the picture show. Nat smoothly skimmed across the pond and became even fancier as he noticed us watching. After a particularly bold maneuver, Nat went down hitting the ice with his nose. I am sure it hurt, but he would not let us know it.

Nat went on to advance as a businessman and became Karl's competitor as a local bank president. Karl wears shoes now, Nat gave up ice-skating a long time ago. But during that week so long ago, the fact that both would be Harvard graduates and bank presidents would not have impressed me as much as Karl's bare feet and Nat's ice-skating.

As with most things, the good in the snow wore out pretty soon. It turned grimy and icy, and the bad of the cold and frozen pipes quickly outweighed the glamour of the snow. Before long, I was thankful that Skippy and the other funny paper characters were Yankees instead of me. Even being out of school was not so wonderful. Chores at Daddy's print shop called for my presence. So when school reopened after two weeks, I felt all right about it. And spring time lay out there waiting two weeks closer than when the snow came.

# CHAPTER 25

# The Humble Beginning
# Of a Football Dynasty

Those of us who wanted to play team sports did it mainly on our own. Planned recreation held a minor spot on the priority scale.

Not much ranks higher on the present day priority list than football. But in Forsyth the pigskin fell victim to the economic panic in the early '30s.

For at least ten years, the old Forsyth High School, the predecessor to Mary Persons High, fielded a team, but that changed when I was right young. I heard various reasons for the abandonment of the gridiron. Mama blamed it on the danger of the sport while some others said it detracted from attention to academics. Most said money was the problem.

Basketball did not cost much. I always heard local people sort of pitched in to build the crude frame gym we had, but I cannot account for the fine hardwood floor.

The uniforms cost little, and back then the players wore simple cheap tennis shoes, a far cry from the mod, high fashion basketball shoes of today. The equipment of that day contrasts with today's the same way the old two-handed set shot contrasts with the slam-dunk.

Basketball, slowed by the center jump after every goal and the designation of a standing guard, would not excite current fans, but it was Forsyth's only organized sport for most of the 1930s so it drew pretty good crowds. People like Walter Bramblett and Sim Rhodes became heroes in our eyes.

As a youngster, I always blamed the absence of football on the school principal, Mr. Theo Rumble. To me he just looked like a killjoy. His arrow-straight posture combined with his deeply serious facial countenance to portray a total picture of sternness. Besides that, he seldom smiled and sang bass in the Methodist choir. I later learned that my dislike for the principal was misplaced. Although no one would accuse Mr. Rumble of such frivolity as being a sports fan, not all the blame rested with him.

Simple logic just dictated that a school system which closed for a time because of a money shortage most certainly ought not to buy expensive football equipment. It did not, and it was no doubt right.

Few other schools in small towns played football during that time. The economy limited the sport to big cities and larger towns. The Atlanta schools, particularly Boys High and Tech High, and schools from cities like Macon, Savannah, Columbus, and Augusta had a league called the Georgia Interscholastic Athletic Association, but known to most folks as the G. I. Double A.

The cities smaller than those but bigger than Forsyth had two leagues, the N.G.I.C. and the S.G.F.A. Those stood for the North Georgia Interscholastic Conference and the South Georgia Football Association. That did not leave any room for little schools like ours, so the few who played football used the congressional districts as a league and all of us used that system for basketball games.

This did not mean, though, that I had no exposure to football in my early youth. About the time football was abandoned in Forsyth, my brother Bubba went to school at Georgia Military College in Milledgeville. In those days, GMC and Gordon Military College in neighboring Barnesville became a sort of farm system for major colleges who wanted to polish up the skills of football players from small towns before they came to places like Georgia, Georgia Tech, Auburn, Alabama, and others.

Although Bubba did not play football (he was a good track runner though), numbers of the GMC football players came to visit with him in Forsyth from time to time. This made me into an ardent fan.

The big game of the year was always on Thanksgiving afternoon when GMC and Gordon played for a kind of state junior college championship. I hardly ever missed one of those. But there was something closer to us that really meant more to me.

Forsyth's black college, State Teachers and Agricultural College, played with a passion, and I watched with equal enthusiasm. Their team was good and won almost all of their games, but one player rose way above the others as the hero for me and about everybody else.

His name was Mann. I do not know his first name, because I never heard it. Instead of a first name, they just called him Big. Being called Big Mann fit him just exactly right. He did it all—run, throw the ball, and, O Lord!, he could kick. He also had a special antic to excite the crowd.

When the game was at a really crucial point and the most important play was about to take place, Big Mann would throw his helmet to the sideline, take the ball and go. He seldom failed, and the fans went crazy over their bareheaded idol. It would be interesting to know how good Big Mann would perform in today's more sophisticated game. I have an idea that those folks endowed with vast talent would excel in any age and in most any environment.

As much as my friends and I enjoyed those games, our disappointment at the lack of high school football continued. This meant we had no opportunity to play ourselves, or at least we thought we did not.

Then came the fall of 1938. Mr. Crooms, who taught in Forsyth for a couple of years, had already started a baseball team at the high school to go along with basketball. When he left, the school needed a coach. That is when Buck Kunde came along.

Nobody had bothered to tell Coach Kunde that the school only intended to play basketball and baseball. So as soon as he showed up in Forsyth, he took it on himself to begin canvassing the town for funds to buy football equipment. He raised some money, but not much. So the scant resources resulted in the purchase of some terribly cheap and inadequate equipment. Put this together with players who had no experience and the coach got about what you would expect—a poor season. No one should count the season a total failure though. Coach Kunde's high tension coaching set the stage for better things to come.

Later, when Swede Olsen, a former Mercer and Redskin star, came to coach, he talked Mercer into giving him some of their discarded equipment. These pads, shoes, and suits had been pretty much used up, but they were a big step forward for the Mary Persons Bulldogs who had been making do with a whole lot less. The Dogs also took a big step forward in performance that year.

With the big team using the Mercer equipment, this meant the old cheap stuff was available for use by a newly created 7th and 8th grade team. I could hardly wait for this new development. I was about to play on a real football team with real, even though pretty sorry, uniforms. When the days finally ran down, practice began but we still lacked something. We had a team with football suits, and we sure had practices and practices and practices. After a while, all the practice became tiresome as we began to realize that we would not play any games because we had no one to play.

All practice and no play did not make us dull boys, it made some of us kind of rebellious. I cannot remember just what straw broke the back of our loyalty to the seventh and eighth grade team, but some of us bolted the team. We formed our own team and acted as our own coaches. Next we challenged the official team to a game. The school officials scoffed at this, but they had not counted on the discontent of the official team. Although the school never gave the game its sanction, it took place one afternoon anyway.

I doubt anyone remembers the details of the game, but I think we won. I sort of expect that the other side remembers it as a victory for them. That is not important though. The important thing is that a game was played.

If we had not pulled out, the same boys would have practiced against each other in virtually the same circumstances as we did in the game. But there is a big difference. When it's us against us, that ain't a game. To have a game, it takes us against them. Without our pullout, we would have all remained us. I enjoyed my role as a them. That simple conflict in the fall of 1939 did not amount to much. Not many people saw it and almost none remember it anymore.

By 1941, the Mary Persons football team had made enormous strides. In fact, they came within a hair of winning the district championship. Even all this success did not take away all of the light moments for the team. One of them occurred when Alfred Seymour came out for football early that fall.

Although a high school senior, Alfred was little. So little that most folks called him Sapsucker after the very little bird of the same name. When Alfred started going through the pile of uniforms and equipment in the gym, he found nothing that would fit a sapsucker-sized ballplayer, so he put on the littlest one he could find.

His entrance onto the field for practice caused a lot of knee-slapping laughter. The helmet wobbled around on his head. The shoulder pads almost came down to his elbows. His pants reached his ankles, and his shoes made his feet look like clown's feet.

Before the practice ended, the coach put Alfred in to carry the ball. Running from the single wing tailback position, he started to his right and then cut back off tackle. Just about that time, Alfred's too-big football pants began slipping down from his waist toward his thighs. Quickly, he switched the ball from his right hand to his left and reached down to grab his pants. The combination of his short stature and the ducking motion caused by reaching for his pants allowed Alfred to run right under the grasp of two defenders. His tugging at the britches created a couple of stutter steps and because of that another tackler missed.

Down the field went Sapsucker, ball in the left hand and pants in the right. Unfortunately, a touchdown was not to be. The oversized shoe on his left foot got caught and tangled with the flapping inside of the right pants leg. So Alfred stumbled and went down.

But nobody laughed. Sapsucker had made his point. With decent equipment, he might have played a pretty fair game of football. But we never knew for sure because the best I remember he quit pretty soon afterwards. Nothing more to prove.

The role of football hero in the fall of 1941 was reserved anyway for Archie Tingle who did most of the running and passing for the Mary Persons Bulldogs. Archie wore the numeral 0 and naturally became known as the "Zero Hero."

All this pales to primitive insignificance in light of the present massive success of Mary Persons High School as a perennial football power in Georgia under Coach Dan Pitts. Nevertheless, I wonder if some of those little threads in Forsyth's sports fabric might not have made some contribution to latter day successes.

# CHAPTER 26
# Visiting, for Better or Worse

When I was little, you visited kinfolk every summer. Visiting did not mean spending an afternoon with somebody. When you did that, you went calling. Visiting means spending a week or so and living the same life the hosts lived.

I "visited" in Marshallville, Vienna, Atlanta, and some other places and, for the most part, would have sooner stayed home. I had plans at home, but on visits I did what was planned for me or, worse still, nothing at all.

"The most dreaded visit of the year" award went to Marshallville. Yet, looking back on it, it probably afforded me the most valuable experience of all. Without realizing it, I learned there about a different life from a different time. As a small boy, though, learning was not what I had in mind for summertime.

When you drive through the beautiful farm lands and onto the oak-lined streets of Marshallville, you look at the substantial houses with wide shady porches and you sense the quiet dignity of the town. Although the adults might think, "How beautiful and how comfortable," an eight- or nine-year-old boy thinks, "Oh me, how boring!"

The town was part of the reason for the boredom, and another was the kinfolks that we visited. Although, looking back on it, Aunt Essie and Cud'n (that means cousin in Marshallville) Frank Murph were interesting, But I did not know it then.

Actually, Aunt Essie was not my aunt, and Cud'n Frank was not my cousin. Essie Murph was my mother's older first cousin, and Frank was her husband. Childless and old, they lived sedately unaccustomed to the noises and confusion caused by a little boy. So Mama said I must not act like a little boy.

They lived in town. Like almost all men in Marshallville, Cud'n Frank called himself a farmer. Yet I never saw him without a coat and tie or with any farm implements. The only times I know of him going out to the farm was in the afternoon when a man named Cliff who worked for them drove him out there. I figured this was because he was sick and took shots all the time (he was diabetic). I think now, though, this was because Aunt Essie "had money" and he did not much like working anyway. Cud'n Frank spent his mornings with a leisurely breakfast and a trip to the post office and the bank and then walking around uptown Marshallville.

I went with Cud'n Frank on lots of his morning routines. The first time I went, as we walked into the post office, a man was coming out.

"Morning Cud'n Frank."

Inside the post office the lady clerk looked up and nodded.

"How you today, Cud'n Frank?"

At the bank, at least two other people spoke to him as Cud'n Frank. By that time I became curious.

"How come all these people call you Cud'n Frank, Cud'n Frank?" I asked.

He chuckled, patted me on the back of the head and answered. "Because they're all my cousins." Marshallville was indeed a close knit town.

Better times in Marshallville came when my visit coincided with that of my cousin Jimmy Lamb from Tampa. Cud'n Frank kept a horse in the barn behind the house in town. Cliff used the horse to plow the garden. When Jimmy and I came at the same time, we rode the horse because Jimmy was big enough to catch it and handle it.

One day while Cliff, the hired man, saddled the old animal, I asked, "What's his name?"

"Just named horse," Cliff grunted. The horse was not a candidate for the Derby, and Cliff was not much of a conversationalist.

Jimmy and I had fun, but other times in Marshallville meant sitting and listening to the quiet old folks' conversation under the admonition of being seen and not heard. Frankly, at the time it would have suited me better not even to be seen. Jimmy died as a pilot in World War II, so our relationship never grew beyond those days on Horse in the fields behind Aunt Essie and Cud'n Frank's house.

The Vienna visits were different. Even though Marshallville and Vienna were not too far apart and shared an agricultural economy, their spirit and tone separated them widely. Perhaps U.S. Highway 41 running through Vienna made a difference.

Where Marshallville resisted change from the ways of another century, Vienna yearned to be modern. When older folks spoke in a hushed way in Marshallville, piety was a likely subject. When voices lowered to a near whisper in Vienna, they likely conveyed bits of gossip. They enjoyed cookouts where the men stole away into the kitchen from time to time for a belt of bourbon.

My sister Rosa Emiline, her husband Bill, and their little boy Billy moved to Vienna where Bill bought a cotton gin. They lived on the main street in an apartment in the home of Mrs. Horne. Dr. Waters, the local dentist who always seemed to wear seersucker suits, lived across the street and presided at most of the cookouts.

Mama used the trips to Vienna as an exposure to friendships of other women in the country newspaper business. The first stop on this pilgrimage came in Perry where we visited *The Houston Home Journal* to pass some time with its editor, Miss Ruby Hodges.

A lady of culture and charm, Miss Ruby ran a paper with good content but produced it in primitive ways. We called the *Home Journal* a handset paper. That meant every letter and every number printed in the paper was picked by hand from a type case and fixed in a type position in a "type stick" until you complete a full line. The line of type was then put between "column rules" in a "chase." When the chase, which enclosed a full newspaper page of type, was full, the type was tightened or "justified" using leads and slugs pried into place with a makeup rule. The whole thing was measured by a line gauge.

Then the printer or compositor locked up the page by twisting a quoin key causing the wedge-like quoins to tighten and thus transformed all of the type into a single form for printing purposes. In most print shops, the most important machine was the Linotype which has become a sort of printing dinosaur these days. The absence of the Linotype in *The Houston Home Journal* shop made the handset process necessary.

I mention all this in hopes some ancient printer of my vintage may read and appreciate it. Miss Ruby would have understood as would the other two women on Mama's itinerary. The others lived in Vienna, Madge Methvin and Emily Woodward.

Along with her husband, Claude Methvin, Miss Madge ran *The Vienna News*. They carried the motto "A good newspaper is never neutral, it is always on the side of truth." I suspect they also followed the country journalism rule of printing all the news fit to print.

The problem is deciding what news is fit to print and what is not.

Their son Eugene Methvin became one of America's top literary and news men as a Senior Editor of the *Reader's Digest* in Washington. He too remembers the tools of the trade I listed above. His capacity to keep his ties with his origin no doubt helps his present success.

Miss Emily (or to some just Miss Em) lived two miles from town on a dirt road. For a time, my sister and her husband and son lived next door. Miss Em gained fame as a writer and expanded it by founding the Georgia Press Institute.

On the left of the house where my sister first lived there was a vacant lot with three or four pecan trees but with enough open space to play a little baseball or football. So on most of the days when I visited Vienna, I played out there with a boy named Sonny Coley. Then sometimes we played at other places just whatever seemed right at the time.

Like Forsyth, Vienna was a town where young boys could roam the streets without danger and without appearing to be vagrants. Various others joined us from time to time with one of the regulars living a couple of blocks away. Time, talent, intellect and hardwork led him to public acclaim in future years. His name is George Busbee, the two-term Governor of Georgia. Sonny married one of George's sisters.

Watermelons and pimento peppers contested with cotton for the leading cash crop around Vienna. Every summer day during the watermelon season, farmers brought their melons to the Vienna depot to be carried by trains to faraway markets. Most times the melons outnumbered the train spaces, so some of the melons stayed behind usually to become feed for hogs. Sonny had a better idea for the leftovers.

"If we look pitiful enough," he explained, "they will give us a watermelon apiece."

We did, and they did. Even the July gnats in Dooly County could not detract from the sweetness of our free feast.

I recall a couple of other eating adventures in Vienna like Sunday dinner at Miss Ollie's Tea Room. Not only did it have good food, Senator Walter George and his wife, Miss Lucy, were usually there. He looked like a Senator ought to look and, in my view, acted like a Senator ought to act. The total gentleman, he always visited with the other diners. I felt honored.

On another visit I ate boiled peanuts for the first time at a baseball game in Cordele. We did not boil peanuts in Forsyth. We parched them. They seemed mushy to me, but I learned to like them later.

In every way my visits in Atlanta with my sister Rachel differed from those others. If Vienna tried for the modernity Marshallville shunned, Atlanta already had it, like it or not.

Instead of a horse without a name and watermelons without a train, Atlanta offered attractions which dazzled me. It had picture shows with stage shows at the Capitol, Paramount, Loew's Grand, Fox, Roxy, and Rialto. It had indoor roller skating at the Rollerdrome on Penn Avenue and hot, just-made doughnuts just around the corner at the little Krispy Kreme place. You could buy fudge even better than Mama could make at the Candy Pan stores around town.

Swimming pools seemed to be everywhere, and from time to time we would go to what seemed like awfully fancy restaurants like the Ship Ahoy, Wisteria Gardens, or Francis Virginia. But I liked the Toddle Houses better.

Best of all, Atlanta had streetcars. These lumbering deep green trolleys clickety clacked over almost every street in town. They ran all the way to Marietta and they ran all the way to Stone Mountain. Even today, MARTA cannot make this claim. The streetcar seats were oak on an iron frame. The seat and back panels were of split cane fancily woven with little octagonal holes. The seat backs were mounted on rollers so by pushing them forward you could reverse the direction the seat faced.

Streetcars had personality, and part of it stemmed from the men who operated them. They were called motormen, but I do not know why because the streetcars ran from electricity transmitted from overhead wires by way of a rod mounted on a swivel on top of the streetcar.

When the streetcar reached the end of the line, the motorman simply moved from what had been the front toward the other end, and, as he did, he pulled the back of each seat so as to turn the seats around. Simply stated, the back of the streetcar became the front. Then the motorman turned the rod around on the wire overhead. He took his place at the end of the car which had been the back, and away he went from whence he had come.

Streetcars gave me the chance to learn Atlanta. I worked out a sort of game using transfers with the idea being to get all the way around Atlanta without paying another fare. It almost worked a few times.

One June afternoon, Baby and I went to the Paramount where a big band played between the showing of the main movie feature. The band was that of Ozzie Nelson and the vocalist was Harriet Hilliard. I do not have to tell you who they were later.

When we left the movie along Peachtree Street, radios could be heard from the stores and people looked sad. One lady came up to us and sobbed.

"Paris has fallen."

The sadness of that day contrasted with the fun and excitement of another bit of history I witnessed the December before. Mama let me miss school and took me to see the *Gone With The Wind* premier festivities but not the premier itself. It was cold, and the press of the crowd obstructed our view; so we paid a woman to let us stand on her porch. From there, we saw Clark Gable, Vivian Leigh, Carol Lombard, Olivia de Havilland, and other people from that world of make believe.

The Golden Age of Hollywood had come to Golden Atlanta. I saw it. I am glad.

CHAPTER 27

# The Better Visitor

We were not the only ones who visited in the summer. Buddy Howard lived in Charlotte, North Carolina, and usually spent some weeks with his Aunt Mary and Uncle Willie Cobb Holland next door. He had a knack for making life interesting. Maybe it ran in his family.

I never knew Buddy's grandfather, but I wish I had. Mr. Ty Holland was elected sheriff in the early 1900s and served with distinction. In fact, even his election campaign was distinctive. He worked out a plan and followed it just right.

Under the plan, he would knock on every door and ask every voter for support. What made this unique was that Mr. Holland intended to walk the whole way. Even though Monroe County was a big county, he covered every foot of every road.

Standing about six feet seven inches tall, even his long legs could not carry him out every morning and get him back home for every meal or even at night. So if he reached a house a meal time, custom and courtesy of the time dictated the voter invite him in for a meal. He always accepted. When he reached a house about dark, he first asked for their vote and then followed with another request.

"Since it's late, would you mind putting me up for the night?"

Again custom and courtesy demanded a yes answer. He had a privately spoken idea.

"If you eat at a man's table or sleep in his bed, he's got an investment in you. Who votes against his own investment?"

They didn't and he won easily.

He served as sheriff with no less flair. Tradition tells that the sheriff's giant size scared the life out of the criminal element, or, as they say today, it intimidated them. He never carried a gun, much less used one. He just told the malefactor, "Come on, you're under arrest." They came on.

Sheriff Holland did run into difficulty when they initiated him into a fraternal order. This took place in Macon and he was supposed to meet his wife after the ceremony in the lobby of that city's finest hotel, the Dempsey. He arrived there first and sat down in one of the old overstuffed mohair upholstered chairs to read the afternoon newspaper.

Suddenly, and right according to the plan of his new lodge fellows, a gaudy young woman with a heavily painted face sat right on his lap. Before the sheriff could register a protest or even surprise, in walked Mrs. Holland with some of her lady friends.

Anger, confusion, and embarrassment flowed all over the lobby, except for the lodge brothers who were hiding behind potted palms and trying to stifle their laughter. I do not know where the painted lady went, but I do know Mrs. Holland left walking with a resolute gait and her jaw set like stone. The fearless and effective sheriff sat there wordless.

The next day, Sheriff Holland called his friends together.

"My wife didn't take kindly to what happened," he began, "She won't talk to me, she won't listen to me, and she won't let me come home.

"I got no place to go. Since you fellas got me into this, you'll just have to take turns putting me up at night," he continued, with a look of despair.

His lodge brothers were distraught that they had brought such misfortune on a friend. Privately they decided to go to explain it all to Mrs. Holland and beg for forgiveness. No luck.

She would not listen to them any more than she would to her husband. The only thing left to do was to offer the sheriff a place to sleep. They did and he accepted, moving to a different house each night. Tension began to mount because the wives of the brothers were not too sure about the innocence of the whole thing themselves.

Just as an interspousal civil war neared eruption in Forsyth, some sort of community gathering took place with husbands and wives all there.

The Holland fuss dominated the conversation. The ladies whispered about the "disgraceful carryings on." The men tried to figure out a solution. In the midst of this, who should walk in arm-in-arm but Sheriff and Mrs. Holland. She then made the grand announcement.

"I knew all along it was a prank, but I just thought you men deserved a little of your own medicine." She had administered a double dose.

Little wonder life became more exciting in our neighborhood when Buddy came to visit, considering his genes. It all started for me when one of us figured out an activity we called "shooting ducks." A duck is a used cigarette. We shot ducks by looking for long clean ones and taking them to the loft above our garage and smoking them. Sometimes I would sneak one or two Chesterfields out of Daddy's pack on his bedroom mantle. I took care not to get greedy for fear he would begin to miss them. One time we secured a whole pack of Wings cigarettes. They carried an extra bonus in the form of pictures of sleek airplanes like the Winnie Mae. Smoking these things made us a little dizzy but not sick since we did not know about inhaling. But we learned soon enough that smoking can make you sick.

Late one Sunday afternoon we found an almost untouched cigar, and eagerly we climbed the ladder to the garage loft.

"Who's going first," I asked hoping Buddy would volunteer. He did.

"Let me have that thing," he said, reaching in his pocket for a wooden kitchen match and lit the old stogie.

I did not want to admit it, but just being in the loft with the cigar smoke pretty near made me sick—let alone puffing on it. As Buddy smoked away, I did not know whether to admire him or pity him. I found out which it should have been soon enough.

A little while later, we went to Sunday night service at the Methodist church. I went with Mama and Daddy, and Buddy went with Lyle Hollis and his fiance Gladys Fambro. They sat a little ways in front of us, and I began to notice Buddy's shoulders making a funny motion. Then I heard Buddy making some funny sounds. Then I learned cigars can make little boys sick. Since seeing Lyle pick little Buddy up and carry him out of the church, I have not seen Buddy smoke too many cigars.

On an early afternoon in August 1941, Buddy caught me at home. The words burst out excitedly.

"I got Uncle Willie Cobb's car."

To appreciate the importance of this statement, you need to know Buddy was a couple of weeks shy of fifteen and I was a month from fourteen. Few things rank as high as driving a car at that age. Particularly without an adult along. Besides there was bound to be a girl or two out there wanting to go to ride.

Buddy's uncle turned the car over to him to run an errand. Our use of it went beyond that.

After wheeling around for awhile, we saw Ann Gilbert who was visiting her aunt and grandmother. She lived in Jacksonville but spent many summers in Forsyth where we had formed a long time friendship. None of us were surprised when she joined us for the ride.

Not wanting to be spotted by Buddy's uncle, we decided a country drive to be the safest. Travelling over a pretty little road north of town, we came upon a washboard section of it, and, thinking it the right thing to do, Buddy mashed down on the accelerator. The car fishtailed one way then the other until it skidded at a crazy angle into the ditch on the right.

Up started being down, and down started being up. As the car tumbled both sideways and end over end, we pitched around the inside like poker chips in a washing machine. The car finally came to a rest on its left side with the three of us scrambled like so many eggs.

Remarkably, we were not hurt and were able to push and pull ourselves through the right hand front window and out into the field where the car settled, having knocked down a substantial length of fence.

"Look at Willie Cobb's car," Buddy stammered.

We did and it was mighty poor looking. Totalled is not a big enough word to describe what was left of that Ford. Somehow Ann did not find the car her greatest concern.

"Don't tell anybody I was with you," she just kept saying.

Her chin kept quivering, and her hands kept shaking. Buddy with his head hanging low kept mumbling something like, "What am I gonna say to Willie Cobb?"

I do not know what I said. I just know that I wanted to get away from that place and be at home. So we headed up the long dusty road parched by August afternoon heat.

Walking was slow, and we hurt a little bit, but just then I heard a familiar sound coming around the curve in the road behind us. It was the distinctive clink of trace chains and plop of mule hooves accompanied by the squeak of wagon wheels. As I looked around, an old man made his way toward town in his weathered one-mule wagon.

At first he seemed suspicious of us but finally took pity. His pity, however, was not boundless because we quickly learned that his compassion for us did not exceed his concern for his mule.

The old man was willing for us to ride downhill in the wagon, but he made us get out and walk up the hills so as not to tire out his mule. Eventually we made it home.

The last thing we heard from Ann as she left us was, "Remember, don't tell anybody I was with you."

I did not hear Buddy's conversation with his Uncle Willie Cobb Holland. I did not want to. From Buddy I learned it went something like this:

"That thing wrecked."

"What thing?"

"Your car."

"Anybody hurt? Who was with you?"

"Just me and Harold. Nobody else, and both of us are all right."

"Oh."

I do not really know what the conversation was between Mama and me, except her expressions of thankfulness that Buddy and I came out uninjured. I do know that I too said that just the two of us occupied the car.

Having weathered the storm of disclosure, I walked out the front door of our house and took a deep breath convinced that I had survived both the wreck and the parental confrontation. About that time, Buddy came along, and we decided to walk up to Willingham's garage and see them pull the car in. As we neared the garage, we again met Ann Gilbert. This time she was with her cousin Gloria Chapman, an ardent conversationalist. Before we could say anything, Gloria was chattering about the wreck and Ann's involvement.

Buddy and I both knew that if Ann had told Gloria she was in the car, everybody in town would know by nightfall. Before we could express our disapproval of Ann's revelation to Gloria, Ann said with a relieved look, "Oh, I told Mama about the whole thing too, so it's all right to tell your folks I was in the car."

So there we were. We had not only wrecked the car, we had lied to our folks. This meant going back and reopening the whole issue. Right then I was more than a little mad with Ann. But I got over it. I have not seen her in some years but I like her, and I understand her concern. The aunt that she visited in Forsyth was Miss Mary Amos, the same teacher I feared so much after my halloween escapade about which I will write later. No wonder Ann did not want to make any ripples around the house.

About three years later, Buddy and I jointly bought a Model T Ford. But on that August afternoon in 1941, I did not ever want to see an automobile again. I truly thought the old man in the beat-up wagon with the worn-out mule "had a better idea."

# CHAPTER 28

# Of Chinaberry
# Horses and Easter Eggs

The Bible proscribes covetousness, and the young boys in the thirties strove mightily to abide by the "shalt nots." But try as we might, we transgressed this commandment regularly when it came to ponies.

Most any boy would commit all sorts of felonies to get a pony. But only a few obtained them. In fact, Charles Hollis was the only boy about my age with a pony in Forsyth, but three girls had them: Kathryn Zellner, Gloria Chapman, and Marilyn Wiley.

The rest of us satisfied ourselves with various substitutes. Mr. Tribble's stable helped because he sometimes had a pony or two in his stalls and did not mind when I came by and petted them. If he did not have a pony there, I contented myself with petting a horse or even a mule. I learned that mules ranked higher in some ways than any of them and that our part of the country owed a heavy debt to the unheralded mule.

All of us in the North Lee Street section shared in the enjoyment of the main pony substitute—the chinaberry horse. Most folks have never heard of one of those, but I owned and had fun with a lot of them.

Chinaberry trees begin their growth as long slender sticks with a soft bark which peels off easily in the face of a pocketknife's attack. To make a horse from this, we cut off the stick about six feet from its pointed end. If all you wanted was a humble mustang like the bit players in the cowboy shows rode, you just put the stick between your legs and held the big end and galloped off.

If you wanted something fancier, you carved designs on the bark. Some boys shaved off all the bark to play like their horse was white like Buck Jones's horse.

One boy even shaved the bark in a spiral to make a chinaberry horse look like a sort of candy stick zebra. As for me, I just cut off a little bark here and a little bark there because I always admired pinto ponies.

Whatever they looked like, the thunderous hoof beat of chinaberry horses echoed around the neighborhood throughout my childhood. The thrill that we experienced when a chinaberry horse rared up stands as a monument to the creative imagination of little boys.

But those four pony owners that I mentioned did not have to content themselves with imagination. They rode the real flesh and blood and, in doing so, made up a diverse group.

Charles Hollis possessed talent in just about every area. He played the piano, but he also stood out as the best athlete around, making him a focal point of admiration. Kathryn was the first feminine object of my admiration, and Gloria was the quintessential friend. Everybody liked her.

Of the four though, Marilyn was the most interesting. She moved easily with a lithe body carrying a freckled face and sandy hair. And when she mounted her steed, that was something else. Missy, as we called her, used no saddle on the animal which was a little bigger than a pony and a little smaller than a horse, a little grayer than white and a little whiter than gray.

When she raced by, hair flowing behind her, she evoked a vision of a blonde Indian princess reigning over the make-believe plains on the streets of Forsyth.

I find it hard to think of Missy in a frilly dress at a party. But like the rest of us, she went to them when the occasion demanded. One such occasion arose when the Ingram sisters issued an invitation for a late winter festivity. The rains came and the weather turned cold, so Mama drove me freshly scrubbed to the Ingram house. I ran through the cold rain from the car to the porch where Mrs. Ingram answered my knock.

"Come in," she invited in a quizzical way.

I sat on the sofa showing every bashful bone in my body because nobody greeted my entrance except the stern-looking Mrs. Ingram.

"Where is everybody?" I thought silently.

"Did you think the party was today, Harold?"

"Yes'm."

"Oh, I'm sorry, it's tomorrow."

The flush of absolute embarrassment rushed through my body causing sweat to burst from every pore.

"Let me drive you home," said Mrs. Ingram, trying for kindness and understanding.

"No'm, I'll be all right," I whispered as I bolted out the door and into the sheets of cold rain, running all the way home.

Home looked good, and I resolved not to leave it for parties again. But time and events changed things so when the warmth of spring brought on the Easter season, I faced another invitation. This one was from Banks Worsham and his cousin Kathryn Zellner who planned an Easter egg hunt at the Cabaniss grove. I liked Banks and I liked Kathryn and I loved the Cabaniss grove, so I agreed to go.

The Cabaniss grove held and still holds an important interest for me.

Captain Tom Cabaniss once owned the place where he built a stately home not long after he returned from his Confederate military service. He built a sort of bandstand or summer house in the grove in front of his home where he hosted important events on summer afternoons. He invited prominent leaders like Alexander Stephens, Bob Toombs, and Ben Hill to lecture to the townspeople. Captain Cabaniss was later elected to the Congress where he developed a friendship with Grover Cleveland and supported the silver standard.

The Captain also built a pond in the rear and right hand side of the house, and it attracted the interest of boys looking for a place to swim. Before the period of my recollection, one of the town's notorious events took place there.

The Rudisill brothers lived near the pond and sneaked back there for swimming often. In the midst of their aquatic sport, one of the Rudisills swam over to what he thought was a log and grabbed it. The object turned over and a human hand extended out of the croker sacks which wrapped a body and reached above the water line.

It does not take much imagination to figure how quick the boys left. The authorities came and determined that the body was the object of a homicide, which they never solved.

Even though they drained the pond before my time, the grove remained a fine place to play and to reflect on the adventures of the old

Captain and the Rudisill boys. So the Easter egg hunt there suited me fine despite the fact that I never hunted eggs too well.

At this hunt, the big deal had nothing to do with the number of eggs you found. Everything turned on finding the golden egg which would make the finder into a hero or heroine. For me this took an added importance because I could make up for the deep shame of the Ingram party faux pas.

I approached the hunt by ignoring anything but the golden egg. But—no golden egg for me. After a long time of looking with no success, I just stood there staring into space. Then Missy Wiley walked up to me, causing me to expect a friendly comment lessening my distress. Instead she gave me a violent shove making me fall to the ground. With a shriek of joy, she picked up the golden egg which had been right between my feet all the time. I lay there in humiliation, thinking of the words of the villain in the Postem ad: "Foiled again."

The world did not look too good, but everything always changes. The World of Commerce had no thought of the Easter bunny as a bearer of gifts for little people then, but Easter did mean new Sunday clothes. Most times that did not mean much to me, but this time it did because I faced a new phase in my life.

Grown men wore long pants while little boys wore short pants in the summer and knickers in the winter. The knickers particularly offended me because I generally wore those made of something they called tweeduroy, a kind of tough corduroy. When you walked the knickers said, "swish, swish, swish," and I did not like that at all. Long pants were objects of desire and ambition, making this Easter a landmark.

Walking into the house after the egg hunt, Mama called me into her room.

"Let's try on your Easter outfit," she smiled.

"By grannies," I thought, "Long pants."

Not just any kind of long pants, but white linen-like pants and a white coat making up a complete suit. So proud was I that I burst across the bedroom and hugged Mama.

Just before leaving for Sunday school the next morning, the telephone rang. My sister Baby rushed to answer it, thinking it might be her boyfriend.

"Harold, it's for you," she said, disappointedly.

"Come by Ma Willingham's house after church," said Billy Hill on the phone. "Me and you are going to look for Easter eggs."

"I'll be there," I answered, happy to hunt eggs in a noncompetitive way.

The Willinghams were Billy's grandparents and lived across the street from us. One of their sons, Harry, was close enough to my age for me to admire him but far enough removed to make me nervous around him as an older boy. Years have erased that age difference. I still admire him, but we now share the same generation and many common memories and sentiments.

Mr. A. L. Willingham, Harry's father and Billy's grandfather, personified the true free enterprise era of America. He owned and operated the Chevrolet place in Forsyth. He also possessed distinct technical talents, having invented a coupling device used nationally by railroads.

Before entering the car business, Mr. A. L. owned a blacksmith shop and still kept the shop equipment under his house. This he did just in case the automobile fad fizzled out.

On top of all this, Mr. A. L. understood politics well, working behind the scenes as well as serving as Mayor of Forsyth.

When I arrived at the Willingham's house after church, everything was ready for Billy and me to hunt eggs. We did. We hunted walking and we hunted crawling. That part of the hunting brought on some extra trouble. I still wore the brand new white long pants. Crawling on new spring grass in white long pants just naturally makes trouble and that is what I had when I went home.

All I could do was look forward to the summer because it had to be better than the times of that winter and spring.

Then a year later a new Easter came along. I lived through the next Easter better able to understand lots of things, but most of all I learned more about the world.

Mama and Gladys Powell spent Saturday getting the Easter dinner ready. In those days fried chicken was the order of the day and not ham. This was the case for a reason. First off, nobody called young chickens broilers or fryers back then. They called them frying-size chickens and had them only in the spring and summer because of the lack of fancy chicken houses. So in the winter we ate baked hens for Sunday dinner. Easter opened the season for fried chicken. For dessert on Easter, strawberry shortcake was mandatory.

This appealed to me, and age had canceled out egg hunting and made long pants seem sort of natural.

Coming home late that Saturday afternoon, I walked in the back door to hear Mama calling me to the library. In that room sat a man of obvious contradictions. His clothes looked like he might have jumped off of a freight train, which may have been a fact. His weatherbeaten face showed the signs of a life of dissipation and disappointment. That same face displayed an underlying handsomeness and sophistication telling of an interesting past.

"This is your cousin George Ray Black," Mama told me.

He came over, smiled, and shook my hand while I looked at him awash in wonder.

Mama had two uncles on her mother's side of the family, Uncle Ray and Uncle Will, both of whom lived in Newnan before Uncle Will moved to Tampa about the turn of the century. Down there he acquired what I had always heard to be a lot of wealth. So when Uncle Will died, George Ray inherited a part of the fortune.

I once heard he chartered a ship and hired the Guy Lomardo Orchestra to entertain a whole bunch of his friends on a trip to Europe. Whether this is true or not, he spent his inheritance in short order, and a hard life followed.

He was living that hard life when he came to visit us. I liked him and wondered at all I had heard.

The next morning I went to Sunday school and church and expected George Ray to join us for fried chicken and strawberry shortcake. But, when I came home, he had left. I never saw him again.

Many, many years later, as an adult, I met his daughter. Our acquaintance spanned a period of only one day, but I pegged her as one of my favorite kinfolks. Perhaps we may meet again sometime.

# CHAPTER 29

# The Ups and Downs of Halloween

In the Forsyth of my childhood, Halloween held a big place for boys in their early teens. We perpetrated many tricks, but the candy companies had not yet come up with the idea of the treats. Minor mischief might better describe the usual activities on Halloween night.

After an early supper, the boys hit the streets armed with a bar of Octagon soap. We used the soap to mark the show windows of the stores with giant swirls. In addition to this, garbage cans and porch furniture were overturned, and the boys derived great pleasure by ringing door bells and running before anyone came to the door.

All this revolved around a sort of Tom and Jerry game being played good naturedly by the boys and the small local police force, which generally counted two night officers on Halloween instead of the usual one. The damage was slight, and young folks found an opportunity to let off steam. As far as I could tell, almost everybody enjoyed it, and no one was much upset over the mischief. After all, the show windows probably needed washing, and the rest of the cleanup required minimum effort.

Now everything I have said was true until the big one came along. It all hit the fan on Halloween when I was in the seventh grade.

As the sun went down that afternoon, the chill of the first cold night of the fall began to make its bite on the young teens and preteens looking forward to the evening's revelry. I hurried to the supper table, wolfed down the ham and eggs that Mama liked on cold fall nights, and begged to be excused before the others finished. Having received this permission from understanding parents, I grabbed my bar of soap, put on my Mackinaw jacket and cap, and headed out the door.

Upon arriving at the courthouse square, I saw two groups assembling to do their thing. My group consisted of twelve- and thirteen-year-old boys while the other group was made up of what we called "big boys."

During the first part of the evening, we followed the traditional Halloween activities . . . soap swirls, doorbells, garbage cans, and porch furniture. Then suddenly we noticed something new was happening. The big boys had found a huge quantity of large rolls of fence wire stored in a lot behind Bramblett's Hardware Store. This presented a new and wonderful opportunity. They rolled and, in some instances, unrolled the fence wire around the various streets of the business section of Forsyth.

In each instance, they were just a step or so ahead of the aging and slower-footed police officers. This appeared to be a wonderful event. Before we younger boys realized it, we became caught up in the excitement of the night and became part of the more imaginative activities.

Just one block north of the courthouse square on Lee Street, James Tribble had a stable where he sometimes sold wagons. A brand new one-horse wagon sat in front of the stable that night on display, and it triggered the making of what seemed like a terrific plan.

With roars of laughter and cries of excitement, the boys both big and small took off pulling and pushing the wagon down the street toward the depot and on to the small lumber yard operated by Mr. Frank Bennett and Mr. T. J. Hughey. There we found piles of shavings which we loaded into the wagon and carried across Main Street to Mary Persons High School.

Load after load was spread on the floors of the halls and auditorium of the school. Only fatigue and a little boredom stopped the procedure.

Upon finishing the shavings job, the problem arose as to what to do with the wagon. Some bright young person in the crowd (or perhaps mob would be a better word) came up with the idea that it should be hung by a rope from the little dome on top of the high school roof. This suggestion met with unanimous approval, and, through an astounding exhibition of juvenile ingenuity and energy, the wagon was hoisted to the roof and left there for all to see.

I lay in bed that night, tired but filled with satisfaction over having been involved with what seemed to be the most exciting evening I had ever spent. I could hardly wait to get to school the next day. Little did I know that the events of the next day would be among the most frightening I ever experienced.

So I went off to sleep still thinking that the world was a place filled with good times for any twelve-year-old boy who had the good fortune to fall in with older, stronger, and more daring boys. The next day would show me better.

In those days, schools in small towns only had eleven grades, and the high school building accommodated grades seven through eleven. A boy in the lowest of all of the grades in the school felt so proud for having been even a small part in the monumental defacing of the building.

This pride lasted through my arrival at school that day and into the first couple of hours. But somewhere about the middle of the morning as I sat in the classroom of Miss Mary Amos who had the well-earned reputation of being the most feared scolder in the school. A person came to the door saying that I was wanted in the principal's office. The lump in my throat was about like a small watermelon as I walked down the hall and found that the principal, Mr. E. E. O'Kelly, was not there, but rather was on the telephone waiting to talk to me.

When I picked up the telephone he said he was at the city hall and he gave me a list of names of other boys to be assembled and brought to the city hall. That list included all of us "little boys" involved in the affair the preceding evening. It seemed that either one of the policemen had recognized all of us who were not smart or quick enough to escape notice, or that some of the big boys had told on us. I never knew which, and right then it did not matter. The immediate future was a whole lot more important than the past.

The first danger of the immediate future was Miss Mary Amos. I had to tell her that I and the other boys had been summonsed to the city hall. If I had trouble swallowing when I went to the principal's office, I now had trouble even breathing.

First we heard the word from Miss Amos. Then this rag-tag group of twelve- and thirteen-year-old "little boys" banded together and headed up the street.

About halfway to the city hall, one of them began to laugh and said, "George thinks we're going to court."

"Where do you think we're going?" said another one of the boys.

At that point, tears began to flow from the eyes of the first speaker. This was a solemn group making its way across the streets of Forsyth on the morning of the first day of November 1939. Solemnity and terror continued as we filed into the meeting room of the city council. In those days, small towns had no recorder's court. The court was presided over by the mayor. A quiet man and somewhat shy, Mayor Alexander, the father of my good friend Carolyn, ordinarily did not scare me. That day he did.

Mayor Alexander looked at us with a steely glare.

"You're charged with disorderly conduct and damage to private and public property. How do you plead, guilty or not guilty?"

Expecting the very worst but not knowing what else to do, we pled guilty, whereupon Mayor Alexander demonstrated some of the best judicial wisdom that I have ever witnessed.

"Boys," he began, "You've made a mess out of your town and you ought to be ashamed. I don't have any choice but to punish you. So, it's my sentence that you young gentlemen spend the night in the city calaboose."

There was a silence that seemed to last forever while most of us wished we could find someway to die on the spot. Mayor Alexander broke the silence.

"Now, I want to say this to you. If you all can get this town absolutely clean and all the mess you've made straightened up before dark this afternoon, you won't have to spend that night in the calaboose. And if you're gonna get it done, you better start now."

He sort of waved his hand as if to say go out and get at it. You better believe we did.

There may have been instances of boys working harder and faster on a cleanup job. There may have been times that Forsyth and Mary Persons High School were cleaner than it was on that November afternoon. But, if there were, I cannot imagine it. The job was done. Most of us felt some relief from that but the shame continued and we still had our parents to face.

The thought of going home after our work was done shook me from my head to my toes. Many years had passed since I hid in the trunk to escape the first grade and the electric spanking machine, but I thought about that and wished that I could be so little again and hide from reality that easily. Understanding that impossibility, I walked in my house as bravely as I could.

There I found a startling thing—normalcy. Nothing different from any other day. Nobody mentioned anything about the activities of the night before or about the punishment received that afternoon. My mother said something about me doing my homework and commented that supper was almost ready.

I wondered at all this and still do. I never knew whether my parents did not know of my involvement in the mischief, or whether they felt adequate punishment had been meted out.

In any event, relief overwhelmed me. I think back now about Mayor Alexander, and I believe that he concluded that the best course was to deal with us in a mature way rather than treating us as children. He was wise, and I believe that we all profited from it.

CHAPTER 30

# This Too Shall Pass

You have to get beyond middle age before you begin to understand that almost nothing lasts forever. In my childhood (and even during much of my adulthood), I harbored no doubts that some things would just go on and on.

During the 1930s I thought nothing could replace the Packard as the ultimate status symbol. The Rolls Royce held no meaning to me. I had never seen one. The Cadillac and the Lincoln seemed like pretenders trying to catch up, but without much hope. If you wanted admiration and envy, the Packard could hand it to you.

The Packard possessed the mantle of immortality. It would last for ages to come. But . . . where is the Packard today? The straight line body and the dignified grill with its vertical chrome gave way to a stream-lining. It did what the Rolls refused to do. As a result, it is gone.

The same can be said of other leading brands like Ipana toothpaste, Shinola shoe polish, and Nash, Studebaker, and Hudson cars. I thought the children of every generation would improve their reading skills by reading aloud the Burma Shave signs. This shaving cream company advertised by spacing little signs along the highway just far enough apart to make you read fast. In sequence the signs conveyed little jingles and always with the Burma Shave logo at the end. An example:

> Although we sold
> Ten million others
> We couldn't sell
> Those cough drop brothers.
> Burma Shave.

That jingle probably does not make sense now because I am not sure you can find Smith Brothers Cough Drops anymore. The box had the picture of the Smith Brothers, both of whom had long beards and obviously did not use shaving cream.

Burma Shave signs no longer make trips shorter for little folks and no longer serve as an aid in learning to read. I attribute this to at least three reasons. Cars became too fast. Highway rights-of-way grew too wide. And then the highway beautifiers decreed that these little efforts at cleverness must go in favor of what they see as the beauties of nature.

When have you seen a big brown bar of Octagon soap with its strong smell and equally strong cleansing power? Most folks do not even remember the famous and valuable Octagon coupons on the wrapper. They offered all sorts of goods in return for coupons, most of them requiring a mail order from the catalog. However, the one "premium" that I really prized was more readily available.

I regularly tiptoed into the kitchen to filch five coupons off the second shelf of the pantry. From there I ran or rode my bicycle to Mr. Ashley Phinazee's City Drug Store. Those five coupons netted me a kite just as fine as any store-bought kite available at that time.

These kites flew easily and with consistency. Homemade kites could not come close in quality. We made them with paper that always seemed too heavy or too fragile, and the wood invariably put the kite out of balance. We often were reduced to trying to put the kite together with paste made from a mixture of water and flour which always came loose in the face of a brisk wind.

(I wonder how many March winds have blown since a little boy has flown an Octagon Soap kite with a tail made of discarded clothes or sheets and using scrap string from the cotton mill down the street. Too many.)

In Forsyth itself, numerous businesses I viewed as immortal have proved their mortality by shutting down. Not only are they gone, they are largely forgotten. The Forsyth Mercantile Company, the E. W. Banks

Company, Bramblett Hardware Company, and, saddest of all to me, the *Monroe Advertiser*. These are only a few representatives of a class of enterprises which faded from the scene for varying reasons.

Society accords no immunity from extinction to institutions. Bank Stephens Institute where I spent the first six grades of my school life has long since ceased to educate children. In my days there, no one doubted the place had an unending future. Wrong again. Nothing lasts forever.

Then there was Bessie Tift College. It certainly could not die. Forsyth without Bessie Tift was unthinkable. Imagine Forsyth without Bessie Tift? Imagine Forsyth without the First Baptist Church? Impossible.

In fact, to most of us outsiders, the college was the church and the church was the college. We saw the Baptists as numbering so many and doing so much that they faced no threat of any sort. Although the members of our little Presbyterian Church and the larger Methodist congregation felt no inferiority in the face of the huge Baptist influence, we held them in awe. Nothing could threaten them or their institutions' existence.

The First Baptist Church lives. But Bessie Tift College lives only in memory and by the influence of its vast service to the community. Somewhere after its beginning in 1848, the Baptists took the college under their wing. Between times of educating young women and adding culture to the little town, it even served as an important hospital for Confederate soldiers in 1864. Its supplied Forsyth an abundance of good teachers when other small southern towns went lacking. As a result Forsyth students excelled in college and the adult world. The college brought to Forsyth an intelligentsia few small towns possessed and it gave the townspeople a taste of music, theater, and literature through its concerts, plays, and lectures.

In my early days, I did not fully understand, much less appreciate, these assets flowing from the college. Like the rest of the boys my age, I did appreciate it in my own way though. What we appreciated without any real understanding of them was the girls.

To begin with, they looked pretty. They were just enough older than us to arouse all sorts of fantasies. After all, mystery grabs the male mind beyond almost anything. At that age, dreams of pulchritude meant a lot more than visions of culture. We were too young to touch but old enough to imagine.

Between Sunday school and church on Sunday mornings, we headed to the corner at Alexander's Drug Store. The college girls had their own Sunday School on campus, but they went to church in town. On the way they walked by the corner where we stood. I am not sure they noticed us at that early stage of life, but we sure noticed them.

Another way to get to see and even know the girls arose on the day they came back to school after summer vacation. Knowing they traveled by bus or train, we studied the rail and bus schedules and met them with gracious offers to carry their bags. If the girls would offer to pay for the service, we declined with a flourish of chivalry.

Unlike the other boys, I had a couple of other avenues for contact with these older women. The print shop at Daddy's newspaper published the campus newspaper called *The Campus Quill.* The girls on the staff brought the copy to the shop and hung around and watched the type-setting and printing.

By the time of my early teens, I had performed enough odd jobs around the shop to know in detail what went on. Nothing could have offered me a better opportunity to show off my knowledge and maturity than sauntering over to explain the process to the girls. They seemed impressed and appreciative. This opportunity had its limits though. Some-times my older brother Bubba would be there. Not only did he know more about printing than I did, he was even older than the girls, and that preempted me entirely. So on those times I just went back to feeding the job press and thinking about the pulchritude.

That brings up the second special way I had to get to know the girls. Bubba sometimes dated them, and on rare times the rules allowed them to come to our house in the afternoon. Maybe Daddy's position as a preacher made this easier. When they came to meet Bubba, I stayed around home. This resulted in at least one thrill and one deep embarrass-ment.

Walking through the dining room on my way to the kitchen one of those afternoons, I chanced to peek through a crack in the folding doors between the dining room and the library. Wonder of wonders, there stood Bubba before the fireplace . . . of all things, kissing a college girl. Wait until the other boys my age hear about that!

The incident of my embarrassment was unmentionable and deeply felt. One afternoon while one of the girls was at the house, I made a quick stop at Mama and Daddy's bathroom. The room had two entrances, one from the bedroom and the other from the hall near the library. In my rush I failed to lock the door.

In the midst of my compliance with one of nature's basic requirements, the hall door flung open. There she stood in all her beauty and dismay looking full faced and unexpectedly at me. There I stood, unable to do otherwise, but almost wanting to jump in the bowl and pull the flush lever. Whatever hope I had for impressing the college girls was decimated forever, I thought.

For what seemed like an eternity, I had visions of the girl telling the story to all the other girls amid gales of laughter. During that time, I thought I detected a derisive snicker on the face of any of the girls I saw. So mostly I just avoided them.

It did not take much effort to avoid the college girls because the rules at Bessie Tift in those days took care of that pretty well. Somebody put together a system which truly overloaded the girls with "thou shalt nots."

Thou shalt not leave the campus except at rare tightly scheduled times. Thou shalt not ride in a car except at even rarer and tighter scheduled times. The idea of drinking alcohol was, of course, so far removed from possibility that it was not even among the remotest considerations.

The most discussed but equally enforced taboos were smoking, dancing, and playing cards. In the eyes of the rulemakers, these three activities had their origin with the devil himself. Most of the girls disagreed, but their opinion was of no import. An interesting difference in that era and today is that while the girls complained to one another, nobody did anything more. A demonstration or even a private protest to the authorities just was not an option.

But those of us in the "too young to participate crowd" talked about this a good deal. The subject almost always came up when the boys our age sat on the green benches on the courthouse square near the Confederate monument. Late one Sunday afternoon, it had a good airing.

"It just ain't right," declared one of the boys, watching the winter sun go down.

"They can't do anything. What's wrong with riding in a car with a boy? Somebody ought to do something about it."

"What difference does it make to you," laughed Billy Hill, "You don't have a car and the girls wouldn't ride with you if you did."

"That's not the point," returned the first boy. Then he pointed to the Confederate soldier on top of the monument.

"I'll betcha that fella didn't own no slaves either, but he fought just the same. It's the principle of the thing."

That statement stumped us.

While this serious discourse was going on, Eldridge Roquemore had wandered into the gathering. As the rest of us pondered the depths of the last comment, Eldridge had a suggestion.

"If the girls need all those rules, they must need some serious protection."

As he said that, his eyes settled on the World War I cannon that had been a fixture on the courthouse square all my life and more. That old weapon was massive with its big wooden wheels held together by steel rims. Although it probably had not felt the jolt of firing since Armistice Day 1918, it served its purpose as it guarded a courthouse that needed no guarding.

Before anybody said anything, we all knew what all of us were thinking. Then Eldridge said it.

"Let's take the cannon down to the college to protect the girls."

We replied not with words but with action. So here we went, five or six thirteen-year-old boys at the first dark of a chilly and quiet Sunday evening, moving down Johnston Street pulling and pushing a cannon. A mixture of grunts and laughter mingled among us until a car pulled up beside us. It was Mr. Buck Smith, Forsyth's only night policeman, driving Forsyth's only police car.

"Where ya'll taking the cannon," asked the aging officer, leaning out of the window of the aging Chevrolet.

"They said to carry it to the college campus," came the answer with an absolutely straight face.

"Oh," said Mr. Buck, as he drove away with a puzzled look on his face.

We did pretty well on the street, since there was no traffic on a late Sunday. In fact, we had no trouble at all until we reached the railroad track. In those days, the space between the tracks was not filled so there was a drop of several inches creating a sort of a trap.

When we pushed and pulled the big wheels of the big gun over the first track, it went, "blump." Then it settled between the tracks and just sat there. We pushed some more. We pulled some more. We tried pulling the heavy wooden spokes. We tried lifting the tongue for leverage. We tried sitting on the barrel for leverage. It did not matter what we did, the cannon just sat there. It seemed to be laughing at us, taunting us for having moved it from its official resting place.

As we stopped for a minute or two for rest, and maybe a little planning, one of the boys uttered one word in that kind of loud guttural whisper when you are overcome by horror.

"Listen."

We all heard it. There was no mistaking it . . . a train whistle. And the cannon sitting on the track. Without a command, but with expressions of terror, we all grabbed the cannon.

"Blimp, blimp," went the cannon this time, almost jumping out of its hole. What our determination and planning could not do after long effort, our fear did in a few seconds.

Once beyond this obstacle, we rolled easily to the campus. We thought our efforts were well rewarded when we looked at the cannon sitting under the arch at the entrance to the college grounds. Its barrel faced outward ready and able to fend off the forces of Satan which might expose the girls to evils like riding in cars with boys, smoking, playing cards, or that even more terrible sin, dancing. We went home with pride.

The next day, other people faced the job of returning the cannon to the courthouse square. Eldridge said it best.

"What us five or six boys did in about fifteen minutes, it took seven city hands and two dump trucks all day to undo."

The cannon is gone. When the scrap drives of World War II came along, the city fathers sacrificed the old artillery piece to the war effort. I sure hope that its metal did something good for the cause of freedom because I miss it on the courthouse square.

Like the cannon, like the Packard and Octagon soap coupons, like the *Monroe Advertiser* and Forsyth Mercantile, Bessie Tift College is gone too. Forsyth feels its loss more than it feels the others.

Maybe nothing has ever been permanent, but there is less permanence today than before. We make everything disposable.

But somehow a disposable college just does not seem right.

# CHAPTER 31

# When College Was Different . . . And I Was Too

I never knew college life of the 1930s, but I always wished I had. It fascinates me because the people who went to college then were just enough older than me so that I looked up to them. Even today, those folks seem to treasure their college memories more than students of other eras. I believe that they enjoyed it so much and developed such strong ties with each other because of the character of the time. College life then lacked the easy frivolity of the twenties, and it lacked the intense rush of the forties. It certainly lacked the sophistication of later years when everybody has a car and many live in apartments.

Back then, simple things sufficed and even excited. Students lived in dormitories or in fraternity and sorority houses. Because the students did not have the means or money to go somewhere else, the social life stayed on the campuses and brought the students closer together.

Although that era escaped me as a student, I did have a couple of brushes with pre-war college campuses. One came from a visit to Mercer with my friend John Heard, and the other from a visit with my sister Baby at Florida State College for Women.

When John invited Barrett Sutton and me to Mercer for a weekend, the thirties had already slipped away. It was the fall of 1941, and John was a new freshman while Barrett and I were high school sophomores viewing the opportunity with widest of eyes. We found cleverness exceeding all expectations.

As we walked into John's dormitory, Sherwood Hall, the only telephone in the whole place rang. A boy grabbed the wall phone in the hall and answered it.

"Sherwood Forest. Robin Hood speaking."

"Now that is college," I thought to myself. I wondered if I might ever get that quick witted. But before my admiration for the phone answerer could grow deeper, John had a suggestion.

"Put down your bags," he said, with eyes twinkling, "There's something on this floor you got to see."

We followed anticipating the eighth wonder of the world. When John led us into a room on the left side of the hall, we truly felt we had beheld it. Heavy cords strung from almost every object in the room through countless pulleys to one master pulley between the bed and the study desk. The designer of all this wonderful maze lay on the bed holding a book. Maybe he was studying, but I really think he was just waiting for us to come in so he could show off.

"Show 'em how it works," commanded John, as we walked in.

The boy pulled a cord.

"Whoop." A window went up with a force.

He pulled another cord.

"Zip." A window blind came down.

Another pull, a drawer opened. Another, the closet door opened. And on and on and on.

When we caught the Greyhound bus home on Sunday afternoon, I thought a lot about the wonders I had seen and heard. Two conclusions resulted. With this kind of brain power and cleverness in college, the world is getting better than anybody ever dreamed. The other conclusion? It sure will be tough to compete when I get to college.

My other college visit came much earlier. Baby spent one year at Bessie Tift College in Forsyth. She then decided to go off to school and, for some reason, picked FSCW. Situated in Tallahassee, this became Florida State University when it turned coed.

Going off to college took a lot of getting ready for a girl in 1935. Some of it was necessary like getting clothes and such, but the rest was more ritual than anything else. This meant saying goodby and expressing good wishes in the proper way—parties and get-togethers.

For Baby it began when she and three of her girlfriends rented a cabin at Indian Springs for a week. These four who had felt a close personal bond for all of their lives probably sensed that this bond would change forever once one of them went away and found a new circle of friends. They knew this would be the last chance for four teenage girls to be to each other what they had been since earliest childhood. So they resolved to make the most of it.

Any such retreat required chaperons. Mama and Mable Alexander were elected. That meant that I was elected too. So one hot morning I helped Mama and Baby load the car with food and so on for the week, and off we went.

Hot August air blew through the car windows doing little to cool us off, and the prickly artificial horsehair finish of the upholstery made my sweaty legs uncomfortable. I was glad when we rounded the sharp bend known as Dead Man's Curve; Indian Springs lay right ahead of us. It reminded everybody of the dangers of car travel.

"Wasn't it horrible about the truckload of children turning over here?" Baby asked, really not wanting an answer.

"I heard they were on their way to a picnic," commented Lula May Tyson. Lula May was Baby's friend and rode with us that day. I liked her because she spent time with me and tried to help me with my reading problems.

"Maybe those precious little folks wouldn't have died if the road hadn't been paved," Mama speculated.

"I know for certain," she continued in that tone of voice that she always had when she issued a warning, "Some people think they can drive as fast as they want just because the road got paved. They ought to realize it's even more dangerous than a bumpy road."

By the time that bit of advice sunk in, we turned left by the swimming pool and headed up the hill toward the cabin. Seeing the creek and the new rock walls bordering the trails, I thought of how much fun all this could be if we had another boy with us. A week in the woods with two middle-aged women and four teenage girls did not fit the plans of an eight-year-old boy.

For generations Indian Springs had attracted mainly older people who came to drink the water. It flows from a spring in a rock formation. Most young folks would not drink it, saying it smelled like rotten eggs. I liked it, and a few years later we made special trips to Indian Springs to get jugs of it. When the city of Forsyth installed its new water system with chlorinated water, I developed a rash and the doctor said it might be a reaction to the water. I doubted that, but I drank the spring water for several months anyway.

To accommodate the older clientele, Indian Springs had three sizeable hotels. A real fancy one, the Wigwam, burned before I could remember, but I heard a lot about it. They said it had an enormous pine tree rooted in the lobby and growing right through the roof. According to legend, the tree dated back to the time when the Creek Indians used Indian Springs as a favorite gathering spot. I wish I had seen all that.

The Foy Hotel was a less expensive place on the highway south of the park. And then there was the Elder Hotel. It had class.

Sitting on a hilltop overlooking the park, the Elder had wide porches wrapping around it. Scores of rocking chairs creaked continuously as the geriatric generation sat, rocked, gossiped, and sipped the water brought fresh from the spring. I suspect some of them put something a little stronger in the water, but, because of the conventions of the times, they probably sat down wind from the more straight laced of the guests.

The older people's grip on Indian Springs began slipping in the middle 1930s though. Three things accounted for this. There was the paving of the road which made it easier for young folks to get there for a few hours stay, and Franklin D. Roosevelt's New Deal triggered the other factors.

In my view, the best of all his alphabet soup bureaucracies was the CCC—the Civilian Conservation Corps. They took young men who need-ed jobs, organized them in semi-military fashion, trained them, and put them to work building the things that America needed.

Some of the fine things they built rose in the valleys and hills of Indian Springs State Park. Where a crude wooden shed once stood over the spring itself, they built a beautiful stone masonry building. Impressive stone steps and walks led down the hill to the spring from a large and handsome pavilion. They remade the whole park and gave it a new attractiveness.

With these public changes came some private ones. Someone put in a commercial swimming pool . . . a big thing to us boys and girls. Even more important to those who reached their teens, two dance halls sprang up. The old, water-driven mill building between the creek and the highway housed one dance hall and the other one sat on the opposite side of the highway just beyond where the creek crosses under it.

The operation of the two varied considerably. The hall in the old mill building filled a special event purpose, mainly dances on Saturday night. On the other hand, the casino (as it was called) opened every night in the summer and boasted several attractions. Its owner, Dan Hoard, installed bowling alleys and a food counter in addition to the dance hall. It depended on a jukebox for music, playing songs like "South" and "Martha."

A lot of the people who went to those dance halls had a distinctive dancing style. We laughingly called it the Indian Springs shuffle. The boy would dance straight ahead and slide his feet with long even steps while the girl backed up till they reached the far end of the hall. Then they would turn around and do the same thing coming in the other direction. Thinking back on it, it was sort of a country style Castle Walk. Whatever it was, Forsyth people made fun of it, and sometimes they mockingly copied it.

The two dance halls drew young folks mainly from Forsyth and Jackson, and that made for a few problems. With the two towns being natural rivals, the boys from each became rivals for the attention of the girls from the other town. All this led the boys from Jackson to dislike the boys from Forsyth and vice versa. This then led to a little fighting now and then.

Most times nobody knew exactly what started the fight, but each side always blamed the other and each side always claimed to have won. My brother Bubba told me about the most famous of the fights when he came down to breakfast one Sunday morning with a swollen lip. It all happened the night before at the old mill dance hall. According to Bubba, our neighbor Durwood Willingham went out on one of the big rocks in front of the hall for a breath of fresh air or maybe a smoke or even a little dram, who knows. Bubba's account continued.

"I heard Durwood's whistle. [Durwood, Bubba, and other boys in the neighborhood had a special five-toned whistle they used to signal one another.] We all ran out on the porch and found that somebody from Jackson had hit Durwood with a bottle and Durwood was fighting back."

A battle royal ensued. Of course the Forsyth boys claimed they won. The Jackson boys probably claimed that they had. One other lingering memory centered around the fact that one of the bigger Forsyth boys ran and hid incurring the undying scorn of his former buddies.

The fresh memory of all this raised some real concerns in Mama's mind, while it gave me at least one reason to think the week might have some excitement connected with it. One thought kept popping into my mind: "Man, wouldn't it be great if I got to see a fight like that."

The swimming pool down the hill from the cabin was the other positive factor about the trip from my point of view. So even before we could get the car unpacked, I began nagging Mama and Baby to let me go to the pool. But before I made any progress with my entreaties, Miss Mable drove up with the other two girls, her daughter Mary Eleanor Alexander and Leila Parks. At that point, whatever I had to say was drowned out by a whole lot of giggling and loud talking about when the boys were going to get there. Finally, Leila took sympathy on me.

"Go on back and put on your bathing suit. We'll all go on down to the pool."

From the little back porch which served as my room for the week, I could hear clearly through the paper-thin walls between me and the room with two double-decked bunks where the girls slept.

"You're not really going to wear it," I heard Baby's voice say.

"I bought it to wear. I'm wearing it." This time it was Mary Eleanor's voice.

"Miss Mable will go into an old fashioned decline," Lula May laughed.

"Well, the boys around the pool sure won't decline," said Leila.

From then on they laughed so much I could not tell what they were saying, but I knew something interesting was about to happen. Not wanting to miss any of it, I rushed into the big room which lay between the two bedrooms and the front porch. Out walked Mary Eleanor.

"Great day in the morning," I thought without making a sound.

"She's stark naked," I exclaimed in total silence.

She was not naked. She was wearing a tight bathing suit made of the same kind of rubber they used for bathing caps. It was darker than white and lighter than tan and so was Mary Eleanor's skin. This created the effect of making it hard to tell where the skin stopped and the rubber started. Even for a boy who grew up with sisters, this sight jolted me.

Then it happened. Miss Mable strolled out of the bedroom where she and Mama stayed.

"My Lord," she stammered, her eyes the size of saucers. At first I thought Miss Mable would either faint or have a seizure. An old fashioned decline just couldn't do justice to her rage. She simply exploded.

"You get back in there and take that thing off."

"Aw, Mama, I want to wear it."

"You will not. Nobody but a common girl or a fast girl would be seen in something like that. Now get rid of that thing."

Miss Mable won the argument like I knew she would, but it disappointed me anyway.

We spent the days at the pool, walking the trails and playing in the creek. When night came, so did the boys . . . Pete, Millard, Hight, and Pleas. That meant the girls went out and I stayed at the cabin with the two Mamas. They tried to entertain me, but I really wanted to go with the girls and their boyfriends. An invitation didn't come though.

So as the week wore on I set about devising a plan for Saturday night. My plan began with casual mention of the Saturday night fights at the dance halls. I commented that boys do not fight when Mamas are around. This led to a meeting. Baby announced they planned to go the dance at the old mill Saturday night. Mama then announced that she, Miss Mable, and I planned to go too. Baby looked crestfallen, but she knew better than to argue. Mama had cast the die. This delighted me. I might get to see a fight after all.

The prospects of a fight pretty much vanished when no Forsyth boys showed up for the dance. Rumor had it that the Butts County sheriff and his deputy lay in wait for them. Having heard the rumor, the Forsyth boys opted for discretion rather than valor, a rare choice for them.

So the dancers were boys and girls from Jackson plus the four Forsyth girls and their boyfriends who all lived in other towns. Against the wall I sat with Mama and Miss Mabel. I guess that is where they get the phrase "wallflowers." Yet we did have our moments. Each of the boys had a "duty dance" with Mama and Miss Mabel, and each of the girls dragged me on the floor to do the Indian Springs shuffle. Mama and Miss Mabel seemed to enjoy it. I didn't. I just wanted to see a fight.

After what seemed like a long and boring time, intermission arrived. Everybody walked across to Dan Hoard's casino for a Coca-Cola. Since the whole evening had been so calm, the Mamas decided it was time for them to go home and miraculously agreed to let me stay with the girls and their beaus.

At Dan's casino, the jukebox blared out with Benny Moten's record of "South". Right off the bat I noticed two boys who had not been at the old mill. They wore deep suntans, carried heavy muscles, and looked neatly fresh scrubbed. They were CCC boys.

One of them took the hand of a Jackson girl to lead her to the dance floor. With no delay, two or three Jackson boys jumped him. The other CCC boy ran to the window and whistled with a volume far beyond anything Bubba and his friends ever did. In response to the whistle, a maze of muscular, khaki-clad boys with short cropped hair swarmed up from the creek and out of the woods. The whole CCC unit covered up the place.

The Jackson boys who had outnumbered the first two CCC members suddenly found themselves completely overwhelmed. They took a sound whipping. As the fight spread, the casino manager climbed on the counter holding a pistol in his trembling hand making threats that he did not carry out.

I do not know how it ended. Baby's date Pete Peterson grabbed me by one hand and Baby by the other and hustled us out of the place. But I realized my dream. I saw the king of fights, and I did not need to see anymore.

Not long after we returned home, Baby's big farewell party took place at our house. Mama opened all the doors including the sliding door to the parlor and the French doors connecting the parlor with the library as well as the folding doors which constituted a sort of wall between the library and the dining room. But the most activity centered around the punch bowl and food on the front porch.

Baby looked good in a white dress with ruffles, and the guests all seemed to have a good time.

In a few days, Baby left for Tallahassee, but I did not go to visit for another year or so. By the time of my trip, she had sort of removed herself from the regular style of college life. Having a talent for writing, she secured a job with the *Tallahassee Daily Democrat* and was dating a young reporter who covered politics.

I particularly looked forward to going to see Baby for several reasons. For one thing, I missed her. I also wanted to see college life, and both politics and newspaper work excited me.

I did not get a taste of college life because Baby had come to view it as juvenile. I did see some of my other interests. Although my whole life had revolved around a country newspaper, daily newspapers seemed like something entirely different. They had glamour. In my mind, all reporters wore felt hats with the brim turned up in front and a card saying PRESS stuck in the hat band. That is what I thought, but I thought wrong.

When Baby's friend picked us up to go to supper, his appearance did not meet my expectations. He looked like almost any young man who worked in almost any office. He revived my expectations though with the way he talked. As he drove toward the restaurant, he explained that Florida's dynamic young United States senator was supposed to show up there. In fact, because of that the reporter could put the supper tab on his expense account. He went on and on about the young senator and his greatness, even saying that one day he might be another FDR. The senator was Claude Pepper (it is hard to think of him as a young man now, since he became the personified "older" congressman, and the foremost champion of the elderly population). Pepper never showed up that night, but the reporter no doubt still included the tab on his expense account.

I remember the restaurant as a rustic place on the edge of a lake. It had a hallway leading from the dining room area to the rest room, and when I walked this way I saw something foreign to me—a row of slot machines. Looking over them, I found the nickel machine and that fell within my budget. Glancing both ways to see nobody watching, I slipped my nickel in the machine and pulled the lever.

"Rrrr, Rrrr, Rrrr—blip, blip, blip," went the machine.

Then.

"Crash, trinkle, trinkle, trinkle, rattle, rattle, rattle," as money flowed almost endlessly.

The noise or perhaps a witness brought a mass of people to see what my first venture into the world of gambling had wrought. One of those who rushed out to see was the restaurant manager.

"Son," pontificated the manager, "we don't allow minors to gamble here so you'll have to give that money to me."

Quickly, Baby's reporter friend stepped forward flashing his press card.

"Would you have given the nickel back to the boy if he had not hit the jackpot?"

"No-o-o-o," responded the crowd.

Cowed, the manager just walked away, and I kept the money. Whether the reporter succeeded in life, I do not know. I do not even remember his name, but he still has my admiration and appreciation.

While Baby never made the best use of her very considerable writing skills, she did write some pretty good things, including radio commercials and occasional newspaper columns. There is one piece that she wrote which I appreciate more than any others. It did not compare in quality with some of her better works, but it meant more to me. I am sorry now that I refused to publish it when I had a little newspaper. It seemed too personal at the time. She died years ago. So in belated appreciation, let me publish it now.

> Being the middle child in a family has many advantages. I had the joy of older sisters and brothers and little sister and brother and then all of a sudden we are grown and are contemporaries.
>
> Harold had supper with us this week and while he and the men in the party talked of baseball, politics and their families it gave me a chance to remember Harold as a little brother.
>
> I first remember him as a tow-head with a dutch bob who liked to eat and talk and who didn't like the first grade. It was the hours wasted inside when there were so many interesting things to do in a six-year old's world.
>
> I remember his pets and especially the bad goat that would chase everybody in the family except Harold. There were the marbles and kite years and the baseball. I remember how he would beg to go barefoot before it was warm enough.
>
> Memory lapses between grammar school and high school. Next I recall his being a tall, skinny boy with a horn. This was the bad year. Harold and one of his buddies next door got trumpets and tried their best to be another Harry James. To say that they didn't make it would be the understatement of the year. It is bad having one ham trumpet player in the neighborhood but having two is unspeakable. Somewhere we got through this but on its heels followed Woody Herman's record called "Jumpin at the Woodside." Hearing this record once is bad but hearing it everyday over and over is awful. It was almost better having Harold and his friend play the trumpet because they had to stop for wind.
>
> Then high school was over and the college years and the time spent in Japan. All these years run together for me. One thing I will always remember. Harold got a dog for graduation from college. The dog was

a tricolor collie and a beauty. Harold named him Rebel and they were great pals. Rebel was hit by a car one day and we took him to Macon to a veterinarian. I was with him when he got the call telling him that Rebel had died. When I looked at Harold's face I thought of the words of Lincoln, "Too big to cry and far too badly hurt to laugh."

With the years I have lost a little brother but I have gained a friend.

# CHAPTER 32

# Family Ties

According to popular belief, family connections controlled Southern towns and the countryside in the 1930s. In the system akin to the clan connections of Scotland, the ancestral homeland of a large portion of early Georgians, families formed alliances reaching into the social, economic, religious, and political life of the community. They viewed nepotism as a desired goal rather than an undesired evil. Family connections meant everything. In today's jargon, it was vital networking.

In this environment I grew up in a family with no local ties. Even though I was born in Forsyth, many saw me as an outsider because my immediate family and my Aunt Rachel Wyly's family constituted my entire blood-related network. Daddy came to Georgia from Virginia with no kin in this state. Although Mama's Georgia connections ran deep and included kinsmen of some importance, she did not come to Forsyth until 1917 making her a newcomer. So in my childhood, Forsyth viewed us as outsiders.

By tradition, this fact amounted to a distinct disadvantage. All my friends had wide local family ties and expressed pride in them, while we wore the badge of newcomers. Yet we wore that badge not with shame or embarrassment but with a certain pride. Much can be said of not being burdened with family connections over which you have no control. Without thinking seriously about that, I believe all of us in my immediate family understood it and sort of liked the idea. It gave to us a degree of independence and an opportunity for individual actions others lacked.

It also gave our family circle a contradictory set of attitudes. The first was a fierce devotion to one another, but this was counterbalanced by an attitude of personal independence and right of privacy. Except for my frequent dependence upon my mother's encouragement, I treasured my independence and privacy as something like a gift from God.

For me personally, all this may have flowed from my position in the family as the youngest child. The death of my sister two years my senior left me as a little boy with no sibling within eleven years of his age. Some amount of isolation naturally resulted. Years later, I developed an understanding for my youngest daughter Beth when she went through her childhood the youngest of four children. I think though that she, like I, learned to appreciate that being the "baby" is not always so bad.

"Youngest child isolation" offers wonderful opportunities for private thoughts, private dreams, and just plain loafing with your psyche.

For about thirteen years, this opportunity abounded. I had close friends, but they could not invade personal relationships of family and home. And I never thought things should be different. My Aunt Rachel's daughter, Emma Lee, lived in Forsyth, but she was a lot younger. Besides that, she was a girl. So our relationship did not develop until later.

Then things did become different. In the fall of 1940, my cousin Lumpkin Coffee, just my age, moved to Forsyth. Within a few months my nephew Billy Crowder, only five years younger than I, came along with his parents to live with us. So I was suddenly with a cousin just my age and a nephew only five years my junior.

Billy was born at our house. More than a year had passed since Sister had married and no longer read Uncle Wiggily to me, but she came home for the birth of her child when I was still just five. I stood in the hall downstairs waiting for word from the room directly above Mama and Daddy's room. After what seemed like an awful long time to me, Dr. George Alexander came down the steps smiling warmly and with his deep voice spoke kindly, "Well, Harold, there's a little boy up there to play cowboy with you."

I do not remember the first time I saw Billy, but I do recall wanting to spend all my time in the room with Rosa Emiline and Billy. When bedtime neared, Mama tried everything to get me out of the room non-violently. When all else failed, she grabbed my ear and led me out.

Maggie Horton, the practical nurse looking after mother and child, viewed this with delight. In those days the mother of a funny paper character called Elmer always pulled him around by the ear. Taking her cue from that, Maggie tagged me Elmer. She laughingly called me by that name for the rest of her days.

For a time Billy and his parents lived in Barnesville followed by Sparta and then Vienna. We visited them some, and they visited us right often. The first time Billy visited by himself came during a period when Rosa Emiline and her husband Bill went to Chicago to the 1934 World's Fair. Mama worried about gangsters in the Windy City and warned them to keep the car doors locked. As a two year old, Billy did not approve of the trip either. Although grandmothers are all right, they do not match mothers.

To overcome the little boy's dissatisfaction, Mama assigned me the task of finding entertainment for him. Simple things like making funny faces and jumping around did pretty well for awhile but failed as long-term interest holders. Something better had to be found.

That is when I remembered Tribble's stable. Located only a block from our house, the stable always had mules, horses, and sometimes ponies. George Tanner's blacksmith shop in the back of the building also held all sorts of interests for me.

So to the stable we went. Billy thought the horses too big while the mules just lacked interest for him. You have to be older than two for a blacksmith to fascinate you. It was beginning to look like the stable flunked out as an entertainment center as we neared the front door to leave.

Billy shrieked. Not the kind of sound caused by fear, but a shriek brought on by a pleasant site. He had seen what we missed and what he wanted to see. In the corner near the opening onto Lee Street, a whole family of tiny piglets played merrily.

From this spot Billy refused to move. The little pigs offered the fun I could not dream up for him. Watching the little creatures try to run and roll over one another caused the little boy to clap his hands and laugh until tears flowed. For the rest of his visit, we reacted to Billy's moments of boredom or unhappiness by going to see the pigs. It always worked. Mama even began calling Billy, "Piggy." She used this as a term of affection for a long time.

I suppose Rosa Emiline and Bill saw some interesting things in Chicago, but they could not have liked them as much as Billy liked the pigs.

I confess to showing less hospitality on some of Billy's other visits. This was before we reached the age where the five year spread between us faded so we could really be close. When he was just old enough to tag along, it cramped my style or, even worse, limited my mischief.

"Look, he's following us" Billy Hill said as he and I headed toward Blue Hole.

Sure enough, a hundred feet or so behind in the woods stood my five-year-old nephew.

"We need to get shed of him," warned Billy Hill.

"Don't worry. I'll just run him off," I replied.

Trouble was, Billy just would not be run off. So then I tried talking him into going home, explaining all sorts of good things that might be happening there. Still no luck.

We then resorted to a more drastic means of preventing an intrusion on our visit to the swimming hole. We had brought a rope with us which we intended to use for swinging out over the water, but it had to be put to another purpose now.

"Billy," I started explaining, patronizingly, "We're gonna play cowboy, and you're gonna be the outlaw that we caught. Now that means I'm gonna have to tie you to this tree where you will be the prisoner."

Using the rope to tie him firmly but not painfully, the scheme worked.

"Now the next part of the game," I explained further, "is that we go look for some more outlaws while you stay right here. We'll be back tereckly."

After we finished our secret swim and dried our hair the best we could, we returned, untied Billy, and went home. I would like to tell you that we tied him up so he would not face the dangers of swimming at Blue Hole so young. Unfortunately, I cannot claim so high a motive. The truth is we did not want him seeing our adventure for fear he might tell on us.

Our mistreatment of little Billy sometimes came without intent. That is what happened in the loft over our garage. The loft was among my favorite places. It served as a kind of private clubhouse where I sometimes just went to sit by myself. Other times friends joined me and we imagined it an outlaw hideout, a castle prison tower, a lookout point for a fort, or whatever childish imagination could turn it into. We sometimes smoked a forbidden cigarette there; even worse we once or twice looked at the little nine-page books there. Those books had crudely done imitations of famous funny paper characters in ridiculous pornographic situations. No wonder Billy wanted mightily to climb the ladder and explore this marvelously mysterious spot.

He begged and begged until Edgar Castleberry and I caved in. I climbed the ladder first so that while Edgar pushed Billy from below, I could pull him through the square hole in the loft floor.

With this done, Edgar turned back to get my half-broken air rifle and started up the ladder. As he climbed, Billy stuck his head in the opening just at the instant the rifle went off. The B-B shot hit Billy in the soft spot between the eyelid and the eyebrow.

Two things saved him from serious injury . . . about a half-inch and the poor power of my worn-out air rifle. Even so we still had a serious problem. Mama did not want Billy in the loft, and she sure did not want us shooting around his eye with an air rifle.

Yet here we were with a little boy in the loft having been shot and crying uncontrollably. If we let him out of the loft, Mama would immediately know what happened. So we made him stay there until he stopped crying and then told him that if he told about this we would not let him come back to the loft. That worked and we all came out without any further damage.


My cousin Lumpkin Coffee lived in Eastman. He visited Forsyth more than I visited Eastman. Going to Eastman had its goods and bads. The bads had to do with the heat and the gnats; the goods had to do with Aunt Emmy's cooking and my relationship with Lumpkin and his sister Virginia.

In the early days, Lumpkin and I developed a liking for building little forts with Lincoln logs and molding lead soldiers. Lumpkin had a set of molds and a little melting pot, and, thanks to Daddy's print shop, I had an endless source of lead. So we molded enough soldiers for big battles. The forts made the battles even more fun.

As little boys, we played the roles of the men who worked in the occupations of our ambition. Lumpkin wanted to grow up as a garbage man, while I aspired to heading the street repair crew for Forsyth. I cannot imagine the reason for Lumpkin's interest in garbage collection. Certainly that could not predict his future as a physician.

My fascination with street repair undoubtedly came from watching Mr. Mays, the Forsyth street superintendent, and his only helper, a man named Bop. The mules, which pulled most of their equipment, lived in a small stable attached to the city hall less than a block from our house. I always enjoyed watching Mr. Mays, Bop, and the mules work together to perform their common tasks.

Bop called the lead mule Bob. To show my appreciation for Mr. Mays, Bop, and Bob, I named my little red tricycle Ear Bob.

My friends wanted to work as firemen, policemen, railroad engineers, ice men, or like jobs. Perhaps some sociological lesson could be drawn from the fact that each of these ambitions involved tasks which provide an essential service but from which the performer receives slight compensation or praise. For some reason, glamorous occupations escaped our attention. I will leave to sociologists the question of why we ignored the rich and famous as objects of imitation.

All I know is that we spent hours on my front porch with me playing like a turned over rocking chair was a piece of street equipment pulled by an imaginary mule while I directed the work of a nonexistent Bop. At the same time, Lumpkin used another rocking chair as his pretended truck in which he gathered garbage seen only in his mind's eye.

Besides these things, we played all the things boys played looking forward to every new visit. The coming of Billy and Lumpkin to live in Forsyth opened a new chapter in my life. Occasional visits became constant associations. Familiarity replaced curiosity. Mutual appreciation turned into true affection, all leading to the discovery that kinfolks can be good friends.

# CHAPTER 33

# Our Very Own Yankee

Forsyth of the 1930s claimed numerous advantages. It had a hotel, a cafe (The Royal Palm), a picture show, a pool hall, a bowling alley for awhile, three drug stores, three banks (they boasted no bank ever failed in Forsyth), two colleges (one for white girls and the other for young blacks), and a thriving community.

But something was missing . . . Forsyth had no Yankee. Oh, a few Yankees stopped by and sojourned and moved on, but they were visitors or transients. A sophisticated New Yorker, Fred Lang married a prominent Forsyth lady who built a log house called Towaliga Lodge. The fact that Fred pronounced Towaliga as ToWALLiga tipped off his lack of permanence.

We faced a kind of deprivation in not knowing or hearing how Yankees talked. They not only talked with accents different from ours, they used words different from ours.

They threw a stone or pebble. We did too, but we called it a rock. They rode a bike. We did too, but we called it a wheel. They licked the hard candy on the end of a stick and called it a lollipop. We licked the same candy and called it a sucker.

Then there were the times when we used the same word while intending a different meaning. When we said barbecue, we talked about a meat cooked very slowly (usually from sundown to sunup) over a pit with coals. The meat was then pulled apart and drenched in a hot vinegar-based sauce. To them barbecue meant almost anything cooked outdoors, even the simple act of grilling a hamburger.

Even our cuss words and obscenities came out different.

Let us take a look at some of the early Yankees who made brief stops in my town. A man named Gates appeared from nowhere wearing fine but well-worn clothes and accompanied by two big white bulldogs. They went everywhere he went. Mr. Gates spoke in scholarly tones and spent so much of his time in a county library that the little widow who ran it seemed smitten. But his shaky hands and roadmap eyes said a lot about his habits.

Rumor had it that Mr. Gates was the son of one of America's wealthiest families which paid him to stay away from home. I remember one Sunday afternoon a group of us were playing on the school ground at Bank Stephens when Mr. Gates and his two dogs walked by. Robert and George Bailey also had a big bulldog named Brandywine. And Thomas and Charles Hollis had a big, mean chow dog named Chan. These two animals attacked Mr. Gates's bulldogs and might have killed them had their owners not pulled them off.

None of this made Mr. Gates very happy. We never knew for sure about his origin because he left as suddenly as he showed up. Only the librarian really seemed to care.

A tall Dane from South Dakota appeared in the late summer of 1938 for the purpose of coaching football, basketball, and baseball at Mary Persons High School in Forsyth. His size, flamboyance, and beautiful wife attracted wide attention for some time. Most of us youngsters liked him because he was different and paid attention to us.

The first time I saw him, he and his wife were moving into their apartment, and, a young friend of mine, M. L. Keith, and I were playing pitch. He immediately saw the defects in my baseball delivery and spent the rest of the afternoon giving me tips on how to improve while his wife had to do all the moving.

The mothers around town did not share our admiration for the coach, mainly because of the sort of language he used. Their disapproval spread to the rest of the community when some of his other exploits surfaced.

First, there was the matter of the Armistice Day barbeque. Someone delegated the coach to get the hogs. So loaded with the money which had been given to him, he took the school truck and headed for the slaughterhouse in Macon. Along the way, he encountered a hog truck which had just been involved in a wreck.

Glory be, there were several dead hogs along the side of the road. Having an eye for a good deal, the coach bought these carcasses for a pittance, had them dressed at the slaughterhouse for a small amount of money. Anyone who knows anything about livestock slaughter knows that hogs killed in a wreck without being properly bled cause problems. They did.

A lot of people became sick. They were sick at their stomachs and sick of their coach. He and his wife left pretty quickly.

This coach was followed by another Yankee who contrasted starkly with the first one. Karl (Swede) Olsen had all the good qualities the first one lacked. Even to this day, he stands as one of my all-time heroes.

He had captained the Washington Redskins football team in the days before pro football became so big. In fact, he began his Redskin career before they moved from Boston to Washington. But the impressive thing was his wide range of interests. I learned a lot of government in his civics class, but I think I learned more shooting a bow and arrow at his home some two or three miles from town on Saturday afternoon. The community lost a great deal when Swede Olsen left. It is a shame he did not stay long enough to be the "Yankee" we needed as our own.

Just as you never own a cat, Forsyth never owned any of these Yankees. They each made a blip on the screen of time but none of them embroidered the fabric of the community.

All that changed in May of 1940. Having formerly housed a Rogers store, an ice cream parlor, and other various activities, the building across from the courthouse at the corner of Lee and Main Streets sat vacant.

That is when two young men opened up a Western Auto store there. This would not have been so unusual except that one of these young fellows was Harold Reeves, formerly of Ohio. Even the fact that he was married to a pretty brown-eyed girl from South Carolina did not soften the fact of his being a Yankee.

They told him that he would not last six months in business in Forsyth. How wrong they were. Six months ran into a year. A year ran into six years. For fifty years Harold Reeves owned and operated the Western Auto store in Forsyth.

Even if that was all that he did, it would be significant enough. But it was not all. Harold became a worker in the community, a pillar of the

Baptist church, an active Boy Scout leader, a civic club stalwart, and generally a willing participant in causes for good.

But really that does not say much because a lot of folks could have filled those slots. The important thing is that only one person can truly be Forsyth's Yankee. He was our very first one, just like George Washington was our very first President.

World War II changed a lot about Southern small towns. It caused a lot of our boys to see Yankee towns. It caused a lot of Yankee boys to see and stay in our town. But Harold Reeves came to Forsyth not because of the war but because it was where he wanted to live. And he stayed because he was determined to prove wrong those who said he could not make it there. He died in Forsyth fifty years after his arrival. They buried him in his adopted soil.

CHAPTER 34

# The Gentle Rebels

"Spring with its rich green of budding foliage, the perfume of flowers and the singing of birds, gives all its charm to this occasion, and nature smiles upon the scene. This is a day which southern people love for its precious memories and have set apart in honor of those noble men who died for the holy convictions of their souls. The celebration of this day loses none of its enthusiasm as years roll by.

"The whole people joined in the commemoration of this day with tears and sorrow during that trying period succeeding the war. They still cling to it with a true devotion and each new year gives evidence that its services of love are held as high and sacred privileges.

"The twenty-sixth day of April will not soon be forgotten. It has a place in the hearts of our people, and its annual recurrence will be marked with pleasure for centuries to come."

Those words and others like them form part of the heritage of many Southerners. They touch me more than others because my grandfather, Judge Hugh Lumpkin, spoke these words at the Memorial Day ceremony in LaFayette, Georgia, in 1882.

At age sixteen he ran away from home in 1862 to join the Confederate Army. He suffered a leg wound and limped slightly for the rest of his life. Mama said that he wore the limp as a badge and, by saying that, raised the possibility that he affected it to remind all of his service to the Lost Cause.

Although I never knew my grandfather, Mama told me so much about him I felt that I did know and love him. My grandmother died when I was little, and I remember her telling me how it scared her as a five year old when the Yankees made an unsuccessful attack on Newnan.

Memories and sentiments of the war ran deep and naturally in the lives and ways of the Southerners of my boyhood. In those pre-World War II days, the Civil War was called simply the War Between The States but never the Civil War. That phrase implies a rebellion within a nation, and my elders carefully instructed me that the Confederacy was not a bunch of rebels but a combine of sovereign states. They also taught me, probably wrongly, that slavery was really a side issue designed to attract sympathy in the North and to create distaste for the Confederacy by the French and English governments.

I never heard anyone defend slavery, but I heard much praise of the Confederacy and criticism of the North, particularly of General William T. Sherman. Throughout the countryside, lonesome chimneys silhouetted against the sky as the only remains of burned houses. Most of these houses undoubtedly burned because of open fires, faulty stoves, and lack of water. Nevertheless, the stark chimneys gained fame—Sherman's fingers.

Into young adulthood the teachings of my upbringing instilled in me a love for the song "Dixie" and a respect for the Stars and Bars with an attitude approaching reverence but totally devoid of militance. This continued well into my mature life with no thoughts of guilt or any idea of these symbols standing for any sort of meanness.

This environment led naturally to observances and organizations honoring the memory of those who participated in the war. The one important observance occurred on the day my grandfather referred to— April 26, Memorial Day. This may strike some as strange because of the common recognition of May 30 as Memorial Day. We did not celebrate that day. For Northern states it occupied the same place as April 26 did for us. Back then if we referred to May 30 at all, we called it Declaration Day, reserving the title Memorial Day for April 26.

Preparation for Memorial Day started in February. The United Daughters of the Confederacy conducted an essay contest each year selecting a subject for papers usually a historic character from the 1860s era. In a spirit of cooperation, our teachers required all of us to compete by writing papers. Among the pupils this added nothing to the popularity of Memorial Day. But looking back, we learned something and honed our writing skills.

The day itself suited us better, mainly because school let out at noon. We called that a half holiday. Earlier than usual, Mama would call me to breakfast on April 26, so I could take care of an annual chore. Custom and personal sentiment directed that I and other young folks gather flowers and tie them together with a string.

Nobody bought flowers. We picked flowers from our gardens or wild flowers from fields or roadsides. I picked mine from Mama's little flower garden lying just back of the kitchen. What the garden lacked in artistic design, it made up for by splashing color over this part of the backyard. A generous supply of sweet peas, ragged robins, and brown-eyed susans offered itself as gifts to the memory of honored ones.

Like the other pupils, I carried my spray of flowers to the high school auditorium and lay it at the foot of the stage. About three hours after school began, we all filed into the auditorium where the annual ceremony took place.

Mrs. Cary Bittick and Mrs. Fred Stokes generally directed the doings. It opened when Mr. George W. Waldrep ascended the stage escorted by two young boys. Mr. Waldrep was the last surviving Confederate veteran in our county, and, because of this and other admirable personal traits, he commanded unquestioned public esteem. Two or three times, I was one of the escorts.

The two things I recall most about this task are the feeling of honor and my amazement and the agility and strength of this old man. He needed no escort as he almost sprung up the steps to the stage. Even to his last days, Mr. Waldrep could be seen riding his horse along the Indian Springs Road near his farm. The erect way the slender old soldier sat on his mount sometimes washed away the appearance of old age and replaced it with a vision of a young man, gallant looking in his gray uniform, on his way to do what he thought was right.

During the ceremony we sang songs, listened to speeches, and clapped for those who won the essay contest. Mrs. Stokes would then tell us to come forward in rows to take up the floral offerings. If you found the one that you brought from home, that was okay. If you did not, that was okay too because we felt no personal pride and most of them were pretty much alike anyway.

Leaving the school, we walked the short distance to the cemetery. Amid solemn tombstones below and cheery singing of birds above, we made our way to the place where three hundred Confederate soldiers and one Confederate nurse lie in eternal repose. First a prayer and then we placed at least one bunch of flowers on each grave.

No battle took place in Forsyth. These casualties came mainly from the Battle of Atlanta. Forsyth's railroad location made it a hospital center with the main facilities located at Monroe Female College, later Bessie Tift College, and at the Snead Home which is still occupied by a member of that family, Velma McCosh. The graves, though, were ours. My grandfather said it better in the same speech quoted earlier:

> But we have left to us the graves of our martyred dead. These graves are sadly, peculiarly ours. Ours to keep and honor. No nation claims them now. And ah! How sacred to us these silent mounds and how our hearts are stirred as we contemplate them. Let us remember that beneath each mound lies all that remains on earth of some noble patriot.

In Forsyth, the United Daughters of the Confederacy (UDC) carried the burden of keeping alive the memory of the Lost Cause. At a meeting in the middle '30s, they decided to organize a Children of the Confederacy chapter. They chartered it as the Stephen Douglas Mobley Chapter. That group met first at Barbara Goggans's house on a cold afternoon. I was one of the twenty or so charter members.

We met monthly during the school year, rotating among the houses of the members. We ate cookies, drank punch or Russian tea, learned a little history and citizenship, and planned social events. I counted it as fun.

The highlight of my Children of the Confederacy experience was the only state convention we ever attended. During the spring of 1941, Mama told me about the convention set for June in Washington, Georgia. This sounded good to me, but I winced a little when she explained the details.

"Only those who compete in one of the literary contests can go."

After some thought, I figured it worthwhile so I started memorizing a speech. I have no idea of the subject, but it certainly must have involved Southern history.

The Forsyth delegation included four girls and two boys: Barbara Goggans, Farice Spangler, Gloria Chapman, Katherine Bittick, Bubba Williams, and me. All sorts of interesting things happened.

For one thing, Bubba and I stayed at the home of a dentist on the main street. On our first morning there, we came down to breakfast to be greeted by the dentist and his wife bringing in breakfast. Neither of us could believe she carried the biggest platter of fried chicken we had ever seen. After gorging ourselves, we walked toward the church where the meeting was to be. Bubba began laughing to himself, "The folks in Washington, Georgia, sure know how to eat breakfast."

The original plan called for all of us to compete in our contests the next morning, as I did. But events of the night before changed it for some. The convention opened that night with a devotional, some comments by adult leaders, and a business meeting. They scheduled a dance for right after the meeting. The trouble was that the meeting ran out of gas too soon.

To fill up the time, one of the ladies announced, "We will go ahead with the young ladies reminiscences competition tonight." That would have suited all right except that our reminiscencer, Farice Spangler, did not come to that meeting. Expecting to perform the next morning, she and some others went somewhere else figuring to show up at the dance as though they had attended the whole thing. The plan backfired.

One by one the other reminiscencers rose and reminisced. One pretty brown-eyed girl evermore reminisced. Her talent, beauty, and personality smote me. When she finished, the ladies told us the winner would be announced the next morning. I harbored not the slightest doubt that the brown-eyed girl had first place going away. I wanted that to happen because I wanted her to be happy.

I left for the dance expecting great fun. The attendance list revealed about three times as many girls as boys and the leaders instituted a girl break. That, of course, means that while you dance, a girl has the right to tap your partner's shoulder and dance with you. A plan spun in my head devised to arrange for me to dance with "Brown Eyes" most of the night.

The first kink in my plan arose when Farice rushed into the dance hall enveloped in tears. She approached the UDC ladies with a heart-rending explanation and entreated them not to deprive her of the chance

to reminisce. The sweetness of their spirit and Farice's earnestness allowed her to prevail.

One of the ladies was sympathetic and patted Farice on the back,
saying, "Don't you worry yourself, honey, you can reminisce in the
morning."

This elated Farice, but Brown Eyes did not share that joy. What had
been a sure winner faced another threat. I think it hurt my chances with
her, too, but I tried anyway. I pursued my plan by asking the Forsyth
girls not to break on me when Brown Eyes and I danced. The plan did
not fall on deaf ears, it fell on mad ears. They made their own plan and
it worked. Mine didn't.

I never danced with Brown Eyes at all. Instead the meanest looking,
biggest girl in the southland broke on me early, and we danced and
danced and danced. Bouncing along to "The Hutsut Song," I edged her
over by my Forsyth "friends" and looked with pleading eyes. They
looked straight at me, then they turned their heads. As my big mean
dancing partner shoved me away, I heard my "friends" laughing.

Following that night of failure, I did not expect much from the next
morning either. I made my speech such as it was and then came Farice
and her delayed performance. At the luncheon they gave the prizes in my
contest to someone else, but, in light of recent events, I did not much
care. When Farice received the first place prize for reminiscences, her
blue eyes shone with appreciation. Across the hall, two brown eyes
flashed, and appreciation had nothing to do with it.

As the meeting ended, one of the UDC ladies announced the new
state officers. To my utter shock I was a vice president and I did not
even know I was a candidate.

"They sure do things strange at Children of the Confederacy conventions," I thought as I stepped into the car to start home. Then I
thought again, "Maybe the big, mean looking girl was on the elections
committee."

Having lived through all this, it would have appalled me to think our
activities or the song "Dixie" or Stars and Bars could possibly have
offended anyone or that anyone could possibly use these symbols as
emblems of hatred. Our little group harbored a deep-seated quiet pride
and wished no harm for anyone.

But sometime in my young adulthood, widely differing forces assault-
ed my sentiments and shocked a core attitude formed through the years.

There appeared on the horizon blacks who viewed these things as insults to their dignity and reminders of that period of indignity imposed upon their race.

About the same time, some whites began to use the song and the flag from another age as rallying symbols for hatred and opportunities to demonstrate poor taste and a lack of understanding of history by the vulgar display of the Stars and Bars on t-shirts, baseball caps, car and truck tags, and other such like. This same group played "Dixie" militantly rather than reverently. To me—and I am sure many others—the actions of the white hate groups stood as the ultimate desecration of the memory of the good things in our history.

Some of us found no place to go. On one hand, the hate groups offended us. But, on the other hand, even understanding the pain of the black community, we found it hard to expunge an important part of our history and teachings.

To this day, the answer to the dilemma eludes me. I want to love the grandfather that I never knew. I want to treasure the recollection of dealing with the sweet ladies who helped the Children of the Confederacy. I want to believe that not all Confederates were bad. But in doing this I want, at the same time, to respect the dignity and feelings of all humanity. Maybe there is no way to do all of this and maybe it is only my generation which seeks to.

In thinking of the Confederate flag and its horrible misuse by those who stir ill will, I recall again the words spoken by my grandfather in 1882:

> The beautiful banner of Stars and Bars which led these brave men to the hour of victory and around which they rallied in the hour of defeat is furled forever unless unfurled by the impartial historian who may write of the true, and the brave in America's past.

Obviously he believed that the flag should not be raised for evil purposes. He also believed that whatever good was in it should be remembered. Maybe we can reach that sort of solution sometime.

The Brown Eyes of the children of the Confederacy Convention did not disappear. Even though no romance ever developed between us, we became friends in college. Her two brothers were also among my friends.

Some will remember her as a person with amazing family connections. Her grandfather was chief justice of the Georgia Supreme Court. He father was a judge on the U.S. Fifth Circuit of Appeals. Her uncle was a powerful United States senator. One of her brothers was a judge on the Georgia Court of Appeals. The other brother has served as a Superior Court judge. Her husband served as governor of Georgia. He led the state through some of her most turbulent times.

Those who know her for these things know her as Mrs. S. Ernest Vandiver. Others of us know her as Betty Russell Vandiver, a woman of enormous charm, strong intellect, outstanding ability . . . and *green* eyes.

# CHAPTER 35

# The Problem We Didn't See

Remembering people and events is easy. Relating the story of those people and events without the distortion caused by changed attitudes and experience is hard.

In the pages that follow, I try to tell the story of my relations with a few of the black people I knew as a youth without filtering it through the altered views of my current thinking. As best I can, I relate what a young boy saw, did, and thought in Middle Georgia of the 1930s.

Sometime before 1927, the year of my birth, Willie Bell came to work at our house. She clothed her frail body in a crisp, white uniform with a white maid's hat. Her capacity for love was as big as her body was small, and from my first days I became a beneficiary of that love.

Mama often told about one of the first times she scolded me for some infantile rebellion, and how I ran directly to Willie throwing myself into her soothing embrace. Mama said I returned to her after hearing Willie's words of sympathy.

"Ivvie says I ain't nussin' but a baby," I said between sobs.

This statement continued as my joking retort for years when I faced discipline. Even now those words remain lodged in my mind as a reminder of the affectionate bond between Willie and me.

Willie left us when I was about five. According to the official line, the work became too much for her, so she took an easier job. I later realized that the Depression forced Mama to do without regular help, and so Willie had to go. Whatever the reason, I did not take it so well. I remember hugging Willie while she explained she would come to see me every now and then. She did too. We stayed in touch until her death about thirty years later.

A succession of cooks or maids, mostly part-time, followed Willie. Mobile stayed until the day we heard a loud noise in the dining room where we found Mobile on the floor unconscious. I think she recovered, but poor health ended our tie. Before her seizure and departure, I went to her house a couple of times where she lived with her husband Cheney and several children.

Arriving at their house one day, I found the children in a little cow pen standing around a yearling calf. The ground went "squosh" under my feet from cow excrement and a summer shower.

"We been ridin' the calf. It's yo turn," called one of the boys.

Because of the gentle appearance of the calf and my ignorance, I climbed on the animal's back. Getting off was quicker than getting on. With one quick twisting buck, the calf threw my legs skyward and my head groundward. The smelly muck of the ground smeared over my face. It even covered my ears so much I barely heard the yelps and giggles from the children. That ended my interest in rodeos.

After Mobile, we had another cook who stayed only briefly because Mama discovered she "toted." That means she took things that did not belong to her. The code of the time allowed for household help to carry food home. Not so with other things. Other things finished the employment of the cook.

While all this was going on, my grandmother Lumpkin came from Lafayette to live with my Aunt Rachel. Because of her age and poor health, a teenage girl did a few odd jobs for her like building fires. Mama worked almost full time at the newspaper by then, so the same young woman saw after me part time. I quickly developed deep admiration for her and with good reason. She ran faster than anybody. She was unbelievably strong. She could do clever things like carving intricate patterns on my chinaberry horses. She probably learned some of this from her father, who was a highly respected preacher and an accomplished carpenter. She also developed her mother's warmth and kindness.

At six, I could not have known that Annie Ruth Goodson would become more of a friend than an employee for Mama for many, many years. Or that she would become a second mother to my children. She has even looked after my grandchildren. This created a warm and deeply personal relationship with five generations of my family.

One of my earliest brushes with true meanness came because of a tragedy in Annie Ruth's family. Some older boys talked Annie Ruth's little brother into acting as a lookout while they stole gasoline. When the police approached, the older boys drove away. The young lookout ran. The police shot him dead.

Shock and grief enveloped our house. I saw the combination of sorrow and anger that Mama and Daddy felt. They talked about it. Mama cried about it. I cannot say they did anything to right the wrong.

"Crazy" was what we called people with mental illness. We put that tag on two of Forsyth's black people.

"Crazy Ella" was one of them. I first saw her walking across the railroad toward Hooks Lumber Yard carrying a croker sack containing bricks (we called them brick bats). She used these as weapons.

Seeing the strange-looking woman, Billy Adams, Norris Sykes, and I knew what was expected of us. We ran toward her hollering, "Crazy Ella, Crazy Ella."

We knew what to expect of her, too. She took the brick bats from the sack and began throwing them at us. We faced no real danger because Crazy Ella did not boast a strong throwing arm.

Not much later, I encountered the other "crazy" black woman. Billy Hill and I went into the woods behind his house to play, hoping to slay some wild beast with my air rifle. Instead we wound up sitting by a little branch eating raw peanuts. Hearing the crunching sound of light footsteps, we turned to see a wizened black woman. Her dress was made of croker sacks, and her shoes of inner tubes. She looked at us through penetrating eyes. Then she fixed her gaze on my brass-barrelled air rifle.

"*You* are the one I'm looking for," she said, to a scared Harold.

"You got the Gold Gun!" she spoke in mystic tones.

"I am the Queen of these woods. Touch my finger and you will be rich," she said, pointing a finger wrinkled by age and crooked by arthritis.

Fear overcame greed, and Billy and I ran all the way to his house.

The woman became known as Queenie. I saw her often after that as she stood in animated conversation with the huge oak trees lining the streets of Forsyth. Only once did I have an isolated conversation with Queenie. Curiosity had supplanted fear by the time I encountered her on a dirt road on the edge of town where I was riding my bicycle.

"I own all of this land through here," she said, with a sweeping gesture. "I gon' build a railroad out here."

I thought this funny. Years later I learned that in the 1830s, railroad men considered that very spot as the possible route for the track to Atlanta. Had Queenie heard that story in her youth? Was her statement a coincidence? Or do troubled minds have a mystic power that other minds lack?

My association with Gene and Robert Blackman remained important for the first fourteen years of my life. That association centered mainly around the print shop at the newspaper office, fishing, and a few special jobs around home. The mores of the time prohibited much beyond that.

Robert went with us to fish at Midville twice. Those times we went by car, and Robert drove. Getting to the river, Robert and I took turns drinking from the pipe through which water flowed freely from underground sources. We walked through the woods with our arms on each other's shoulders. We sat on the same log and ate sandwiches that Mama had made for us.

That night we went to the little town where we walked the streets separately. I drank from the water fountain labeled "White." Robert drank from one labeled "Colored." At Mr. Drew's cafe, Daddy and I ate at a table in the part of the building facing the main street. Robert ate at a table in a different part of the same building, facing a back alley. A common kitchen between the two seating areas supplied each of them. We ate the same food from the same kitchen, but in separate places. That night Daddy and I slept in the extra room at Mr. Drew's house. Robert slept in the car.

After school on a Monday afternoon, I came by the newspaper office to see what was expected of me. Walking back to the shop, I stopped in shock. Robert's face was swollen to grotesque proportions. Ugly cuts ran from his forehead to his chin.

"What happened?"

"The police beat me."

"Why?"

He offered no answer.

I learned the story from Daddy. On Saturday, Robert drank too much whiskey and then walked toward town. As he reached to the street beside the Methodist church, the police stopped him.

"Jes lemme go home," Robert said, pulling away from the official grasp. The police grabbed him again. He pushed the officer away. The policeman began beating Robert with a blackjack. He beat. He beat, and he beat, until Robert fell senseless on the street.

None of us did anything. I guess we did not know what to do.

As Daddy and I readied things for an afternoon of fishing, John Ham, the black undertaker, joined us. Daddy shook his hand. That night after supper, Daddy sat down before the fireplace in his room. I watched as he untangled some balled-up fishing lines, displaying his enormous patience and attention to unimportant details. I failed to appreciate the mental therapy this oft-repeated ritual afforded because I fell into an attempt to untangle some balled-up thoughts in my own mind. I thought about the inconsistency of our lives recalling some of the events related here and many more. I knew those produced different reactions and emotions in different people. In some, they aroused passion. In others, compassion. The big questions of fairness and logic lay beyond my reach at that time. So I asked Daddy a little question.

"You shake hands with colored folks. Most people don't. Why?"

"Big boy, it goes deeper than that. Some people who won't shake hands with colored folks will sometimes hug them. Why?"

"I don't know."

"Well, there's a difference between affection and respect. You can feel affection for an inferior. You can only respect an equal. Hugging is a sign of affection. A handshake is a sign of respect."

# CHAPTER 36

# An Age Ends

The fall of 1941 followed on the heels of a good summer. That summer saw the first full season of the Forsyth swimming pool, lots of fishing, a trip or two, and the Children of the Confederacy meeting in Washington, Georgia. Including the car wreck with Buddy Howard and Ann Gilbert, the summer was a memory builder.

The fall held even more promise. As a high school sophomore, I finally liked school and began to do well. Besides that the girls began looking prettier, particularly the brunette in my biology class.

Then there was football which had replaced baseball in my heart. The Mary Persons High School team looked like the best ever with Archie Tingle and Billy Reeves starring, supported by Marion Dorner, Possum O'Neal, and a number of others. Georgia stepped to the threshold of national football honors with Frank Sinkwich beginning his junior year, just one year away from the Heismann Trophy. I saw Georgia and Sinkwich three times that year, including their 21-0 win over Tech which opened the door to the Orange Bowl. In the bowl game they beat TCU handily.

Back home, fun abounded. Every Friday night "our crowd" went to someone's house where we played records, danced, talked about sports and politics, and lived through the experience of moving from adolescence to young adulthood. Sunday afternoons no longer involved boisterous games. Now we headed for Mr. Ashley Pinnazee's drug store for a gathering of our crowd. Puberty and imagined sophistication had made their marks.

When Halloween rolled around this time, the games and mischiefs of earlier years seemed awfully childish. Instead we went to a party at Bubba William's house several miles from town. The best part was a hayride with hand holding and maybe a little bit of snuggling.

During November someone came up with the idea of a big Christmas dance, and we decided to use the Children of the Confederacy as the organizational vehicle for the event. Plans called for the girls to wear long dresses and the boys to wear their Sunday best.

We rented the American Legion Hall and decided to splurge on a jukebox rather than just using somebody's record player. This posed a problem though because jukeboxes in that era had no more than eighteen records. Selecting the records frayed the edges of good humor. So the officers met one afternoon in late November at Mack Tribble's house to thrash it out. I was dead set on "Chattanooga Choo Choo" and others had equally strong feelings for their favorites. Somehow we reached a consensus, and "Chattanooga Choo Choo" was part of it.

That fall had a dark side, too, and it absorbed more interest than anything else. A new principal had succeeded Miss Florrie Childs at Banks Stephens grammar school a year or two earlier. And just as everybody thought things were going along fine, the lid blew off. Some person or persons accused the new principal of mismanagement of the lunchroom.

People chose up sides. One side demanded the principal leave. The other side demanded she stay. She decided to leave and her friend, the commercial teacher Miss Vivian Harris, said, "If she goes, I go." Then the high school principal, Mr. E. E. O'Kelly, jumped in, "If they go, I go." They all three went.

The high school students did not take any of this lightly. Although we really did not know the grammar school principal, we knew and liked Miss Harris and Mr. O'Kelly. I understand Miss Harris was a fine teacher and I know she was beautiful. Mr. O'Kelly was fair in his dealings with all of us.

Things grew so intense, a large group of students began organizing a strike. Placards for picketing were painted and leaflets were secretly printed on the school's mimeograph machine. We set a day for the strike —then we chickened out. In fact, because of the depth of our cowardice,

we had William Graham to throw the placards and leaflets in the Ocmulgee River to destroy the evidence.

The adult community did not surrender that easily though. They called a mass meeting at the courthouse for the next Monday. That coming
event commanded every ounce of interest in Forsyth. On the Sunday
morning before the Monday meeting, I went to Sunday school at the
Methodist church as I had for some time because of the shortage of
young people at the Presbyterian church at that time. Young and old alike
were absorbed in talk of the school fuss and the meeting. The same thing
was true when I went over to our church for the regular Sunday morning
service.

After church I pled with Mama to let me practice driving when we
finished Sunday dinner. Being fourteen, my parents only let me drive in
the country and then only if Mama was with me. After dinner, Mama, my
nephew Billy Crowder, and I left for the spin which excited me, but
scared Billy. After Billy begged to be let out of the incompetently driven
car, Mama and I stopped at Alexander's Drug Store for a Coca-Cola. The
drug stores had curb service so we parked and placed our order. While
we waited, Homer Dungan, who had left Daddy's employment to work
for the newspaper in Barnesville, came out to the car and told us the
ultimate news.

"The Japanese bombed Pearl Harbor."

At one stroke, our entire sense of values changed. The school fuss
really did not matter much anymore. The Christmas dance became an
embarrassingly insignificant event. Georgia's pending first bowl game
was no longer historic.

The Japanese bombed Pearl Harbor. War!

Everyday the world turns on its axis, but some turns are different.
This one marked not just the change from one day to another, it marked
the change from one age to another.

Puberty had changed our interests. The Japanese had changed everything. Neither the simple world that I had known nor the simple life I had
lived would ever be again. I miss them, and I treasure the memory of
them.

# EPILOGUE

Many, many years after the events I have related, I drove through the edge of Forsyth. On the way to a busy day of modern problems, my thoughts were far from those old times. Then I glanced down the little street that led to the path we trod to Blue Hole so long ago. A solitary figure was walking toward me with a pole in one hand and a tin can in the other. The scene warmed my heart with the belief that some things never change—like simple folks fishing the simple way.

As the figure drew closer, I saw clearer. The pole was a cue stick and the can was a beer can. That told me something. The events of days long passed will not come walking up the street physically. They walk only in your memory. But that is all right.

Suppose we did not have memories? A joy unremembered is a joy lost and a tragedy unremembered is a tragedy likely repeated.

Just like the Queen said to Alice.